The Story of a Common Soldier

Leander Stillwell

EAST INDIA
PUBLISHING COMPANY
PREMIER CLASSICS

Published by the East India Publishing Company
Ottawa, Ontario.

9781989201428

CONTENTS

PREFACE

When I began writing these reminiscences it did not occur to me that anything in the nature of a preface was necessary. It was thought that the dedication to my son Jerry contained sufficient explanation. But I have now finished writing these recollections, and in view of all that they set forth, I believe that a few brief prefatory remarks may now be appropriate. In the first place it will be said that when I began the work it was only to gratify my son, and without any thought or expectation that it would ever be published. I don't know yet that such will be done, but it may happen. The thought occurred to me after I had written some part of it, and it is possible that about at that point some change began to take place in the style, and phraseology, and which perhaps may be observed. So much for that. Next I will say that all statements of fact herein made, based upon my own knowledge, can be relied on as absolutely true. My mother most carefully preserved the letters I wrote home from the army to her and to my father. She died on February 6, 1894, and thereafter my father (who survived her only about three years) gave back to me these old letters. In writing to my parents I wrote, as a rule, a letter every week when the opportunity was afforded, and now in this undertaking with these letters before me it was easy to follow the regiment every mile of its way from Camp Carrollton in January, 1862, to Camp Butler, in September, 1865. Furthermore, on June 1, 1863, at Memphis, Tennessee, as we passed through there on our way to join Grant's army at Vicksburg, I bought a little blank book about four inches long, three inches wide, and half an inch thick. From that time until we were mustered out, I kept a sort of very brief diary in this little book, and have it yet. The old letters and this book have been invaluable to me in writing my recollections, and having been written at or near the time of the happening of the events they mention, can be relied on as accurate and truthful.

Though I attained the rank of a commissioned officer while in the service, yet that did not occur until near the end of my time, and after the war was over. So it is submitted that the title given these sketches, "The Story of a Common Soldier," is warranted by the facts.

If this manuscript should ever be published, it will go to the world without any apology or commendation from me whatever. It is, though, only fair to say that I make no pretensions to being a "literary" man. This is simply the story of a common soldier who served in the army during the great war, and who faithfully tried to do his duty.

L. STILLWELL.
December 30, 1916.

CHAPTER I

THE BEGINNING OF THE WAR. LIFE AT CAMP CARROLLTON, JANUARY AND FEBRUARY, 1862

I was born September 16, 1843, on a farm, in Otter Creek precinct, Jersey County, Illinois. I was living with my parents, in the little old log house where I was born, when the Civil war began. The Confederates fired on Fort Sumter on April 12, 1861, and thus commenced the war. On April 15, 1861, President Lincoln issued a call for 75,000 men, to aid in putting down the existing rebellion. Illinois promptly furnished her quota, and in addition, thousands of men were turned away, for the reason that the complement of the State was complete, and there was no room for them. The soldiers under this call were mustered in for three months' service only, for the government then seemed to be of the opinion that the troubles would be over by the end of that time. But on May 3, 1861, Mr. Lincoln issued another call for volunteers, the number specified being a little over 42,000, and their term of service was fixed at three years, unless sooner discharged. The same call provided for a substantial increase in the regular army and navy. I did not enlist under either of these calls. As above stated, the belief then was almost universal throughout the North that the "war" would amount to nothing much but a summer frolic, and would be over by the 4th of July. We had the utmost confidence that Richmond would be taken by that time, and that Jeff Davis and his cabinet would be prisoners, or fugitives. But the battle of Bull Run, fought on July 21, 1861, gave the loyal people of the Nation a terrible awakening. The result of this battle was a crushing disappointment and a bitter mortification to all the friends of the Union. They realized then that a long and bloody struggle was before them. But Bull Run was probably all for the best. Had it been a Union victory, and the Rebellion then been crushed, negro slavery would have been retained, and the "irrepressible conflict" would have been fought out likely in your time, with doubtless tenfold the loss of life and limb that ensued in the war of the sixties.

The day after the battle of Bull Run Congress passed a law authorizing Mr. Lincoln to call for five hundred thousand three-years volunteers. It was under this law, supplemented by authority from the Secretary of War, that the regiment was organized in which I subsequently enlisted. I was then only a boy, but somehow I felt that the war was going to be a long one, and that it was the duty of every young fellow of the requisite physical ability to "go for a soldier," and help save the Nation. I had some talk with my father on the subject. He was a strong Union man, and in sympathy with my feelings, but I could see that naturally he dreaded the idea of his boy going to the war, with the result that maybe he would be killed, or come home a cripple for life. But I gave him to understand that when they began organizing a regiment in our vicinity, and which would contain a fair proportion of my neighbor boys and acquaintances, I intended then to volunteer. It was simply intolerable to think that I could stay at home, among the girls, and be pointed at by the soldier boys as a stay-at-home coward.

The work of organizing and recruiting for a regiment in our corner of the State began early in the autumn of 1861. The various counties in that immediate locality were overwhelmingly Democratic in politics, and many of the people were strong "Southern sympathizers," as they were then called, and who later developed into virulent Copperheads and Knights of the Golden Circle. Probably 90 per cent of the inhabitants of Greene, Jersey, Scott, Morgan, and adjoining counties came from the Southern States, or were the direct descendants of people from that part of the country. Kentuckians, Tennesseeans, and North and South Carolinians were especially numerous. But it is only fair and the truth to say that many of the most prominent and dangerous of this Copperhead element were men from remote Eastern States. What caused these persons to pursue this shameful course I do not know. President Lincoln was personally well aware of these political conditions in our locality, as his old home, at Springfield, the State Capital, was not far away, and he doubtless knew every man of reasonable prominence in our entire Congressional District. He wanted soldiers, regardless of politics, but it was necessary, in that locality, to hold out some special inducements to his constituents of the Democratic faith. So, for that reason, (with others,) as was well understood at the time, Gen. Jacob Fry of Greene County, a Kentuckian by birth and a life-long Democrat, was selected as the one to recruit and organize, and to be the colonel of the regiment to be raised from the counties above named and their vicinity. Aside from the political consideration, this selection of Gen. Fry was regarded at the time as a very good and appropriate one. He was an old-timer, having been a resident of Greene county from his boyhood, had been sheriff of the county, and had held other responsible offices. And, what was considered still more important, he had served with credit and distinction in the "Black Hawk War" in 1831-2, where he held the rank of Colonel. Soon after the close of this Indian disturbance, he was made Brigadier-General, and subsequently Major-General, of the Illinois militia. He was a grand old man, of temperate habits, strict integrity, and unflinching bravery. But he was sixty-two years old, and that proved to be a handicap that eventually resulted in his resignation, as will appear later.

The Fair Grounds, about half a mile east of Carrollton, the county seat of Greene County, were designated as the "Camp of Instruction" for Col. Fry's regiment. Recruiting for it began about the last of September, but it proceeded very slowly. Several of the boys from my neighborhood had previously enlisted in other regiments, and it looked as if the "wiry edge" of volunteering had somewhat worn off. Co. F of the 14th Illinois Infantry had been raised almost entirely in Jersey county, and several of my old schoolmates were in that company. And there were little squads that had joined other regiments. The 22nd and the 27th Illinois Infantry and the 9th Missouri Infantry, (afterwards designated as the 59th Illinois Infantry,) each had some men and boys from our part of the county.

Up in the northwest corner of Jersey County and close to the Greene county line lived an old farmer by the name of John H. Reddish. He, too, had served in the Black Hawk War, and under the command of Col. Fry. The highest position he attained in that scrap, as shown by the records, was that of corporal, but, regardless of his rank, it is entirely safe to say that he was a fighter. As soon as it was announced that Col. Fry was raising a regiment, and was to be its colonel, Uncle John Reddish forthwith took the field to recruit a company for this organization. The fact that he had been a Black Hawk war soldier gave him immense prestige, and settled in his favor the question of his military qualifications without further evidence. The truth is that at that time almost any man of good repute and fair intelligence, who had seen service in this Black Hawk racket, or the Mexican war, was regarded as fit and desirable for a commissioned officer, or, at the least, pretty high up in the non-commissioned line. But, as it afterwards turned out, that was an erroneous notion. There were exceptions, of course, but in any event, as regards the Black Hawk episode, service during it was of no practical benefit whatever to a man who became thereby an officer in the Civil war. Capt. Reddish was kind hearted, and as brave an old fellow as a reckless and indiscriminating bull dog, but, aside from his personal courage, he had no military qualities whatever, and failed to acquire any during his entire service. He never could learn the drill, except the most simple company movements. He was also very illiterate, and could barely write his name. And his commands on drill were generally laughable. For instance, in giving the command of right or left wheel, he would supplement it by saying, "Swing around, boys, just like a gate." Such directions would mortify us exceedingly, and caused the men of the other companies to laugh at and twit us about our Captain. He would have made a first-class duty sergeant, and that was as high a rank as he was capable of properly filling. But he was a good old man, and furiously patriotic. He loved a fighter and abominated a coward, and, on the whole, his men couldn't help but like him. Capt. Reddish selected for his first, or orderly sergeant, as the position was generally designated, Enoch W. Wallace, of my neighborhood. Enoch, as we usually called him, was an old acquaintance and intimate friend of my parents, and I too had known him from the time I was quite a little boy. Take him all in all, he was just one of the best men I ever knew. He had seen service as a Mexican war soldier, but owing to his youth, being only about sixteen when that war began, I think he did not get in till towards the last, and hence his service was short. But he learned something about company drill. When I heard that Wallace was to be the first sergeant of Capt. Reddish's company, I made up my mind, right then, that I would enlist in that company, and told my father I was going to do so. He listened in silence, with his eyes fixed on the ground. Finally he said, "Well, Leander, if you think it's your duty to go, I shall make no objection. But you're the only boy I now have at home big enough to work, so I wish you'd put it off until we get the wheat sowed, and the corn gathered. Then, if you're still of the same mind, it'll be all right." I felt satisfied that the regiment would not leave for the front until after we had done that work, so I at once consented to my father's request.

An incident happened about this time that greatly stimulated my desire to get into the army. Harvey Edsall, a neighbor boy some four or five years my senior, had enlisted that summer in the 22nd Illinois Infantry. Harvey, with his regiment, was in the battle of Belmont on November 7, 1861, and in the action received a rather severe gun shot wound in the calf of one of his legs. As soon as he was able to stand the travel, he was sent home on furlough, and I met him soon after his arrival at his father's house, where the people had gathered to listen to "the preaching of the word" by Elder Harrison Rowden. (We had no regular church building in our immediate neighborhood then, and religious services were held at private houses.) Harvey was rapidly recovering, but his wounded leg was still swathed in bandages, and he walked on crutches. I well remember how we boys stood around and looked at him with wide-eyed admiration. And he had to tell us the story of the fight, and all about the circumstances connected with the shot he got in his leg, until he probably was sick and tired of the subject. But, for my part, I thought Harvey's story was just grand, and it somehow impressed me with the idea that the only life worth living was that of a soldier in time of war. The idea of staying at home and turning over senseless clods on the farm with the cannon thundering so close at hand that the old men said that when the wind was from the south they sometimes smelled the powder!--was simply intolerable.

Remember all the time, as you read these recollections of an old man, that I am trying to give you merely some conception of the thoughts, feelings, hopes, and ambitions of one who, at the time of which I am now speaking, was only an eighteen year old boy.

In the meantime, I went on helping my father do the fall work on the farm. In due time the wheat was sowed, the corn gathered, and a huge stack of firewood for winter cut and brought in, and piled near the dwelling-house. By this time the holiday season was approaching, which I wanted to spend at home, thinking, maybe, it might be the last. And the regiment was doing nothing but recruit, and drill at Camp Carrollton, and, as I looked at it, there was no special need to hurry. But Christmas and New Year's Day soon came, and went, and one evening I told my parents I intended to go to Carrollton the next day, and "maybe" would come back a soldier. Early next morning, which was Monday, January 6, 1862, I saddled and bridled Bill, the little black mule, and struck out. Carrollton was about twenty miles from our home, almost due north, and the road ran mainly through big woods, with an occasional farm on either side of the road. It is likely those woods are all gone now. I reached the camp about the middle of the afternoon, went to the quarters of Reddish's company, found Enoch Wallace, and told him I had come to enlist. He took me to Capt. Reddish, gave me a short introduction to him, and told him my business. The old Captain gave me a hearty greeting, and was so plain, kind and natural in his manner and talk, that I took a liking to him at once. He told me that the first step necessary was to be examined by the regimental surgeon as to my physical fitness, so we at once went to the surgeon's tent. I had previously heard all sorts of stories as to the thoroughness of this examination, that sometimes the prospective recruits had to strip, stark naked, and jump about, in order to show that their limbs were perfect. But I was agreeably disappointed in that regard. The surgeon, at that time, was a fat, jolly old doctor by the name of Leonidas Clemmons. I was about scared to death when the Captain presented me to him, and requested him to examine me. I reckon the good old doctor saw I was frightened, and he began laughing heartily and saying some kind things about my general appearance. He requested me to stand up straight, then gave me two or three little sort of "love taps" on the chest, turned me round, ran his hands over my shoulders, back, and limbs, laughing and talking all the time, then whirled me to the front, and rendered judgment on me as follows: "Ah, Capt. Reddish! I only wish you had a hundred such fine boys as this one! He's all right, and good for the service." I drew a long breath, and felt much relieved. Then we went to the adjutant's tent, there I signed something, and was duly sworn in. Then to the quartermaster's tent, where I drew my clothing. I got behind a big bale of stuff, took off my citizen's apparel and put on my soldier clothes then and there,--and didn't I feel proud! The clothing outfit consisted of a pair of light-blue pantaloons, similar colored overcoat with a cape to it, dark blue jacket, heavy shoes and woolen socks, an ugly, abominable cocky little cap patterned after the then French army style, gray woolen shirt, and other ordinary under-clothing. Was also given a knapsack, but I think I didn't get a haversack and canteen until later. Right here I will say that the regimental records give the date of my enlistment as the 7th of January, which is wrong. The date was the 6th. It was a day I did not forget, and never shall. How the authorities happened to get the date wrong I do not know, but it is a matter of only one day, and never was of any importance.

It was the custom then in the regiment to give each recruit when he enlisted a two-days furlough, but I deferred asking for mine until the next morning. I spent that afternoon in the camp, and the night at the quarters of my company. As already stated, the camp was on the county Fair Grounds. They contained forty acres, and were thickly studded with big native trees, mainly white and black oak and shag-bark hickory. The grounds were surrounded by an inclosure seven or eight feet high, consisting of thick, native timber planks with the lower ends driven in the ground, and the upper parts firmly nailed to cross-wise stringers. There was only one opening, which was at the main gate about the center of the north side of the grounds. A line of guards was maintained at the gate and all round the inside of the inclosure, with the beat close to the fence, for the purpose of keeping the men in camp. No enlisted man could go out except on a pass signed by his captain, and approved by the colonel. The drilling of the men was conducted principally inside the grounds, but on skirmish drill we went outside, in order to have room enough. The quarters or barracks of the men were, for each company, a rather long, low structure, crudely built of native lumber and covered with clapboards and a top dressing of straw, containing two rows of bunks, one above and one below. These shacks looked like a Kansas stable of early days,--but they were abodes of comfort and luxury compared to what we frequently had later.

Next morning, after an early breakfast, I pulled out for home, with my two-days furlough in my pocket. I was accompanied by John Jobson, one of Reddish's company, and who had enlisted about a month previous. He had obtained a short furlough for some purpose or other, and had hired a horse on which to make the trip. Prior to his enlistment he had been working as a farm hand for Sam Dougherty, one of our nearest neighbors, and I had become well acquainted with him. He was about twenty-five years old, of English birth, a fine, sensible young fellow, and made a good soldier. I well remember our high spirits on this journey home. We were young, glowing with health and overflowing with liveliness and animation. There was a heavy snow on the ground, but the sky was clear, and the air was keen and bracing. Occasionally, when we would strike a stretch of level road, we would loose all the buttons of our overcoats save the top one, put the gad to our steeds, and waving our caps, with our long coat tails streaming in the wind, would yell like Comanches, and "let on" that we were making a cavalry charge. I have no doubt that we believed we presented a most terror-striking appearance.

Happy is man that to him the future is a sealed book. In the summer of 1863, while we were stationed near Vicksburg, Jobson was taken seriously ill, and was put on a transport to be taken to a general hospital at Mound City, Illinois. He died en route, on the boat, and was hastily buried in a sand bar at the mouth of White River. The changing currents of the mighty Mississippi have long since swallowed up that sand bar, and with it all that may have been left of the mortal remains of poor Jobson.

I reached home sometime in the afternoon, relieved Bill of his equipments, put him in the stable, and fed him. No one was stirring about outside, and I walked into the house unannounced. My mother was seated in an old rocking-chair, engaged in sewing. She looked up, saw me in the uniform of a soldier, and she knew what that meant. Her work dropped in her lap, she covered her face with her hands, and the tears gushed through her fingers and she trembled in her chair with the intensity of her emotions. There was no sobbing, or other vocal manifestation of feeling, but her silence made her grief seem all the more impressive. I was distressed, and didn't know what to say, so I said nothing, and walked out into the kitchen, thence back to the barn. There I met father, who had come in from some out-door work. He looked at me gravely, but with an impassive countenance, and merely remarked, "Well, I reckon you've done right."

Next morning everybody seemed more cheerful, and I had much to say at breakfast about things at Camp Carrollton.

On the expiration of my furlough I promptly reported at the camp and entered on my duties as a soldier. The absorbing duty was the drill, and that was persistent, and consumed the most of the time. I knew nothing about it when I enlisted, and had never seen any except on the previous Monday afternoon. The system we then had was Hardee's Infantry Tactics. It was simple, and easily learned. The main things required were promptness, care, and close attention. All day long, somewhere in the camp, could be heard the voice of some officer, calling, "Left! left! left, right, left!" to his squad or company, to guide them in the cadence of the step. We were drilled at Carrollton in the "school of the soldier," "school of the company," and skirmish drill, with dress parade at sunset. We had no muskets, and did not receive them until we went to Benton Barracks, at St. Louis. I do not remember of our having any battalion drill at Camp Carrollton. The big trees in the fair grounds were probably too thick and numerous to permit that. Our fare consisted of light bread, coffee, fresh meat at some meals, and salt meat at others, Yankee beans, rice, onions, and Irish and sweet potatoes, with stewed dried apples occasionally for supper. The salt meat, as a rule, was pickled pork and fat side meat, which latter "table comfort" the boys called "sow-belly." We got well acquainted with that before the war was over. On the grub question I will say now that the great "stand-bys" of the Union soldiers during the war, at least those of the western armies, were coffee, sow-belly, Yankee beans, and hardtack. It took us, of course, some time to learn how to cook things properly, especially the beans, but after we had learned how, we never went back on the above named old friends. But the death of many a poor boy, especially during our first two or three months in the field, is chargeable to the bad cooking of his food.

At Carrollton the jolliest time of the day was from the close of dress parade until taps sounded "Lights out." There was then a good deal of what you might call "prairie dogging," that is, the boys would run around and visit at the quarters of other companies. And Oh, how they would sing! All sorts of patriotic songs were in vogue then, and what was lacking in tone we made up in volume. The battle of Mill Springs, in Kentucky, was fought on January 19, 1862, resulting in a Union victory. A Confederate general, Felix K. Zollicoffer, was killed in the action. He had been a member of Congress from Tennessee, and was a man of prominence in the South. A song soon appeared in commemoration of this battle. It was called "The Happy Land of Canaan," and I now remember only one stanza, which is as follows:

"Old Zolly's gone,
And Secesh will have to mourn,
For they thought he would do to depend on;
But he made his last stand
On the rolling Cumberland,
And was sent to the happy land of Canaan."

There was a ringing, rolling chorus to each verse, of course, and which was not at all germane to the text, and, moreover, as the newspapers sometimes say, is "not adapted for publication,"--so it will be omitted. Well, I can now shut my eyes and lean back in my chair and let my memory revert to that far away time, and it just seems to me that I can see and hear Nelse Hegans, of Co. C, singing that song at night in our quarters at old Camp Carrollton. He was a big, strong six-footer, about twenty-one years of age, with a deep bass voice that sounded when singing like the roll of distant thunder. And he was an all-around good fellow. Poor Nelse! He was mortally wounded by a musket ball in the neck early in the morning of the first day at Shiloh, and died a few days thereafter.

The health of the boys while at Camp Carrollton was fine. There were a few cases of measles, but as I remember, none were fatal. Once I caught a bad cold, but I treated it myself with a backwoods remedy and never thought of going to the surgeon about it. I took some of the bark of a hickory tree that stood near our quarters, and made about a quart of strong hickory-bark tea. I drank it hot, and all at once, just before turning in for the night. It was green in color, and intensely bitter, but it cured the cold.

A few weeks after my enlistment, I was appointed to the position of corporal. There are, or were in my time, eight corporals in an infantry company, each designated by a number, in numerical order. I was fifth. I owed this appointment to the friendship and influence of Enoch Wallace, and this was only one of the countless acts of kindness that he rendered me during my term of service. I just cannot tell you how proud I was over this modest military office. I am telling you the truth when I say that I felt more pride and pleasure in being a "Corporal of Co. D" than I ever did later in the possession of any other office, either military or civil. The boys framed up a story on me, to the effect that soon after my appointment I was seen in the rear of the company quarters, stooping over an empty barrel, with my head projected into it as far as possible, and exclaiming in a deep, guttural tone, "CORPORAL STILLWELL!" "CORPORAL STILLWELL!" This was being done, so the boys said, in order that I might personally enjoy the sound. In order to be strictly accurate, I will state that, although the appointment was made while we were at Carrollton, my official warrant was not issued until our arrival at Benton Barracks.

The only thing recalled now that was sort of disagreeable at Camp Carrollton was the utter absence of privacy. Even when off duty, one couldn't get away by himself, and sit down in peace and quiet anywhere. And as for slipping off into some corner and trying to read, alone, a book or paper, the thing was impossible. To use a modern expression, there was always "something doing." Many a time after supper, on very cold nights, when the boys would all be in the barracks, singing or cutting up, I would sneak out and walk around under the big trees, with the snow crackling under my feet, for no other purpose whatever than just to be alone a while. But that condition of things changed for the better after we got down South, and were no longer cooped up in a forty acre lot.

General Grant gained his great victory at Fort Donelson on February 16, 1862, and the news reached us a few days later. The boys talked about it with feelings of mingled exultation,--and mortification. Exultation, of course, over the "glorious victory," but mortification in regard to its effects and consequences on our future military career. We all thought, from the officers down, that now the war would end, that we would see no actual service, and never fire a shot. That we would be discharged, and go home just little "trundle-bed soldiers," and have to sit around and hear other sure-enough warriors tell the stories of actual war and fighting. If we only had known, we were borrowing unnecessary trouble,--as we found out later.

CHAPTER II

BENTON BARRACKS. ST. LOUIS, MARCH, 1862.

Sometime during the last of February, the welcome news was given out from regimental headquarters that we were soon to leave Camp Carrollton. Our first objective point was to be St. Louis, Mo., and what next nobody knew. Definite orders for the movement were issued later, and it then occurred to us that possibly all our recent apprehensions about not seeing any fighting were somewhat premature.

Right here I will say that in the brief sketch of the regiment published in the reports of the Adjutant-General of the State of Illinois, the date of our leaving Carrollton is given as February 21, which is wrong. That date is either a mistake of the person who wrote that part of the sketch, or a typographical error. I have in my possession, and now lying before me, a letter I wrote to my father from Benton Barracks, of date March 2, 1862, in which the date of our arrival at St. Louis is given as February 28th. And I well know that we were only two days on the trip. And besides the date given in my letter, I distinctly remember several unwritten facts and circumstances that satisfy me beyond any doubt, that the day we left Carrollton was February 27, 1862. Early in the morning of that day, the regiment filed out at the big gate, and marched south on the dirt road. Good-bye to old Camp Carrollton! Many of the boys never saw it again, and I never have seen it since but once, which was in the summer of 1894. I was back then in Jersey county, on a sort of a visit, and was taken with a desire to run up to Carrollton and look at the old camp. There was then a railroad constructed during the last years of the war, (or about that time), running south from the town, and less than an hour's ride from Jerseyville, where I was stopping, so I got on a morning train, and, like Jonah when moved to go to Tarshish, "paid the fare and went." I found the old camp still being used as a county fair ground, and the same big trees, or the most of them, were there yet, and looked about as they did thirty-two years before. Of course, every vestige of our old barracks was gone. I stood around and looked at things awhile,--and thought--then left, and have never been there again.

The regiment arrived at Jerseyville about sunset. The word had gone out, all through the country, that Fry's regiment was leaving for the front, and the country people had come to town, from miles around, in their farm wagons, to have one last look, and bid us good-bye. The regiment, in column by companies, company distance, marched up the main street running south, and on reaching the center of the little town, we wheeled into line, dressed on the colors, and stood at attention. The sidewalks were thronged with the country people all intently scanning the lines, each little family group anxiously looking for their boy, brother, husband or father, as the case may have been. (But right here it will be said that the overwhelming majority of the enlisted men of the regiment, and the most of the line officers, were unmarried.) I was satisfied that my parents were somewhere among the crowd of spectators, for I had specially written them as to when we would pass through Jerseyville. I was in the front rank, and kept my face rigidly fixed to the front, but glanced as best I could up and down the sidewalk, trying to locate father and mother. Suddenly I saw them, as they struggled to the edge of the walk, not more than ten feet from me. I had been somewhat dreading the meeting, and the parting that was to come. I remembered the emotion of my mother when she first saw me in my uniform, and I feared that now she might break down altogether. But there she stood, her eyes fixed on me intently, with a proud and happy smile on her face! You see, we were a magnificent-looking body of young fellows, somewhere between 800 and 900 strong. Our uniforms were clean and comparatively new, and our faces were ruddy and glowing with health. Besides the regimental colors, each company, at that time, carried a small flag, which were all fluttering in the breeze, and our regimental band was playing patriotic tunes at its best. I reckon it was a somewhat inspiring sight to country people like those who, with possibly very few exceptions, had never seen anything like that before. Anyhow, my mother was evidently content and glad to see me there, under the shadow of the flag, and going forth to fight for the old Union, instead of then being sneaking around at home, like some great hulking boys in our neighborhood who were of Copperhead sympathies and parentage.

Arrangements had been made to quarter the regiment that night in different public buildings in the town, and the companies were soon marched to their respective places. Co. D had been assigned to the Baptist church, and there my parents and I met, and had our final interview. They were nine miles from home, in the old farm wagon, the roads (in the main) were through dense woods, and across ridges and hollows, the short winter day was drawing to a close and night approaching, so our farewell talk was necessarily brief. Our parting was simple and unaffected, without any display of emotion by anybody. But mother's eyes looked unusually bright, and she didn't linger after she had said, "Good-bye Leander." As for my father,--he was an old North Carolinian, born and reared among the Cherokee Indians at the base of the Great Smoky Mountains, and with him, and all other men of his type, any yielding to "womanish" feelings was looked on as almost disgraceful. His farewell words were few, and concise, and spoken in his ordinary tone and manner, he then turned on his heel, and was gone.

Mother left with me a baked chicken, the same being a big, fat hen full of stuffing, rich in sage and onions; also some mince pie, old time doughnuts, and cucumber pickles. I shared it all with Bill Banfield (my chum), and we had plenty for supper and breakfast the next day, with the drum-sticks and some other outlying portions of the chicken for dinner.

Early the next morning we pulled out for Alton, on the Mississippi River. But we did not have to march much that day. The country people around and near Jerseyville turned out in force with their farm wagons, and insisted on hauling us to Alton, and their invitations were accepted with pleasure. A few miles north of Alton we passed what was in those days (and may be yet) a popular and celebrated school for girls, called the "Monticello Female Seminary." The girls had heard of our coming, and were all out by the side of the road, a hundred or more, with red, white and blue ribbons in their hair and otherwise on their persons. They waved white handkerchiefs and little flags at us, and looked their sweetest. And didn't we cheer them! Well, I should say so. We stood up in the wagons, and swung our caps, and just whooped and hurrahed as long as those girls were in sight. We always treasured this incident as a bright, precious link in the chain of memory, for it was the last public manifestation, of this nature, of good-will and patriotism from girls and women that was given the regiment until we struck the soil of the State of Indiana, on our return home some months after the close of the war.

We arrived at Alton about sundown, and at once marched aboard the big side-wheel steamboat, "City of Alton," which was lying at the wharf waiting for us, and guards were promptly stationed to prevent the men leaving the boat. But "some one had blundered," and no rations had been provided for our supper. We were good and hungry, too, for our dinner, at least that of Co. D, consisted only of the left-over scraps of breakfast. But the officers got busy and went up town and bought, with their own money, something for us to eat. My company was furnished a barrel of oyster crackers, called in those days "butter crackers," and our drink was river water.

The novelty and excitement of the last two days had left me nerveless and tired out, and to tell the truth, I was feeling the first touch of "home-sickness." So, after supper I went up on the hurricane deck of the boat, spread my blanket on the floor, and with my knapsack for a pillow, laid down and soon fell asleep. The boat did not leave Alton until after dark, and when it pulled out, the scream of the whistle, the dashing of the paddles, and the throbbing and crash of the engines, aroused me from my slumber. I sat up and looked around and watched the lights of Alton as they twinkled and glimmered in the darkness, until they were lost to sight by a bend in the river. Then I laid down and went to sleep again, and did not wake until daylight the next morning, and found that our boat was moored to the wharf at St. Louis. We soon debarked, and marched out to Benton Barracks, which were clear out of town and beyond the suburbs. The shape of Benton Barracks, as I now remember, was a big oblong square.

The barracks themselves consisted of a continuous connected row of low frame buildings, the quarters of each company being separated from the others by frame partitions, and provided with two rows of bunks around the sides and ends. At the rear of the quarters of each company was the company kitchen. It was a detached, separate frame structure, and amply provided with accommodations for cooking, including a brick furnace with openings for camp kettles, pots, boilers and the like. Both barracks and kitchen were comfortable and convenient, and greatly superior to our home-made shacks at Carrollton. The barracks inclosed a good sized tract of land, but its extent I do not now remember. This space was used for drilling and parades, and was almost entirely destitute of trees. The commander of the post, at that time, was Colonel Benjamin L. E. Bonneville, an old regular army officer, and who had been a noted western explorer in his younger days. I frequently saw him riding about the grounds. He was a little dried-up old Frenchman, and had no military look about him whatever. All the same, he was a man who had, as a soldier, done long and faithful service for his adopted country. Should you ever want to post up on him (if you have not already done so), read "Adventures of Captain Bonneville, U.S.A., in the Rocky Mountains and the Far West," by Washington Irving. You will find it deeply interesting.

We remained at Benton Barracks about four weeks. Life there was monotonous and void of any special interest. We drilled but little, as I now remember, the reason for that being it rained the most of the time we were there and the drill grounds were oceans of mud. The drainage was wretched, and the most of the rain that fell stayed on the surface until the ground soaked it up. And how it did rain at Benton Barracks in March, 1862! While there, I found in some recently vacated quarters an old tattered, paper bound copy of Dickens' "Bleak House," and on those rainy days I would climb up in my bunk (an upper one), and lie there and read that book. Some of the aristocratic characters mentioned therein had a country residence called "Chesney Wold," where it seemed it always rained. To quote (in substance) from the book, "The rain was ever falling, drip, drip, drip, by day and night," at "the place in Lincolnshire." 'Twas even so at Benton Barracks. When weary of reading, I would turn and look a while through the little window at the side of my bunk that gave a view of the most of the square which the barracks inclosed. The surface of the earth was just a quagmire of mud and water, and nothing stirring abroad could be seen save occasionally a mounted orderly, splashing at a gallop across the grounds. Since then I have frequently read "Bleak House," and whenever that chapter is reached depicting the rainy weather at the Dedlock place, I can again see, and smell, and hear, and feel, those gloomy wearisome conditions at Benton Barracks of over half a century ago. I have read, somewhere in Gen. Sherman's Memoirs, a statement in substance to the effect that rain in camp has a depressing effect upon soldiers, but is enlivening to them on a march. From personal experience I know that observation to be true. Many a time while on a march we would be caught in heavy rains. The dirt road would soon be worked into a loblolly of sticky yellow mud. Thereupon we would take off our shoes and socks, tie them to the barrel of our muskets a little below the muzzle and just above the end of the stock, poise the piece on the hammer on either shoulder, stock uppermost, and roll up our breeches to the knees. Then like Tam O'Shanter, we "skelpit on through dub and mire, despising wind, and rain, and fire," and singing "John Brown's Body," or whatever else came handy. But rainy days in camp, especially such as we had at Benton Barracks, engender feelings of gloom and dejection that have to be experienced in order to be realized. They are just too wretched for any adequate description.

One day while strolling around the grounds sight seeing, I fell in with a soldier who said he belonged to the 14th Wisconsin Infantry. He was some years older than me, but was quite sociable, and seemed to be a sensible, intelligent fellow. He was full of talk about his regiment,--said they were nearly all young men, big stalwart lumbermen from the pine woods of Wisconsin, and urged me to come around some evening when they were on dress parade, and look at them. I had found out by this time that almost every soldier would brag about his regiment, so allowance was made for what he said. But he excited my curiosity to see those Wisconsin boys, so one evening when I was at liberty, I did go and view them while they were on dress parade, and found that the soldier had not exaggerated. They were great, tall fellows, broad across the shoulders and chest, with big limbs. Altogether, they simply were, from a physical standpoint, the finest looking soldiers I ever saw during my entire term of service. I speak now of this incident and of these men, for the reason that later I may say something more about this 14th Wisconsin.

While at Benton Barracks we were given our regimental number,--Sixty-first--and thenceforth the regiment was known and designated as the Sixty-first Illinois Infantry. We also drew our guns. We were furnished with the Austrian rifle musket. It was of medium length, with a light brown walnut stock,--and was a wicked shooter. At that time the most of the western troops were armed with foreign-made muskets, imported from Europe. Many regiments had old Belgian muskets, a heavy, cumbersome piece, and awkward and unsatisfactory every way. We were glad to get the Austrians, and were quite proud of them. We used these until June, 1863, when we turned them in and drew in lieu thereof the Springfield rifle musket of the model of 1863. It was not as heavy as the Austrian, was neater looking, and a very efficient firearm. No further change was made, and we carried the Springfield thenceforward until we were mustered out.

It was also here at Benton Barracks that the mustering of the regiment into the service of the United States was completed. Ten companies, at that time, constituted a regiment of infantry, but ours had only nine. We lacked Company K, and it was not recruited, and did not join the regiment until in March, 1864. On account of our not having a full regiment, Col. Fry (as we always called him) was commissioned as Lieutenant Colonel only, which was his rank all the time he was with us, and Capt. Simon P. Ohr, of Co. A, was commissioned Major. Owing to our lack of one company, and the further fact that when that company did join us the other companies had become much depleted in numbers, the regiment therefore never had an officer of the full rank of Colonel until the summer of 1865, when it became entitled to one under the circumstances which will be stated further on.

CHAPTER III

OFF FOR THE SEAT OF WAR. THE BATTLE OF SHILOH. MARCH AND APRIL, 1862.

On March 25th we left Benton Barracks for the front. We marched through St. Louis and onto the steamboat that day, but from some cause I never knew, the boat did not leave the wharf until about dark the next evening. My company was quartered on the hurricane deck of the boat. Soon after the boat started down the river an incident befell me that looks somewhat comical now, but at that time it was to me a serious matter, and one that troubled my conscience a good deal. I had piled my knapsack, with the blanket strapped on the outside, and my other stuff, at the foot of the gun stack which included my musket. Suddenly I discovered, to my great consternation, that my blanket was gone! Yes, my lords and gentlemen, some "false Scot" had deliberately and feloniously appropriated my indispensable equipment for a night's repose. And a long, raw March night was coming on, and the damp and chilly air was rising, like a fog, from the cold surface of the river. All signs, too, portended a rainy night. The thunder was muttering off in the southwest, intermittent flashes of lightning lit up the sky, and scattering drops of rain were even then beginning to patter on the hurricane deck and ripple the bosom of the stream. What should I do? I must have a blanket, that was certain. But all my life the belief had been instilled into me that stealing was well-nigh the most disgraceful of all crimes, and that a thief was a most odious and contemptible wretch. Moreover, one of the ten commandments "pintedly" declared. "Thou shalt not steal." But something had to be done, and speedily. At last it occurred to me that being a soldier, and belonging for the time being to Uncle Sam, I was a species of government property, which it was my duty to protect at all hazards. That settled the question, and conscience and honesty withdrew. Without going into the demoralizing details, suffice it to say that I stole a blanket from some hapless victim belonging to another company, and thus safeguarded the health and military efficiency of a chattel of the Nation. How the other fellow got along, I don't know. I made no impertinent inquiries, and, during the day time, indefinitely thereafter, kept that blanket in my knapsack, carefully concealed from prying eyes. But it will be recorded here that this was the only act of downright larceny that I committed during my entire term of service, except the gobbling of a couple of onions, which maybe I'll mention later. Of course I helped myself many times, while on the march, or on picket, to roasting ears, sweet potatoes, apples, and the like, but that came under the head of legitimate foraging, and was sanctioned by the military authorities.

The night we left St. Louis I had my first impressive object lesson showing the difference between the conditions of the commissioned officers and the enlisted men. I had spread my blanket at the base of the little structure called the "Texas," on which the pilot house stands. All around the bottom of the "Texas" was a row of small window lights that commanded a view of the interior of the boat's cabin below, and I only had to turn my head and look in and down, to see what was passing. The officers were seated in cushioned chairs, or sauntering around over the carpeted and brilliantly lighted room, while their supper was being prepared. Colored waiters dressed in white uniforms were bringing in the eatables, and when all was ready, a gong was sounded and the officers seated themselves at the table. And just look at the good things they had to eat! Fried ham and beefsteak, hot biscuits, butter, molasses, big boiled Irish potatoes steaming hot, fragrant coffee served with cream, in cups and saucers, and some minor goodies in the shape of preserves and the like. And how savory those good things smelled!--for I was where I could get the benefit of that. And there were the officers, in the warm, lighted cabin, seated at a table, with nigger waiters to serve them, feasting on that splendid fare! Why, it was the very incarnation of bodily comfort and enjoyment! And, when the officers should be ready to retire for the night, warm and cozy berths awaited them, where they would stretch their limbs on downy quilts and mattresses, utterly oblivious to the wet and chill on the outside.

Then I turned my head and took in my surroundings! A black, cold night, cinders and soot drifting on us from the smoke stacks, and a drizzling rain pattering down. And my supper had consisted of hardtack and raw sow-belly, with river water for a beverage, of the vintage, say, of 1541. And to aggravate the situation generally, I was lying on a blanket which a military necessity had compelled me to steal. But I reflected that we couldn't all be officers,--there had to be somebody to do the actual trigger-pulling. And I further consoled myself with the thought that while the officers had more privileges than the common soldiers, they likewise had more responsibilities, and had to worry their brains about many things that didn't bother us a particle. So I smothered all envious feelings as best I could, and wrapping myself up good in my blanket, went to sleep, and all night long slept the unbroken, dreamless sleep of youth and health.

The weather cleared up that night, and the next day was fine, and we all felt in better spirits. Our surroundings were new and strange, and we were thrilling with excitement and bright hopes of the future. The great majority of us were simple country boys, who had so far passed our lives in a narrow circle in the backwoods. As for myself, before enlisting in the army I had never been more than fifty miles from home, had not traveled any on a steamboat, and my few short railroad trips did not amount, in the aggregate, to more than about seventy-five miles, back and forth. But now the contracted horizon of the "Whippoorwill Ridges" adjacent to the old home had suddenly expanded, and a great big wonderful world was unfolding to my view. And there was the daring, heroic life on which we were entering! No individual boy expected that he would be killed, or meet with any other adverse fate. Others might, and doubtless would, but he would come out safe and sound, and return home at the end of a victorious war, a military hero, and as such would be looked up to, and admired and reverenced, all the rest of his life. At any rate, such were my thoughts, and I have no doubt whatever that ninety-nine out of a hundred of the other boys thought the same.

On the afternoon of this day (March 27th) we arrived at Cairo, rounded in at the wharf, and remained a short time. The town fronted on the Ohio river, which was high at the time, as also was the Mississippi. The appearance of Cairo was wretched. Levees had been constructed to protect it from high water, but notwithstanding the streets and the grounds generally were just a foul, stagnant swamp. Engines were at work pumping the surface water into the river through pipes in the levee; otherwise I reckon everybody would have been drowned out. Charles Dickens saw this locality in the spring of 1842 when on a visit to America, and it figures in "Martin Chuzzlewit," under the name of "Eden." I never read that book until after the close of the war, but have several times since, and will say that if the Eden of 1842 looked anything like the Cairo of twenty years later, his description thereof was fully warranted.

Our boat had hardly got moored to the wharf before the word went round that some Confederate prisoners were on the transport on our right, and we forthwith rushed to that side to get our first look at the "Secesh," as we then called them. It was only a small batch, about a hundred or so. They were under guard, and on the after part of the lower deck, along the sides and the stern of the boat. We ascertained that they were about the last installment of the Fort Donelson prisoners, and were being shipped to a northern military prison. Naturally, we scanned them with great curiosity, and the boys soon began to joke and chaff them in a perfectly good natured way. They took this silently, with no other manifestation than an occasional dry grin. But finally, a rather good looking young fellow cocked his eyes toward us and in a soft, drawling tone called out, "You-all will sing a different tune by next summah." Our boys responded to this with bursts of laughter and some derisive whoops; but later we found out that the young Confederate soldier was a true prophet.

Our halt at Cairo was brief; the boat soon cast off and proceeded up the Ohio to the mouth of the Tennessee, and from thence up that river. Some time the next day we passed Fort Henry. We had read of its capture the month previous by the joint operations of our army and navy, and were all curious to see this Confederate stronghold, where a mere handful of men had put up such a plucky fight. My ideas of forts at that time had all been drawn from pictures in books which depicted old-time fortresses, and from descriptions in Scott's "Marmion" of ancient feudal castles like "Tantallon strong," and the like. And when we approached Fort Henry I fully expected to see some grand, imposing structure with "battled towers," "donjon keep," "portcullis," "drawbridges," and what not, and perhaps some officer of high rank with a drawn sword, strutting about on the ramparts and occasionally shouting, at the top of his voice, "What, warder, ho!" or words to that effect. But, to my utter amazement and disgust, when we steamed up opposite Fort Henry I saw only a little squatty, insignificant looking mud affair, without the slightest feature of any of the "pride, pomp, and circumstance of glorious war." It had been built on the low bottom ground near the bank of the Tennessee river, the stream was now high, and the adjacent land was largely covered with water, while the inside of the fort looked a good deal like a hog pen. I couldn't imagine how such a contemptible looking thing had stood off our gunboats as long as it did. But I did not know then that just such works, with earthen walls, were the strongest and best defenses against modern artillery that could be constructed. In fact, what I didn't know about war, at that stage of the proceedings, was broad and comprehensive, and covered the whole field.

As we journeyed up the Tennessee we began to notice queer-looking green bunches of something on the trees. As the forest had not yet put forth its foliage, we knew that growth could not be leaves, and were puzzled to imagine what it could be. But we finally learned from some of the boat's crew that it was mistletoe. So far as I knew none of the private soldiers had ever before seen that curious evergreen, and it was to us a strange curiosity. But we got well acquainted with it later.

We arrived at Pittsburg Landing on the evening of March 31, about sundown. On going into camp in our position upon the line, for the first time in our service we dwelt in tents. We had what was called the Sibley tent, an affair of a conical shape, rather large, and capable of accommodating about twelve men, with their accoutrements. As a circumstance bearing on our ignorance of life in tents, I will say that we neglected to ditch around them, and on the very first night we slept in them there came a heavy rain, and the next morning found us lying more or less in the water, and our blankets and other stuff sopping wet. But after that, on pitching our tents one of the first things we did was to dig around them a sufficient ditch with a lateral extension.

I retain a vivid recollection of the kind of army cooking we had for the first few months in Tennessee. At Camp Carrollton and Benton Barracks we had company cooks who prepared the food for the entire company. They were merely enlisted men, detailed for that purpose, and while their cooking was nothing to brag about, it was vastly superior to what now ensued. We divided up into messes, of four, eight, or twelve men, or thereabouts, to the mess, and generally would take turns in the culinary line. Very few of us knew anything whatever about cooking, and our exploits in that regard would have been comical if the effects had not been so pernicious. Flour was issued to us after our arrival at Pittsburg Landing, but we had no utensils in which we could cook biscuits, or loaves. So we would make a batter out of flour, water, grease, and salt, and cook it in a mess pan, the product being the army "flapjack." It invariably was tough as a mule's ear, about as heavy as lead, and very indigestible. Later we learned to construct ovens of wood, daubed with mud, or of stone, and in them, in the course of time, we acquired the knack of baking good bread. But with us in the west the hardtack was generally our standard bread diet, and nothing could beat it.

And for some time our cooking of "Yankee beans," as we called them, was simply atrocious. As you know, beans should be cooked until they are thoroughly done; otherwise they are decidedly harmful. Well, we would not cook them much more than half enough, the result being a sloppy, slimy mess, its looks alone being well-nigh sufficient to extinguish one's appetite. And as for the rice--the horrible messes we would make of that defy description. I know that one consequence with me was I contracted such an aversion to rice that for many years afterwards, while in civil life, I just couldn't eat it in any form, no matter how temptingly it was prepared.

Owing to improperly cooked food, change of climate and of water, and neglect of proper sanitation measures in the camps, camp diarrhea became epidemic at Pittsburg Landing, especially among the "green" regiments like ours. And for about six weeks everybody suffered, more or less, the difference being only in degree. The fact is, the condition of the troops in that quarter during the prevalence of that disorder was simply so bad and repulsive that any detailed description thereof will be passed over. I never saw the like before, and never have seen it since. I always thought that one thing which aggravated this trouble was the inordinate quantity of sugar some of the men would consume. They would not only use it to excess in their coffee and rice, but would frequently eat it raw, by handfuls. I happen to think, right now, of an incident that illustrates the unnatural appetite of some of the men for sugar. It occurred in camp one rainy day during the siege of Corinth. Jake Hill, of my company, had covered the top of a big army hardtack with sugar in a cone-like form, piling it on as long as the tack would hold a grain. Then he seated himself on his knapsack and proceeded to gnaw away at his feast, by a system of "regular approaches." He was even then suffering from the epidemic before mentioned, and so weak he could hardly walk. Some one said to him, "Jake, that sugar ain't good for you in your condition." He looked up with an aggrieved air and responded in a tone of cruelly injured innocence, "Haven't I the right to eat my r-a-a-tion?" Strange to say, Jake got well, and served throughout the war. He was a good soldier, too.

For my part, I quit using sugar in any form, early in my army service, (except a little, occasionally, with stewed fruit, or berries,) and didn't resume its general use until some years after my discharge from the army.

In consequence of the conditions at Pittsburg Landing that have been alluded to, men died by the score like rotten sheep. And a great many more were discharged for disability and thereby were lost to the service. It is true that some of these discharged men, especially the younger ones, subsequently re-enlisted, and made good soldiers. But this loss to the Union armies in Tennessee in the spring of '62 by disease would undoubtedly surpass the casualties of a great battle, but, unlike a battle, there was no resulting compensation whatever.

The battle of Shiloh was fought on April 6 and 7. In 1890 I wrote an article on the battle which was published in the New York Tribune, and later it appeared in several other newspapers. It has also been reprinted in book form in connection with papers by other persons, some about the war, and others of a miscellaneous nature. The piece I wrote twenty-five years ago is as good, I reckon, if not better than anything on that head I can write now, so it will be set out here.

IN THE RANKS AT SHILOH.

By Leander Stillwell,
late First Lieutenant, 61st Illinois Volunteer Infantry.

There has been a great deal said and written about the battle of Shiloh, both by Rebel and Union officers and writers. On the part of the first there has been, and probably always will be, angry dispute and criticism about the conduct of General Beauregard in calling off his troops Sunday evening while fully an hour of broad, precious daylight still remained, which, as claimed by some, might have been utilized in destroying the remainder of Grant's army before Buell could have crossed the Tennessee. On the part of Union writers the matters most discussed have been as to whether or not our forces were surprised, the condition of Grant's army at the close of the first day, what the result would have been without the aid of the gunboats, or if Buell's army had not come, and kindred subjects. It is not my purpose, in telling my story of the battle of Shiloh, to say anything that will add to this volume of discussion. My age at the time was but eighteen, and my position that of a common soldier in the ranks. It would therefore be foolish in me to assume the part of a critic. The generals, who, from reasonably safe points of observation, are sweeping the field with their glasses, and noting and directing the movements of the lines of battle, must, in the nature of things, be the ones to furnish the facts that go to make history. The extent of a battlefield seen by the common soldier is that only which comes within the range of the raised sights of his musket. And what little he does see is as "through a glass, darkly." The dense banks of powder smoke obstruct his gaze; he catches but fitful glimpses of his adversaries as the smoke veers or rises.

Then, too, my own experience makes me think that where the common soldier does his duty, all his faculties of mind and body are employed in attending to the details of his own personal part of the work of destruction, and there is but little time left him for taking mental notes to form the bases of historical articles a quarter of a century afterward. The handling, tearing, and charging of his cartridge, ramming it home (we used muzzle loaders during the Civil War), the capping of his gun, the aiming and firing, with furious haste and desperate energy,--for every shot may be his last,--these things require the soldier's close personal attention and make him oblivious to matters transpiring beyond his immediate neighborhood. Moreover, his sense of hearing is well-nigh overcome by the deafening uproar going on around him. The incessant and terrible crash of musketry, the roar of the cannon, the continual zip, zip, of the bullets as they hiss by him, interspersed with the agonizing screams of the wounded, or the death shrieks of comrades falling in dying convulsions right in the face of the living,--these things are not conducive to that serene and judicial mental equipoise which the historian enjoys in his closet.

Let the generals and historians, therefore, write of the movements of corps, divisions, and brigades. I have naught to tell but the simple story of what one private soldier saw of one of the bloodiest battles of the war.

The regiment to which I belonged was the 61st Illinois Infantry. It left its camp of instruction (a country town in southern Illinois) about the last of February, 1862. We were sent to Benton Barracks, near St. Louis, and remained there drilling (when the weather would permit) until March 25th. We left on that day for the front. It was a cloudy, drizzly, and most gloomy day, as we marched through the streets of St. Louis down to the levee, to embark on a transport that was to take us to our destination. The city was enveloped in that pall of coal smoke for which St. Louis is celebrated. It hung heavy and low and set us all to coughing. I think the colonel must have marched us down some by-street. It was narrow and dirty, with high buildings on either side. The line officers took the sidewalks, while the regiment, marching by the flank, tramped in silence down the middle of the street, slumping through the nasty, slimy mud. There was one thing very noticeable on this march through St. Louis, and that was the utter lack of interest taken in us by the inhabitants. From pictures I had seen in books at home, my idea was that when soldiers departed for war, beautiful ladies stood on balconies and waved snowy-white handkerchiefs at the troops, while the men stood on the sidewalks and corners and swung their hats and cheered.

There may have been regiments so favored, but ours was not one of them. Occasionally a fat, chunky-looking fellow, of a German cast of countenance, with a big pipe in his mouth, would stick his head out of a door or window, look at us a few seconds, and then disappear. No handkerchiefs nor hats were waved, we heard no cheers. My thoughts at the time were that the Union people there had all gone to war, or else the colonel was marching us through a "Secesh" part of town.

We marched to the levee and from there on board the big sidewheel steamer, Empress. The next evening she unfastened her moorings, swung her head out into the river, turned down stream, and we were off for the "seat of war." We arrived at Pittsburg Landing on March 31st. Pittsburg Landing, as its name indicates, was simply a landing place for steamboats. It is on the west bank of the Tennessee river, in a thickly wooded region about twenty miles northeast of Corinth. There was no town there then, nothing but "the log house on the hill" that the survivors of the battle of Shiloh will all remember. The banks of the Tennessee on the Pittsburg Landing side are steep and bluffy, rising about 100 feet above the level of the river. Shiloh church, that gave the battle its name, was a Methodist meeting house. It was a small, hewed log building with a clapboard roof, about two miles out from the landing on the main Corinth road. On our arrival we were assigned to the division of General B. M. Prentiss, and we at once marched out and went into camp. About half a mile from the landing the road forks, the main Corinth road goes to the right, past Shiloh church, the other goes to the left. These two roads come together again some miles out. General Prentiss' division was camped on this left-hand road at right angles to it. Our regiment went into camp almost on the extreme left of Prentiss' line. There was a brigade of Sherman's division under General Stuart still further to the left, about a mile, I think, in camp near a ford of Lick Creek, where the Hamburg and Purdy road crosses the creek; and between the left of Prentiss' and General Stuart's camp there were no troops. I know that, for during the few days intervening between our arrival and the battle I roamed all through those woods on our left, between us and Stuart, hunting for wild onions and "turkey peas."

The camp of our regiment was about two miles from the landing. The tents were pitched in the woods, and there was a little field of about twenty acres in our front. The camp faced nearly west, or possibly southwest.

I shall never forget how glad I was to get off that old steamboat and be on solid ground once more, in camp out in those old woods. My company had made the trip from St. Louis to Pittsburg Landing on the hurricane deck of the steamboat, and our fare on the route had been hardtack and raw fat meat, washed down with river water, as we had no chance to cook anything, and we had not then learned the trick of catching the surplus hot water ejected from the boilers and making coffee with it. But once on solid ground, with plenty of wood to make fires, that bill of fare was changed. I shall never again eat meat that will taste as good as the fried "sowbelly" did then, accompanied by "flapjacks" and plenty of good, strong coffee. We had not yet got settled down to the regular drills, guard duty was light, and things generally seemed to run "kind of loose." And then the climate was delightful. We had just left the bleak, frozen north, where all was cold and cheerless, and we found ourselves in a clime where the air was as soft and warm as it was in Illinois in the latter part of May. The green grass was springing from the ground, the "Johnny-jump-ups" were in blossom, the trees were bursting into leaf, and the woods were full of feathered songsters. There was a redbird that would come every morning about sunup and perch himself in the tall black-oak tree in our company street, and for perhaps an hour he would practice on his impatient, querulous note, that said, as plain as a bird could say, "Boys, boys! get up! get up! get up!" It became a standing remark among the boys that he was a Union redbird and had enlisted in our regiment to sound the reveille.

So the time passed pleasantly away until that eventful Sunday morning, April 6, 1862. According to the Tribune Almanac for that year, the sun rose that morning in Tennessee at 38 minutes past five o'clock. I had no watch, but I have always been of the opinion that the sun was fully an hour and a half high before the fighting began on our part of the line. We had "turned out" about sunup, answered to roll-call, and had cooked and eaten our breakfast. We had then gone to work, preparing for the regular Sunday morning inspection, which would take place at nine o'clock. The boys were scattered around the company streets and in front of the company parade grounds, engaged in polishing and brightening their muskets, and brushing up and cleaning their shoes, jackets, trousers, and clothing generally. It was a most beautiful morning. The sun was shining brightly through the trees, and there was not a cloud in the sky. It really seemed like Sunday in the country at home. During week days there was a continual stream of army wagons going to and from the landing, and the clucking of their wheels, the yells and oaths of the drivers, the cracking of whips, mingled with the braying of mules, the neighing of the horses, the commands of the officers engaged in drilling the men, the incessant hum and buzz of the camps, the blare of bugles, and the roll of drums,--all these made up a prodigious volume of sound that lasted from the coming-up to the going-down of the sun. But this morning was strangely still. The wagons were silent, the mules were peacefully munching their hay, and the army teamsters were giving us a rest. I listened with delight to the plaintive, mournful tones of a turtle-dove in the woods close by, while on the dead limb of a tall tree right in the camp a woodpecker was sounding his "long roll" just as I had heard it beaten by his Northern brothers a thousand times on the trees in the Otter Creek bottom at home.

Suddenly, away off on the right, in the direction of Shiloh

church, came a dull, heavy "Pum!" then another, and still another. Every man sprung to his feet as if struck by an electric shock, and we looked inquiringly into one another's faces. "What is that?" asked every one, but no one answered. Those heavy booms then came thicker and faster, and just a few seconds after we heard that first dull, ominous growl off to the southwest, came a low, sullen, continuous roar. There was no mistaking that sound. That was not a squad of pickets emptying their guns on being relieved from duty; it was the continuous roll of thousands of muskets, and told us that a battle was on.

What I have been describing just now occurred during a few seconds only, and with the roar of musketry the long roll began to beat in our camp. Then ensued a scene of desperate haste, the like of which I certainly had never seen before, nor ever saw again. I remember that in the midst of this terrible uproar and confusion, while the boys were buckling on their cartridge boxes, and before even the companies had been formed, a mounted staff officer came galloping wildly down the line from the right. He checked and whirled his horse sharply around right in our company street, the iron-bound hoofs of his steed crashing among the tin plates lying in a little pile where my mess had eaten its breakfast that morning. The horse was flecked with foam and its eyes and nostrils were red as blood. The officer cast one hurried glance around him, and exclaimed: "My God! this regiment not in line yet! They have been fighting on the right over an hour!" And wheeling his horse, he disappeared in the direction of the colonel's tent.

I know now that history says the battle began about 4:30 that morning; that it was brought on by a reconnoitering party sent out early that morning by General Prentiss; that General Sherman's division on the right was early advised of the approach of the Rebel army, and got ready to meet them in ample time. I have read these things in books and am not disputing them, but am simply telling the story of an enlisted man on the left of Prentiss' line as to what he saw and knew of the condition of things at about seven o'clock that morning.

Well, the companies were formed, we marched out on the regimental parade ground, and the regiment was formed in line. The command was given: "Load at will; load!" We had anticipated this, however, as the most of us had instinctively loaded our guns before we had formed company. All this time the roar on the right was getting nearer and louder. Our old colonel rode up close to us, opposite the center of the regimental line, and called out, "Attention, battalion!" We fixed our eyes on him to hear what was coming. It turned out to be the old man's battle harangue.

"Gentlemen," said he, in a voice that every man in the regiment heard, "remember your State, and do your duty today like brave men."

That was all. A year later in the war the old man doubtless would have addressed us as "soldiers," and not as "gentlemen," and he would have omitted his allusion to the "State," which smacked a little of Confederate notions. However, he was a Douglas Democrat, and his mind was probably running on Buena Vista, in the Mexican war, where, it is said, a Western regiment acted badly, and threw a cloud over the reputation for courage of the men of that State which required the thunders of the Civil War to disperse. Immediately after the colonel had given us his brief exhortation, the regiment was marched across the little field I have before mentioned, and we took our place in line of battle, the woods in front of us, and the open field in our rear. We "dressed on" the colors, ordered arms, and stood awaiting the attack. By this time the roar on the right had become terrific. The Rebel army was unfolding its front, and the battle was steadily advancing in our direction. We could begin to see the blue rings of smoke curling upward among the trees off to the right, and the pungent smell of burning gun-powder filled the air. As the roar came travelling down the line from the right it reminded me (only it was a million times louder) of the sweep of a thunder-shower in summer-time over the hard ground of a stubble-field.

And there we stood, in the edge of the woods, so still, waiting for the storm to break on us. I know mighty well what I was thinking about then. My mind's eye was fixed on a little log cabin, far away to the north, in the backwoods of western Illinois. I could see my father sitting on the porch, reading the little local newspaper brought from the post-office the evening before. There was my mother getting my little brothers ready for Sunday-school; the old dog lying asleep in the sun; the hens cackling about the barn; all these things and a hundred other tender recollections rushed into my mind. I am not ashamed to say now that I would willingly have given a general quit-claim deed for every jot and tittle of military glory falling to me, past, present, and to come, if I only could have been miraculously and instantaneously set down in the yard of that peaceful little home, a thousand miles away from the haunts of fighting men.

The time we thus stood, waiting the attack, could not have exceeded five minutes. Suddenly, obliquely to our right, there was a long, wavy flash of bright light, then another, and another! It was the sunlight shining on gun barrels and bayonets--and--there they were at last! A long brown line, with muskets at a right shoulder shift, in excellent order, right through the woods they came.

We began firing at once. From one end of the regiment to the other leaped a sheet of red flame, and the roar that went up from the edge of that old field doubtless advised General Prentiss of the fact that the Rebels had at last struck the extreme left of his line. We had fired but two or three rounds when, for some reason,--I never knew what,--we were ordered to fall back across the field, and did so. The whole line, so far as I could see to the right, went back. We halted on the other side of the field, in the edge of the woods, in front of our tents, and again began firing. The Rebels, of course, had moved up and occupied the line we had just abandoned. And here we did our first hard fighting during the day. Our officers said, after the battle was over, that we held this line an hour and ten minutes. How long it was I do not know. I "took no note of time."

We retreated from this position as our officers afterward said, because the troops on our right had given way, and we were flanked. Possibly those boys on our right would give the same excuse for their leaving, and probably truly, too. Still, I think we did not fall back a minute too soon. As I rose from the comfortable log from behind which a bunch of us had been firing, I saw men in gray and brown clothes, with trailed muskets, running through the camp on our right, and I saw something else, too, that sent a chill all through me. It was a kind of flag I had never seen before. It was a gaudy sort of thing, with red bars. It flashed over me in a second that that thing was a Rebel flag. It was not more than sixty yards to the right. The smoke around it was low and dense and kept me from seeing the man who was carrying it, but I plainly saw the banner. It was going fast, with a jerky motion, which told me that the bearer was on a double-quick. About that time we left. We observed no kind of order in leaving; the main thing was to get out of there as quick as we could. I ran down our company street, and in passing the big Sibley tent of our mess I thought of my knapsack with all my traps and belongings, including that precious little packet of letters from home. I said to myself, "I will save my knapsack, anyhow;" but one quick backward glance over my left shoulder made me change my mind, and I went on. I never saw my knapsack or any of its contents afterwards.

Our broken forces halted and re-formed about half a mile to the rear of our camp on the summit of a gentle ridge, covered with thick brush. I recognized our regiment by the little gray pony the old colonel rode, and hurried to my place in the ranks. Standing there with our faces once more to the front, I saw a seemingly endless column of men in blue, marching by the flank, who were filing off to the right through the woods, and I heard our old German adjutant, Cramer, say to the colonel, "Dose are de troops of Sheneral Hurlbut. He is forming a new line dere in de bush." I exclaimed to myself from the bottom of my heart, "Bully for General Hurlbut and the new line in the bush! Maybe we'll whip 'em yet." I shall never forget my feelings about this time. I was astonished at our first retreat in the morning across the field back to our camp, but it occurred to me that maybe that was only "strategy" and all done on purpose; but when we had to give up our camp, and actually turn our backs and run half a mile, it seemed to me that we were forever disgraced, and I kept thinking to myself: "What will they say about this at home?"

I was very dry for a drink, and as we were doing nothing just then, I slipped out of ranks and ran down to the little hollow in our rear, in search of water. Finding a little pool, I threw myself on the ground and took a copious draught. As I rose to my feet, I observed an officer about a rod above me also quenching his thirst, holding his horse meanwhile by the bridle. As he rose I saw it was our old adjutant. At no other time would I have dared accost him unless in the line of duty, but the situation made me bold. "Adjutant," I said, "What does this mean--our having to run this way? Ain't we whipped?" He blew the water from his mustache, and quickly answered in a careless way: "Oh, no; dat is all ride. We yoost fall back to form on the reserve. Sheneral Buell vas now crossing der river mit 50,000 men, and vill be here pooty quick; and Sheneral Lew Vallace is coming from Crump's Landing mit 15,000 more. Ve vips 'em; ve vips 'em. Go to your gompany." Back I went on the run, with a heart as light as a feather. As I took my place in the ranks beside my chum, Jack Medford, I said to him: "Jack, I've just had a talk with the old adjutant, down at the branch where I've been to get a drink. He says Buell is crossing the river with 75,000 men and a whole world of cannon, and that some other general is coming up from Crump's Landing with 25,000 more men. He says we fell back here on purpose, and that we're going to whip the Secesh, just sure. Ain't that just perfectly bully?" I had improved some on the adjutant's figures, as the news was so glorious I thought a little variance of 25,000 or 30,000 men would make no difference in the end. But as the long hours wore on that day, and still Buell and Wallace did not come, my faith in the adjutant's veracity became considerably shaken.

It was at this point that my regiment was detached from Prentiss' division and served with it no more that day. We were sent some distance to the right to support a battery, the name of which I never learned. It was occupying the summit of a slope, and was actively engaged when we reached it. We were put in position about twenty rods in the rear of the battery, and ordered to lie flat on the ground. The ground sloped gently down in our direction, so that by hugging it close, the rebel shot and shell went over us.

It was here, at about ten o'clock in the morning, that I first saw Grant that day. He was on horseback, of course, accompanied by his staff, and was evidently making a personal examination of his lines. He went by us in a gallop, riding between us and the battery, at the head of his staff. The battery was then hotly engaged; shot and shell were whizzing overhead, and cutting off the limbs of trees, but Grant rode through the storm with perfect indifference, seemingly paying no more attention to the missiles than if they had been paper wads.

We remained in support of this battery until about 2 o'clock in the afternoon. We were then put in motion by the right flank, filed to the left, crossed the left-hand Corinth road; then we were thrown into the line by the command: "By the left flank, march." We crossed a little ravine and up a slope, and relieved a regiment on the left of Hurlbut's line. This line was desperately engaged, and had been at this point, as we afterwards learned, for fully four hours. I remember as we went up the slope and began firing, about the first thing that met my gaze was what out West we would call a "windrow" of dead men in blue; some doubled up face downward, others with their white faces upturned to the sky, brave boys who had been shot to death in "holding the line." Here we stayed until our last cartridge was shot away. We were then relieved by another regiment. We filled our cartridge boxes again and went back to the support of our battery. The boys laid down and talked in low tones. Many of our comrades alive and well an hour ago, we had left dead on that bloody ridge. And still the battle raged. From right to left, everywhere, it was one never-ending, terrible roar, with no prospect of stopping.

Somewhere between 4 and 5 o'clock, as near as I can tell, everything became ominously quiet. Our battery ceased firing; the gunners leaned against the pieces and talked and laughed. Suddenly a staff officer rode up and said something in a low tone to the commander of the battery, then rode to our colonel and said something to him. The battery horses were at once brought up from a ravine in the rear, and the battery limbered up and moved off through the woods diagonally to the left and rear. We were put in motion by the flank and followed it. Everything kept so still, the loudest noise I heard was the clucking of the wheels of the gun-carriages and caissons as they wound through the woods. We emerged from the woods and entered a little old field. I then saw to our right and front lines of men in blue moving in the same direction we were, and it was evident that we were falling back. All at once, on the right, the left, and from our recent front, came one tremendous roar, and the bullets fell like hail. The lines took the double-quick towards the rear. For awhile the attempt was made to fall back in order, and then everything went to pieces. My heart failed me utterly. I thought the day was lost. A confused mass of men and guns, caissons, army wagons, ambulances, and all the debris of a beaten army surged and crowded along the narrow dirt road to the landing, while that pitiless storm of leaden hail came crashing on us from the rear. It was undoubtedly at this crisis in our affairs that the division of General Prentiss was captured.

I will digress here for a minute to speak of a little incident connected with this disastrous feature of the day that has always impressed me as a pathetic instance of the patriotism and unselfish devotion to the cause that was by no means uncommon among the rank and file of the Union armies.

There was in my company a middle-aged German named Charles Oberdieck. According to the company descriptive book, he was a native of the then kingdom of Hanover, now a province of Prussia. He was a typical German, flaxen-haired, blue-eyed, quiet and taciturn, of limited and meager education, but a model soldier, who accepted without question and obeyed without a murmur the orders of his military superiors. Prior to the war he had made his living by chopping cord-wood in the high, timbered hills near the mouth of the Illinois river, or by working as a common laborer in the country on the farms at $14 a month. He was unmarried, his parents were dead, and he had no other immediate relatives surviving, either in his fatherland or in the country of his adoption. He and I enlisted from the same neighborhood. I had known him in civil life at home, and hence he was disposed to be more communicative with me than with the other boys of the company. A day or two after the battle he and I were sitting in the shade of a tree, in camp, talking over the incidents of the fight. "Charley," I said to him, "How did you feel along about four o'clock Sunday afternoon when they broke our lines, we were falling back in disorder, and it looked like the whole business was gone up generally?" He knocked the ashes from his pipe and, turning his face quickly towards me, said: "I yoost tells you how I feels. I no care anydings about Charley; he haf no wife nor children, fadder nor mudder, brudder nor sister; if Charley get killed, it makes no difference; dere vas nobody to cry for him, so I dinks nudding about myselfs; but I tells you, I yoost den feels bad for de Cause!"

Noble, simple-hearted old Charley! It was the imminent danger only to the Cause that made his heart sink in that seemingly fateful hour. When we heard in the malignant and triumphant roar of the Rebel cannon in our rear what might be the death-knell of the last great experiment of civilized men to establish among the nations of the world a united republic, freed from the curse of pampered kings and selfish, grasping aristocrats--it was in that moment, in his simple language, that the peril to the Cause was the supreme and only consideration.

It must have been when we were less than half a mile from the landing on our disorderly retreat before mentioned, that we saw standing in line of battle, at ordered arms, extending from both sides of the road until lost to sight in the woods, a long, well-ordered line of men in blue. What did that mean? and where had they come from? I was walking by the side of Enoch Wallace, the orderly sergeant of my company. He was a man of nerve and courage, and by word and deed had done more that day to hold us green and untried boys in ranks and firmly to our duty than any other man in the company. But even he, in the face of this seemingly appalling state of things, had evidently lost heart. I said to him: "Enoch, what are those men there for?" He answered in a low tone: "I guess they are put there to hold the Rebels in check till the army can get across the river." And doubtless that was the thought of every intelligent soldier in our beaten column. And yet it goes to show how little the common soldier knew of the actual situation. We did not know then that this line was the last line of battle of the "Fighting Fourth Division" under General Hurlbut; that on its right was the division of McClernand, the Fort Donelson boys; that on its right, at right angles to it, and, as it were, the refused wing of the army, was glorious old Sherman, hanging on with a bulldog grip to the road across Snake Creek from Crump's Landing by which

Lew Wallace was coming with 5,000 men. In other words, we still had an unbroken line confronting the enemy, made up of men who were not yet ready, by any manner of means, to give up that they were whipped. Nor did we know then that our retreating mass consisted only of some regiments of Hurlbut's division, and some other isolated commands, who had not been duly notified of the recession of Hurlbut and of his falling back to form a new line, and thereby came very near sharing the fate of Prentiss' men and being marched to the rear as prisoners of war. Speaking for myself, it was twenty years after the battle before I found these things out, yet they are true, just as much so as the fact that the sun rose yesterday morning. Well, we filed through Hurlbut's line, halted, re-formed, and faced to the front once more. We were put in place a short distance in the rear of Hurlbut, as a support to some heavy guns. It must have been about five o'clock now. Suddenly, on the extreme left, and just a little above the landing, came a deafening explosion that fairly shook the ground beneath our feet, followed by others in quick and regular succession. The look of wonder and inquiry that the soldiers' faces wore for a moment disappeared for one of joy and exultation as it flashed across our minds that the gunboats had at last joined hands in the dance, and were pitching big twenty-pound Parrott shells up the ravine in front of Hurlbut, to the terror and discomfiture of our adversaries.

The last place my regiment assumed was close to the road coming up from the landing. As we were lying there I heard the strains of martial music and saw a body of men marching by the flank up the road. I slipped out of ranks and walked out to the side of the road to see what troops they were. Their band was playing "Dixie's Land," and playing it well. The men were marching at a quick step, carrying their guns, cartridge-boxes, haversacks, canteens, and blanket-rolls. I saw that they had not been in the fight, for there was no powder-smoke on their faces. "What regiment is this?" I asked of a young sergeant marching on the flank. Back came the answer in a quick, cheery tone, "The 36th Indiana, the advance guard of Buell's army."

I did not, on hearing this, throw my cap into the air and yell. That would have given those Indiana fellows a chance to chaff and guy me, and possibly make sarcastic remarks, which I did not care to provoke. I gave one big, gasping swallow and stood still, but the blood thumped in the veins of my throat and my heart fairly pounded against my little infantry jacket in the joyous rapture of this glorious intelligence. Soldiers need not be told of the thrill of unspeakable exultation they all have felt at the sight of armed friends in danger's darkest hour. Speaking for myself alone, I can only say, in the most heart-felt sincerity, that in all my obscure military career, never to me was the sight of reinforcing legions so precious and so welcome as on that Sunday evening when the rays of the descending sun were flashed back from the bayonets of Buell's advance column as it deployed on the bluffs of Pittsburg Landing.

My account of the battle is about done. So far as I saw or heard, very little fighting was done that evening after Buell's advance crossed the river. The sun must have been fully an hour high when anything like regular and continuous firing had entirely ceased. What the result would have been if Beauregard had massed his troops on our left and forced the fighting late Sunday evening would be a matter of opinion, and a common soldier's opinion would not be considered worth much.

My regiment was held in reserve the next day, and was not engaged. I have, therefore, no personal experience of that day to relate. After the battle of Shiloh, it fell to my lot to play my humble part in several other fierce conflicts of arms, but Shiloh was my maiden fight. It was there I first saw a gun fired in anger, heard the whistle of a bullet, or saw a man die a violent death, and my experiences, thoughts, impressions, and sensations on that bloody Sunday will abide with me as long as I live.

CHAPTER IV

SOME INCIDENTS of the BATTLE of SHILOH.

There were many little incidents at Shiloh that came under my personal observation that I did not mention in the foregoing sketch. The matter of space was important, so I passed them over. But that consideration does not arise now, and as I am writing this for you, I will say something here about several things that I think may be of some interest.

I distinctly remember my first shot at Shiloh. It was fired when we were in our first position, as described in my account of the battle. I think that when the boys saw the enemy advancing they began firing of their own motion, without waiting for orders. At least, I don't remember hearing any. I was in the front rank, but didn't fire. I preferred to wait for a good opportunity, when I could take deliberate aim at some individual foe. But when the regiment fired, the Confederates halted and began firing also, and the fronts of both lines were at once shrouded in smoke. I had my gun at a ready, and was trying to peer under the smoke in order to get a sight of our enemies. Suddenly I heard someone in a highly excited tone calling to me from just in my rear,--"Stillwell! shoot! shoot! Why don't you shoot?" I looked around and saw that this command was being given by Bob Wylder, our second lieutenant, who was in his place, just a few steps to the rear. He was a young man, about twenty-five years old, and was fairly wild with excitement, jumping up and down "like a hen on a hot griddle." "Why, lieutenant," said I, "I can't see anything to shoot at." "Shoot, shoot, anyhow!" "All right," I responded, "if you say shoot, shoot it is;" and bringing my gun to my shoulder, I aimed low in the direction of the enemy, and blazed away through the smoke. I have always doubted if this, my first shot, did any execution--but there's no telling. However, the lieutenant was clearly right. Our adversaries were in our front, in easy range, and it was our duty to aim low, fire in their general direction, and let fate do the rest. But at the time the idea to me was ridiculous that one should blindly shoot into a cloud of smoke without having a bead on the object to be shot at. I had shot squirrels and rabbits, and other small game, in the big woods adjacent to our backwoods home, from the time I was big enough to carry a gun. In fact, I began when I was too small to shoot "off hand," but had to fire from a "rest,"--any convenient stump, log, or forked bush. The gun I used was a little old percussion lock rifle, with a long barrel, carrying a bullet which weighed about sixty to the pound. We boys had to furnish our own ammunition,--lead (which we moulded into bullets), gun-caps, and powder. Our principal source of revenue whereby we got money to buy ammunition was hazel-nuts, which we would gather, shuck, and sell at five cents a quart. And the work incident to the gathering and shucking of a quart of hazel nuts was a decidedly tedious job. But it made us economical in the use of our ordnance stores, so we would never throw away a shot carelessly or unnecessarily. And it was a standing rule never to shoot a squirrel anywhere except in the head, save as a last resort, when circumstances compelled one to fire at some other part of the body of the little animal. And so I thought, at the beginning of my military career, that I should use the same care and circumspection in firing an old musket when on the line of battle that I had exercised in hunting squirrels. But I learned better in about the first five minutes of the battle of Shiloh. However, in every action I was in, when the opportunity was afforded, I took careful and deliberate aim, but many a time the surroundings were such that the only thing to do was to hold low, and fire through the smoke in the direction of the enemy. I will say here that the extent of wild shooting done in battle, especially by raw troops, is astonishing, and rather hard to understand. When we fell back to our second line at Shiloh, I heard an incessant humming sound away up above our heads, like the flight of a swarm of bees. In my ignorance, I at first hardly knew what that meant, but it presently dawned on me that the noise was caused by bullets singing through the air from twenty to a hundred feet over our heads. And after the battle I noticed that the big trees in our camp, just in the rear of our second line, were thickly pock-marked by musket balls at a distance of fully a hundred feet from the ground. And yet we were separated from the Confederates only by a little, narrow field, and the intervening ground was perfectly level. But the fact is, those boys were fully as green as we were, and doubtless as much excited. The Confederate army at Shiloh was composed of soldiers the great majority of whom went under fire there for the first time, and I reckon they were as nervous and badly scared as we were.

I never shall forget how awfully I felt on seeing for the first time a man killed in battle. This occurred on our second position, above mentioned. Our line of battle here was somewhat irregular, and the men had become mixed up. The trees and stumps were thick, and we availed ourselves of their protection whenever possible. I had a tree, it was embarrassingly small, but better than none. I took to a log later. But there was a man just on my right behind a tree of generous proportions, and I somewhat envied him. He was actively engaged in loading and firing, and was standing up to the work well when I last saw him alive. But, all at once, there he was lying on his back, at the foot of his tree, with one leg doubled under him, motionless,--and stone dead! He probably had been hit square in the head while aiming, or peeking around the tree. I stared at his body, perfectly horrified! Only a few seconds ago that man was alive and well, and now he was lying on the ground, done for, forever! The event came nearer completely upsetting me than anything else that occurred during the entire battle--but I got used to such incidents in the course of the day.

After rallying at our third position, we were moved a short distance to the rear, and formed in line at right angles to the road from our camp to the landing. While standing there I casually noticed a large wall tent at the side of the road, a few steps to my rear. It was closed up, and nobody stirring around it. Suddenly I heard, right over our heads, a frightful "s-s-wis-sh,"--and followed by a loud crash in this tent. Looking around, I saw a big, gaping hole in the wall of the tent, and on the other side got a glimpse of the cause of the disturbance--a big cannon ball ricochetting down the ridge, and hunting further mischief. And at the same moment of time the front flaps of the tent were frantically thrown open, and out popped a fellow in citizen's clothes. He had a Hebrew visage, his face was as white as a dead man's, and his eyes were sticking out like a crawfish's. He started down the road toward the landing at probably the fastest gait he had ever made in his life, his coat tails streaming behind him, and the boys yelling at him. We proceeded to investigate the interior of that tent at once, and found that it was a sutler's establishment, and crammed with sutler goods. The panic-struck individual who had just vacated it was of course the proprietor. He had adopted ostrich tactics, had buttoned himself up in the tent, and was in there keeping as still as a mouse, thinking, perhaps, that as he could see nobody, nobody could see him. That cannon ball must have been a rude surprise. In order to have plenty of "han' roomance," we tore down the tent at once, and then proceeded to appropriate the contents. There were barrels of apples, bologna sausages, cheeses, canned oysters and sardines, and lots of other truck. I was filling my haversack with bologna when Col. Fry rode up to me and said: "My son, will you please give me a link of that sausage?" Under the circumstances, I reckon I must have been feeling somewhat impudent and reckless, so I answered rather saucily, "Certainly, Colonel, we are closing out this morning below cost;" and I thrust into his hands two or three big links of bologna. There was a faint trace of a grin on the old man's face as he took the provender, and he began gnawing at once on one of the hunks, while the others he stowed away in his equipments. I suspected from this incident that the Colonel had had no breakfast that morning, which perhaps may have been the case. Soon after this I made another deal. There were some cavalry in line close by us, and one of them called out to me, "Pardner, give me some of them apples." "You bet;" said I, and quickly filling my cap with the fruit, handed it to him. He emptied the apples in his haversack, took a silver dime from his pocket, and proffered it to me, saying, "Here." "Keep your money--don't want it;" was my response, but he threw the coin at my feet, and I picked it up and put it in my pocket. It came agreeably handy later.

Jack Medford of my company came up to me with a most complacent look on his face, and patting his haversack, said,

"Lee, I just now got a whole lot of paper and envelopes, and am all fixed for writing home about this battle." "Seems to me, Jack," I suggested, "you'd better unload that stuff, and get something to eat. Don't worry about writing home about the battle till it's done fought." Jack's countenance changed, he muttered, "Reckon you're right, Lee;" and when next I saw him, his haversack was bulging with bologna and cheese. All this time the battle was raging furiously on our right, and occasionally a cannon ball, flying high, went screaming over our heads. Walter Scott, in "The Lady of the Lake," in describing an incident of the battle of Beal' an Duine, speaks of the unearthly screaming and yelling that occurred, sounding--

"As if all the fiends from heaven that fell
Had pealed the banner-cry of hell."

That comparison leaves much for the imagination, but, speaking from experience, I will say that of all the blood-curdling sounds I ever heard, the worst is the terrific scream of a cannon ball or shell passing close over one's head; especially that kind with a cavity in the base that sucks in air. At least, they sounded that way till I got used to them. As a matter of fact, artillery in my time was not near as dangerous as musketry. It was noisy, but didn't kill often unless at close range and firing grape and canister.

As stated in the preceding sketch, sometime during the forenoon the regiment was sent to the support of a battery, and remained there for some hours. The most trying situation in battle is one where you have to lie flat on the ground, under fire more or less, and without any opportunity to return it. The constant strain on the nerves is almost intolerable. So it was with feelings of grim but heart-felt relief that we finally heard the Colonel command, "Attention, battalion!" Our turn had come at last. We sprang to our feet with alacrity, and were soon in motion, marching by the flank diagonally towards the left, from whence, for some hours, had been proceeding heavy firing. We had not gone far before I saw something which hardly had an inspiring effect. We were marching along an old, grass-grown country road, with a rail-fence on the right which enclosed a sort of woods pasture, and with a dense forest on our left, when I saw a soldier on our left, slowly making his way to the rear. He had been struck a sort of glancing shot on the left side of his face, and the skin and flesh of his cheek were hanging in shreds. His face and neck were covered with blood and he was a frightful sight. Yet he seemed to be perfectly cool and composed and wasn't "taking on" a bit. As he came opposite my company, he looked up at us and said, "Give 'em hell, boys! They've spoiled my beauty." It was manifest that he was not exaggerating.

When we were thrown into line on our new position and began firing, I was in the front rank, and my rear rank man was Philip Potter, a young Irishman, who was some years my senior. When he fired his first shot, he came very near putting me out of action. I think that the muzzle of his gun could not have been more than two or three inches from my right ear. The shock of the report almost deafened me at the time, and my neck and right cheek were peppered with powder grains, which remained there for years until finally absorbed in the system. I turned to Phil in a fury, exclaiming, "What in the hell and damnation do you mean?" Just then down went the man on my right with a sharp cry, and followed by the one on the left, both apparently severely wounded. The thought of my shocking conduct, in thus indulging in wicked profanity at such a time, flashed upon me, and I almost held my breath, expecting summary punishment on the spot. But nothing of the kind happened. And, according to history, Washington swore a good deal worse at the battle of Monmouth,--and Potter was more careful thereafter.

Poor Phil! On December 7, 1864, while fighting on the skirmish line near Murfreesboro, Tennessee, and just a few paces to my left, he was mortally wounded by a gun-shot in the bowels and died in the hospital a few days later. He was a Catholic, and in his last hours was almost frantic because no priest was at hand to grant him absolution.

Right after we began firing on this line I noticed, directly in my front and not more than two hundred yards away, a large Confederate flag flapping defiantly in the breeze. The smoke was too dense to enable me to see the bearer, but the banner was distinctly visible. It looked hateful to me, and I wanted to see it come down. So I held on it, let my gun slowly fall until I thought the sights were about on a waist line, and then fired. I peered eagerly under the smoke to see the effect of my shot,--but the blamed thing was still flying. I fired three or four more shots on the same line as the first, but with no apparent results. I then concluded that the bearer was probably squatted behind a stump, or something, and that it was useless to waste ammunition on him. Diagonally to my left, perhaps two hundred and fifty yards away, the Confederate line of battle was in plain sight. It was in the open, in the edge of an old field, with woods to the rear. It afforded a splendid mark. Even the ramrods could be seen flashing in the air, as the men, while in the act of loading, drew and returned the rammers. Thereupon I began firing at the enemy on that part of the line, and the balance of the contents of my cartridge box went in that direction. It was impossible to tell if any of my shots took effect, but after the battle I went to the spot and looked over the ground. The Confederate dead lay there thick, and I wondered, as I looked at them, if I had killed any of those poor fellows. Of course I didn't know, and am glad now that I didn't. And I will say here that I do not now have any conclusive knowledge that during my entire term of service I ever killed, or even wounded, a single man. It is more than probable that some of my shots were fatal, but I don't know it, and am thankful for the ignorance. You see, after all, the common soldiers of the Confederate Armies were American boys, just like us, and conscientiously believed that they were right. Had they been soldiers of a foreign nation,--Spaniards, for instance,--I might feel differently.

When we "went in" on the above mentioned position old Capt. Reddish took his place in the ranks, and fought like a common soldier. He had picked up the musket of some dead or wounded man, and filled his pockets with cartridges and gun caps, and so was well provided with ammunition. He unbuckled his sword from the belt, and laid it in the scabbard at his feet, and proceeded to give his undivided attention to the enemy. I can now see the old man in my mind's eye, as he stood in ranks, loading and firing, his blue-gray eyes flashing, and his face lighted up with the flame of battle. Col. Fry happened to be near us at one time, and I heard old Capt. John yell at him: "Injun fightin,' Colonel! Jest like Injun fightin'!" When we finally retired, the Captain shouldered his musket and trotted off with the rest of us, oblivious of his "cheese-knife," as he called it, left it lying on the ground, and never saw it again.

There was a battery of light artillery on this line, about a quarter of a mile to our right, on a slight elevation of the ground. It was right flush up with the infantry line of battle, and oh, how those artillery men handled their guns! It seemed to me that there was the roar of a cannon from that battery about every other second. When ramming cartridge, I sometimes glanced in that direction. The men were big fellows, stripped to the waist, their white skins flashing in the sunlight, and they were working like I have seen men doing when fighting a big fire in the woods. I fairly gloated over the fire of that battery. "Give it to them, my sons of thunder!" I would say to myself; "Knock the ever-lastin' stuffin' out of 'em!" And, as I ascertained after the battle, they did do frightful execution.

In consideration of the fact that now-a-days, as you know, I refuse to even kill a chicken, some of the above expressions may sound rather strange. But the fact is, a soldier on the fighting line is possessed by the demon of destruction. He wants to kill, and the more of his adversaries he can see killed, the more intense his gratification. Gen. Grant somewhere in his Memoirs expresses the idea (only in milder language than mine) when he says:

"While a battle is raging one can see his enemy mowed down by the thousand, or the ten thousand, with great composure."

The regiment bivouacked for the night on the bluff, not far from the historic "log house." Rain set in about dark, and not wanting to lie in the water, I hunted around and found a little brush-pile evidently made by some man from a sapling he had cut down and trimmed up some time past when the leaves were on the trees. I made a sort of pillow out of my gun, cartridge box, haversack and canteen, and stretched myself out on the brush-pile, tired to death, and rather discouraged over the events of the day. The main body of Buell's men,--"the army of the Ohio,"--soon after dark began ascending the bluff at a point a little above the landing, and forming in line in the darkness a short distance beyond. I have a shadowy impression that this lasted the greater part of the night. Their regimental bands played continuously and it seemed to me that they all played the tune of "The Girl I Left Behind Me." And the rain drizzled down, while every fifteen minutes one of the big navy guns roared and sent a ponderous shell shrieking up the ravine above in the direction of the enemy. To this day, whenever I hear an instrumental band playing "The Girl I Left Behind Me," there come to me the memories of that gloomy Sunday night at Pittsburg Landing. I again hear the ceaseless patter of the rain, the dull, heavy tread of Buell's marching columns, the thunderous roar of the navy guns, the demoniacal scream of the projectile, and mingled with it all is the sweet, plaintive music of that old song. We had an army version of it I have never seen in print, altogether different from the original ballad. The last stanza of this army production was as follows:

"If ever I get through this war,
And a Rebel ball don't find me,
I'll shape my course by the northern star,
To the girl I left behind me."

I have said elsewhere that the regiment was not engaged on Monday. We remained all that day at the place where we bivouacked Sunday night. The ends of the staffs of our regimental flags were driven in the ground, the banners flapping idly in the breeze, while the men sat or lay around with their guns in their hands or lying by them, their cartridge-boxes buckled on, and all ready to fall in line at the tap of the drum. But for some reason that I never knew, we were not called on. Our division commander, General B. M. Prentiss, and our brigade commander, Col. Madison Miller, were both captured on Sunday with the bulk of Prentiss' division, so I reckon we were sort of "lost children." But we were not alone. There were also other regiments of Grant's command which were held in reserve and did not fire a shot on Monday.

After the battle I roamed around over the field, the most of the following two days, looking at what was to be seen. The fearful sights apparent on a bloody battlefield simply cannot be described in all their horror. They must be seen in order to be fully realized. As Byron, somewhere in "Don Juan," truly says:

"Mortality! Thou hast thy monthly bills,
Thy plagues, thy famines, thy physicians, yet tick,
Like the death-watch, within our ears the ills
Past, present, and to come; but all may yield
To the true portrait of one battlefield."

There was a small clearing on the battlefield called the "Peach Orchard" field. It was of irregular shape, and about fifteen or twenty acres in extent, as I remember. However, I cannot now be sure as to the exact size. It got its name, probably, from the fact that there were on it a few scraggy peach trees. The Union troops on Sunday had a strong line in the woods just north of the field, and the Confederates made four successive charges across this open space on our line, all of which were repulsed with frightful slaughter. I walked all over this piece of ground the day after the close of the battle, and before the dead had been buried. It is the simple truth to say that this space was literally covered with the Confederate dead, and one could have walked all over it on their bodies. Gen. Grant, in substance, makes the same statement in his Memoirs. It was a fearful sight. But not far from the Peach Orchard field, in a westerly direction, was a still more gruesome spectacle. Some of our forces were in line on an old, grass-grown country road that ran through thick woods. The wheels of wagons, running for many years right in the same ruts, had cut through the turf, so that the surface of the road was somewhat lower than the adjacent ground. To men firing on their knees this afforded a slight natural breastwork, which was substantial protection. In front of this position, in addition to the large timber, was a dense growth of small under-brush, post-oak and the like, which had not yet shed their leaves, and the ground also was covered with layers of dead leaves. There was desperate fighting at this point, and during its progress exploding shells set the woods on fire. The clothing of the dead Confederates lying in these woods caught fire, and their bodies were burned to a crisp. I have read, somewhere, that some wounded men were burned to death, but I doubt that. I walked all over the ground looking at these poor fellows, and scrutinized them carefully to see the nature of their hurts and they had evidently been shot dead, or expired in a few seconds after being struck. But, in any event, the sight was horrible. I will not go into details, but leave it to your imagination.

I noticed, at other places on the field, the bodies of two Confederate soldiers, whose appearance I shall never forget. They presented a remarkable contrast of death in battle. One was a full grown man, seemingly about thirty years of age, with sandy, reddish hair, and a scrubby beard and mustache of the same color. He had been firing from behind a tree, had exposed his head, and had been struck square in the forehead by a musket ball, killed instantly, and had dropped at the foot of the tree in a heap. He was in the act of biting a cartridge when struck, his teeth were still fastened on the paper extremity, while his right hand clutched the bullet end. His teeth were long and snaggy, and discolored by tobacco juice. As just stated, he had been struck dead seemingly instantaneously. His eyes were wide open and gleaming with Satanic fury. His transition from life to death had been immediate, with the result that there was indelibly stamped on his face all the furious rage and lust of battle. He was an ill-looking fellow, and all in all was not an agreeable object to contemplate. The other was a far different case. He was lying on a sloping ridge, where the Confederates had charged a battery, and had suffered fearfully. He was a mere boy, not over eighteen, with regular features, light brown hair, blue eyes, and, generally speaking, was strikingly handsome. He had been struck on his right leg, above the knee, about mid-way the thigh, by a cannon ball, which had cut off the limb, except a small strip of skin. He was lying on his back, at full length, his right arm straight up in the air, rigid as a stake, and his fist tightly clinched. His eyes were wide open, but their expression was calm and natural. The shock and the loss of blood doubtless brought death to his relief in a short time. As I stood looking at the unfortunate boy, I thought of how some poor mother's heart would be well-nigh broken when she heard of the sad, untimely fate of her darling son. But, before the war was over, doubtless thousands of similar cases occurred in both the Union and Confederate armies.

I believe I will here speak of a notion of mine, to be considered for whatever you may think it worth. As you know, I am not a religious man, in the theological sense of the term, having never belonged to a church in my life. Have just tried, to the best of my ability, to act according to the Golden Rule, and let it go at that. But, from my earliest youth, I have had a peculiar reverence for Sunday. I hunted much with a gun when a boy, and so did the people generally of my neighborhood. Small game in that backwoods region was very plentiful, and even deer were not uncommon. Well, it was a settled conviction with us primitive people that if one went hunting on Sunday, he would not only have bad luck in that regard that day, but also all the rest of the week. So, when the Confederates began the battle on Sunday, I would keep thinking, throughout its entire progress, "You fellows started this on Sunday, and you'll get licked." I'll admit that there were a few occasions when things looked so awful bad that I became discouraged, but I quickly rallied, and my Sunday superstition--or whatever it may be called--was justified in the end. In addition to Shiloh, the battles of New Orleans in 1815, Waterloo, and Bull Run were fought on a Sunday, and in each case the attacking party was signally defeated. These results may have been mere coincidences, but I don't think so. I have read somewhere an authentic statement that President Lincoln entertained this same belief, and always was opposed to aggressive movements on Sundays by the Union troops.

The wildest possible rumors got into circulation at home, about some of the results of the battle. I have now lying before me an old letter from my father of date April 19th, in answer to mine (which I will mention later) giving him the first definite intelligence about our regiment and the neighborhood boys. Among other things he said: "We have had it here that Fry's regiment was all captured that was not killed; pretty much all given up as lost. That Beauregard had run you all down a steep place into the Tennessee river, *** that Captain Reddish had his arm shot off, that Enoch Wallace was also wounded;"-

-and here followed the names of some others who (the same as Reddish and Wallace) hadn't received even a scratch. My letter to my father, mentioned above, was dated April 10, and was received by him on the 18th. It was brief, occupying only about four pages of the small, sleazy note paper that we bought in those days of the sutlers. I don't remember why I didn't write sooner, but it was probably because no mail-boat left the landing until about that time. The old mail hack ordinarily arrived at the Otter Creek post-office from the outside world an hour or so before sundown, and the evening my letter came, the little old post-office and general store was crowded with people intensely anxious to hear from their boys or other relatives in the 61st Illinois. The distribution of letters in that office in those times was a proceeding of much simplicity. The old clerk who attended to that would call out in a stentorian tone the name of the addressee of each letter, who, if present, would respond "Here!" and then the letter would be given a dexterous flip, and went flying to him across the room. But on this occasion there were no letters from the regiment, until just at the last the clerk called my father's name--"J. O. Stillwell!" and again, still louder, but there was no response. Whereupon the clerk held the letter at arm's length, and carefully scrutinized the address. "Well," said he finally, "this is from Jerry Stillwell's boy, in the 61st, so I reckon he's not killed, anyhow." A murmur of excitement went through the room at this, and the people crowded up to get a glimpse of even the handwriting of the address. "Yes, that's from Jerry's boy, sure," said several. Thereupon William Noble and Joseph Beeman, who were old friends of father's, begged the postmaster to "give them the letter, and they would go straight out to Stillwell's with it, have him read it, and then they would come right back with the news." Everybody seconded the request, the postmaster acceded, and handed one of them the letter. They rushed out, unfastened their horses, and left in a gallop for Stillwell's, two miles away, on the south side of Otter Creek, out in the woods. As they dashed up to the little old log cabin they saw my father out near the barn; the one with the letter waved it aloft, calling at the top of his voice: "Letter from your boy, Jerry!" My mother heard this, and she came running from the house, trembling with excitement. The letter was at once opened and read,--and the terrible reports which to that time had prevailed about the fate of Fry's regiment vanished in the air. It's true, it contained some sad news, but nothing to be compared with the fearful accounts which had been rife in the neighborhood. I have that old letter in my possession now.

Soon after the battle Gov. Richard Yates, of Illinois, Gov. Louis P. Harvey, of Wisconsin, and many other civilians, came down from the north to look after the comfort of the sick and wounded soldiers of their respective states. The 16th Wisconsin Infantry was camped next to us, and I learned one afternoon that Gov. Harvey was to make them a speech that evening, after dress parade, and I went over to hear him. The Wisconsin regiment did not turn out in military formation, just gathered around him in a dense group under a grove of trees. The Governor sat on a horse while making his speech. He wore a large, broad-brimmed hat, his coat was buttoned to the chin, and he had big buckskin gauntlets on his hands. He was a fine looking man, heavy set, and about forty-two years old. His remarks were not lengthy, but were patriotic and eloquent. I remember especially how he complimented the Wisconsin soldiers for their good conduct in battle, that their state was proud of them, and that he, as Governor, intended to look after them, and care for them to the very best of his ability, as long as he was in office, and that when the time came for him to relinquish that trust, he would still remember them with interest and the deepest affection. His massive frame heaved with the intensity of his feelings as he spoke and he impressed me as being absolutely sincere in all that he said. But he little knew nor apprehended the sad and lamentable fate then pending over him. Only a few evenings later, as he was crossing the gang-plank between two steamboats at the Landing, in some manner he fell from the plank, and was sucked under the boats by the current, and drowned. Some days later a negro found his body, lodged against some drift near our side of the river, and he brought it in his old cart inside our lines. From papers on the body, and other evidence, it was conclusively identified as that of Gov. Harvey. The remains were shipped back to Wisconsin, where they were given a largely attended and impressive funeral.

CHAPTER V

THE SIEGE of CORINTH. IN CAMP at OWL CREEK. APRIL and MAY, 1862.

A few days after the battle Gen. H. W. Halleck came down from St. Louis, and assumed command of the Union forces in the field near Pittsburg Landing. Then, or soon thereafter, began the so-called siege of Corinth. We mighty near dug up all the country within eight or ten miles of that place in the progress of this movement, in the construction of forts, long lines of breast-works, and such like. Halleck was a "book soldier," and had a high reputation during the war as a profound "strategist," and great military genius in general. In fact, in my opinion (and which, I think, is sustained by history), he was a humbug and a fraud. His idea seemed to be that our war should be conducted strictly in accordance with the methods of the old Napoleonic wars of Europe, which, in the main, were not at all adapted to our time and conditions. Moreover, he seemed to be totally deficient in sound, practical common sense. Soon after the Confederates evacuated Corinth he was transferred to Washington to serve in a sort of advisory capacity, and spent the balance of the war period in a swivel-chair in an office. He never was in a battle, and never heard a gun fired, except distant cannonading during the Corinth business,--and (maybe) at Washington in the summer of 1864.

During the operations against Corinth, the 61st made some short marches, and was shifted around, from time to time, to different places. About the middle of May we were sent to a point on Owl creek, in the right rear of the main army. Our duty there was to guard against any possible attack from that direction, and our main employment was throwing up breast-works and standing picket. And all this time the sick list was frightfully large. The chief trouble was our old enemy, camp diarrhea, but there were also other types of diseases--malaria and the like. As before stated, the boys had not learned how to cook, nor to take proper care of themselves, and to this ignorance can be attributed much of the sickness. And the weather was rainy, the camps were muddy and gloomy, and about this time many of the boys had home-sickness bad. A genuine case of downright home-sickness is most depressing. I had some touches of it myself, so I can speak from experience. The poor fellows would sit around in their tents, and whine, and talk about home, and what good things they would have there to eat, and kindred subjects, until apparently they lost every spark of energy. I kept away from such cases all I could, for their talk was demoralizing. But one rainy day while in camp at Owl creek I was in our big Sibley tent when some of the boys got well started on their pet topics. It was a dismal day, the rain was pattering down on the tent and dripping from the leaves of the big oak trees in the camp, while inside the tent everything was damp and mouldy and didn't smell good either. "Jim," says one, "I wish I could jest be down on Coon crick today, and take dinner with old Bill Williams; I'll tell you what I'd have: first, a great big slice of fried ham, with plenty of rich brown gravy, with them light, fluffy, hot biscuits that Bill's wife could cook so well, and then I'd want some big baked Irish 'taters, red hot, and all mealy, and then----" "Yes, Jack," interrupted Jim, "I've et at old Bill's lots of times, and wouldn't I like to be with you? You know, old Bill always mast-fed the hogs he put up for his own eatin', they jest fattened on hickory nuts and big white- and bur-oak acorns, and he'd smoke his meat with hickory wood smoke, and oh, that meat was jest so sweet and nutty-like!--why, the meat of corn-fed hogs was nowhere in comparison." "Yes, Jim," continued Jack, "and then I'd want with the biscuits and 'taters plenty of that rich yaller butter that Bill's wife made herself, with her own hands, and then you know Bill always had lots of honey, and I'd spread honey and butter on one of them biscuits, and----" "And don't you remember, Jack," chimed in Jim, "the mince pies Bill's wife could make? They were jest stuffed with reezons, and all manner of goodies, and----" But here I left the tent in disgust. I wanted to say, "Oh, hell!" as I went out, but refrained. The poor fellows were feeling bad enough, anyhow, and it wouldn't have helped matters to make sarcastic remarks. But I preferred the shelter of a big tree, and enduring the rain that filtered through the leaves, rather than listen to this distracting talk of Jack and Jim about the flesh-pots of old Bill Williams. But while on this subject, I believe I'll tell you about a royal dinner I had myself while the regiment was near Pittsburg Landing. It was a few days after the battle, while we were still at our old camp. I was detailed, as corporal, to take six men and go to the Landing and load three or four of our regimental wagons with army rations for our regiment. We reached the Landing about ten o'clock, reported to the proper officer, who showed us our stuff, and we went to piling it into the wagons. It consisted of big slabs of fat side-bacon ("sow-belly"), boxes of hardtack, sacks of rice, beans, coffee, sugar, and soap and candles. I had an idea that I ought to help in the work, and was trying to do so, altho so weak from illness that it required some effort to walk straight. But a big, black haired, black bearded Irishman, Owen McGrath of my company, one of the squad, objected. He laid a big hand kindly on my shoulder, and said: "Carparral, yez is not sthrong enough for this worrk, and yez don't have to do it, ayether. Jist give me the 't'ority to shupirintind it, and you go sit down." "I guess you're right, McGrath," I answered, and then, in a louder tone, for the benefit of the detail, "McGrath, you see to the loading of the grub. I am feeling a little out of sorts," (which was true,) "and I believe I'll take a rest." McGrath was about thirty years old, and a splendid soldier. He had served a term in the British army in the old country, and was fully onto his present job. (I will tell another little story about him later.) I sat down in the shade a short distance from my squad, with my back against some big sacks full of something. Suddenly I detected a pungent, most agreeable smell. It came from onions, in the sack behind me. I took out my pocket knife and stealthily made a hole in that sack, and abstracted two big ones and slipped them into my haversack. My conscience didn't trouble me a bit over the matter. I reckon those onions were hospital goods, but I thought I needed some just as much as anybody in the hospital, which was probably correct. I had asked Capt. Reddish that morning if, when the wagons were loaded, I could send them on to camp, and return at my leisure in the evening, and the kindhearted old man had given a cheerful consent. So, when the teams were ready to start back, I told McGrath to take charge, and to see that the stuff was delivered to our quartermaster, or the commissary sergeant, and then I shifted for myself, planning for the good dinner that was in prospect. There were many steamboats lying at the Landing, I selected one that looked inviting, went on board, and sauntered aft to the cook's quarters. It was near dinner time, and the grub dispenser was in the act of taking from his oven a number of nice cakes of corn bread. I sidled up to him, and displaying that dime the cavalryman gave me for those apples, asked him in a discreetly low tone, if he would let me have a cake of corn bread. He gave a friendly grin, pushed a cake towards me, I slipped it in my haversack, and handed him the dime. Now I was fixed. I went ashore, and down the river for a short distance to a spring I knew of, that bubbled from the ground near the foot of a big beech tree. It did not take long to build a little fire and make coffee in my oyster can of a quart's capacity, with a wire bale attachment. Then a slice of sow-belly was toasted on a stick, the outer skin of the onions removed--and dinner was ready. Talk about your gastronomic feasts! I doubt if ever in my life I enjoyed a meal better than this one, under that old beech, by the Tennessee river. The onions were big red ones, and fearfully strong, but my system craved them so much that I just chomped them down as if they were apples. And every crumb of the corn bread was eaten, too. Dinner over, I felt better, and roamed around the rest of the afternoon, sight-seeing, and didn't get back to camp till nearly sundown. By the way, that spring and that beech tree are there yet, or were in October, 1914, when I visited the Shiloh battlefield. I hunted them up on this occasion and laid down on the ground and took a long, big drink out of the spring for the sake of old times.

Taking up again the thread of our life in camp at Owl creek, I will say that when there I was for a while in bad physical condition, and nearly "all in." One day I accidentally overheard two intelligent boys of my company talking about me, and one said, "If Stillwell aint sent north purty soon, he's goin' to make a die of it;" to which the other assented. That scared me good, and set me to thinking. I had no use for the hospital, wouldn't go there, and abominated the idea of taking medicine. But I was so bad off I was not marked for duty, my time was all my own, so I concluded to get out of camp as much as possible, and take long walks in the big woods. I found a place down on the creek between two picket posts where it was easy to sneak through and get out into the country, and I proceeded to take advantage of it. It was where a big tree had fallen across the stream, making a sort of natural bridge, and I "run the line" there many a time. It was delightful to get out into the clean, grand old woods, and away from the mud, and filth, and bad smells of the camp, and my health began to improve. On some of these rambles, Frank Gates, a corporal of my company, was my companion. He was my senior a few years, a lively fellow, with a streak of humor in him, and was good company. One day on one of our jaunts we came to a little old log house near the foot of a densely timbered ridge. There was nobody at home save some women and children, and one of the women was engaged on an old-fashioned churn, churning butter. Mulberries were ripe, and there was a large tree in the yard fairly black with the ripe fruit. We asked the women if we could eat some of the berries, and they gave a cheerful consent. Thereupon Frank and I climbed the tree, and proceeded to help ourselves. The berries were big, dead ripe, and tasted mighty good, and we just stuffed ourselves until we could hold no more. The churning was finished by the time we descended from the tree, and we asked for some buttermilk. The women gave us a gourd dipper and told us to help ourselves, which we did, and drank copiously and greedily. We then resumed our stroll, but before long were seized with most horrible pains in our stomachs. We laid down on the ground and rolled over and over in agony. It was a hot day, we had been walking rapidly, and it is probable that the mulberries and the buttermilk were in a state of insurrection. But Frank didn't think so. As he rolled over the ground with his hands on his bulging stomach he exclaimed to me, "Lee, by ----, I believe them ---- Secesh wimmen have pizened us!" At the time I hardly knew what to think,--but relief came at last. I will omit the details. When able to navigate, we started back to camp, almost as weak and helpless as a brace of sick kittens.

After that I steered clear of any sort of a combination of berries and buttermilk.

Soon after this Frank and I had another adventure outside the picket lines, but of an amusing nature only. We came to an old log house where, as was usual at this time and locality, the only occupants were women and children. The family consisted of the middle-aged mother, a tall, slab-sided, long legged girl, seemingly sixteen or seventeen years old, and some little children. Their surname was Leadbetter, which I have always remembered by reason of the incident I will mention. The house was a typical pioneer cabin, with a puncheon floor, which was uneven, dirty, and splotched with grease. The girl was barefooted and wearing a dirty white sort of cotton gown of the modern Mother Hubbard type, that looked a good deal like a big gunny sack. From what came under my observation later, it can safely be stated that it was the only garment she had on. She really was not bad looking, only dirty and mighty slouchy. We wanted some butter, and asked the matron if she had any she could sell us. She replied that they were just going to churn, and if we'd wait until that was done, she could furnish us a little. We waited, and when the job was finished, handed the girl a pint tin cup we had brought along, which she proceeded to fill with the butter. As she walked towards us to hand over the cup, her bare feet slipped on a grease spot on the floor, and down she went on her back, with her gown distinctly elevated, and a prodigal display of limbs. At the same time the cup fell from her grasp, and the contents rolled out on the dirty floor, like melted lard. The girl arose to a sitting posture, surveyed the wreck, then laid down on one side, and exploded with laughter--and kicked. About this time her mother appeared on the scene. "Why, Sal Leadbetter!" she exclaimed, "you dirty slut! Git a spoon and scrape that butter right up!" Sal rose (cow fashion) to her feet, still giggling over the mishap, and the butter was duly "scraped" up, restored to the cup, and this time safely delivered. We paid for the "dairy product," and left, but I told Frank I wanted none of it in mine. Frank responded in substance, that it was all right, every man had to eat his "peck of dirt" in his life time anyway,--and the incident was closed. I never again saw nor heard of the

Leadbetter family from that day, but have often wondered what finally became of poor "Sal."

While we were at Owl creek the medical authorities of the army put in operation a method for the prevention and cure of malaria that was highly popular with some of the boys. It consisted of a gill of whisky, largely compounded with quinine, and was given to each man before breakfast. I drank my first "jigger," as it was called, and then quit. It was too intensely bitter for my taste, and I would secretly slip my allowance to John Barton, or Frank Burnham, who would have drunk it, I reckon, if it had been one-half aqua fortis. I happened to be mixed up in an incident rather mortifying to me, when the first whisky rations were brought to the regimental hospital in our camp for use in the above manner. The quartermaster came to Capt. Reddish and handed him a requisition for two camp kettlefuls of whisky, and told him to give it to two non-commissioned officers of his company who were strictly temperate and absolutely reliable, and order them to go to the Division commissary headquarters, get the whisky, bring it to camp, and deliver it to him, the quartermaster. Capt. Reddish selected for this delicate duty Corporal Tim Gates (a brother of Frank, above mentioned) and myself. Tim was about ten years my senior, a tall, slim fellow, and somewhat addicted to stuttering when he became nervous or excited. Well, we each procured a big camp kettle, went and got the whisky, and started back with it to camp. On the way we passed through a space where a large number of army wagons were parked, and when we were in about the middle of the park were then out of sight of everybody. Here Tim stopped, looked carefully around to see if the coast was clear, and then said, "Sti-Sti-Stillwell, l-l-less t-t-take a swig!" "All right," I responded. Thereupon Tim poised his camp-kettle on a wagon hub, inclined the brim to his lips, and took a most copious draught, and I followed suit. We then started on, and it was lucky, for me at any rate, that we didn't have far to go. I hadn't previously during my army career taken a swallow of whisky since one time at Camp Carrollton; I was weak and feeble, and this big drink of the stuff went through my veins like electricity. Its effects were felt almost instantly, and by the time we reached camp, and had delivered the whisky, I was feeling a good deal like a wild Indian on the war path. I wanted to yell, to get my musket and shoot, especially at something that when hit would jingle--a looking-glass, an eight-day clock, or a boat's chandelier, or something similar But it suddenly occurred to me that I was drunk, and liable to forever disgrace myself, and everybody at home, too. I had just sense enough left to know that the thing to do was to get out of camp at once, so I struck for the woods. In passing the tent of my squad, I caught a glimpse of Tim therein. He had thrown his cap and jacket on the ground, rolled up his sleeves, and was furiously challenging another fellow to then and there settle an old-time grudge by the "ordeal of battle." I didn't tarry, but hurried on the best I could, finally got into a secluded patch of brush, and tumbled down. I came to my senses along late in the evening, with a splitting headache, and feeling awful generally, but reasonably sober.

And such was the conduct, when trusted with whisky, of the two non-commissioned officers of Co. D, "men who were strictly temperate and absolutely reliable." But Tim had no trouble about his break. I suppose he gave some plausible explanation, and as for me, I had lived up to the standard, so far as the public knew, and maintained a profound silence in regard to the episode. Tim and I in private conversation, or otherwise, both carefully avoided the subject until the time came when we could talk and laugh about it without any danger of "tarnishing our escutcheons."

In the meantime the alleged siege of Corinth was proceeding in the leisurely manner that characterized the progress of a suit in chancery under the ancient equity methods. From our camp on Owl creek we could hear, from time to time, sporadic outbursts of cannonading, but we became so accustomed to it that the artillery practice ceased to excite any special attention. The Confederates began quietly evacuating the place during the last days of May, completed the operation on the 30th of the month, and on the evening of that day our troops marched into the town unopposed.

CHAPTER VI

BETHEL. JACKSON. JUNE and JULY, 1862.

Soon after our occupation of Corinth a change in the position of our forces took place, and all the command at Owl creek was transferred to Bethel, a small station on the Mobile and Ohio railroad, some twenty or twenty-five miles to the northwest. We left Owl creek on the morning of June 6th, and arrived at Bethel about dark the same evening. Thanks to my repeated long walks in the woods outside of our lines, I was in pretty fair health at this time, but still somewhat weak and shaky. On the morning we took up the line of march, while waiting for the "fall in" call, I was seated at the foot of a big tree in camp, with my knapsack, packed, at my side. Enoch Wallace came to me and said: "Stillwell, are you going to try to carry your knapsack?" I answered that I reckoned I had to, that I had asked Hen. King (our company teamster) to let me put it in his wagon, and he wouldn't,--said he already had too big a load. Enoch said nothing more, but stood silently looking down at me a few seconds, then picked up my knapsack and threw it into our wagon, which was close by, saying to King, as he did so, "Haul that knapsack;"--and it was hauled. I shall never forget this act of kindness on the part of Enoch. It would have been impossible for me to have made the march carrying the knapsack. The day was hot, and much of the road was over sandy land, and through long stretches of black-jack barrens, that excluded every breath of a breeze. The men suffered much on the march, and fell out by scores. When we stacked arms at Bethel that evening, there were only four men of Co. D in line, just enough to make one stack of guns,--but my gun was in the stack.

There was no earthly necessity for making this march in one day. We were simply "changing stations;" the Confederate army of that region was down in Mississippi, a hundred miles or so away, and there were no armed foes in our vicinity excepting some skulking bands of guerrillas. Prior to this our regiment had made no marches, except little short movements during the siege of Corinth, none of which exceeded two or three miles. And nearly all the men were weak and debilitated by reason of the prevailing type of illness, and in no condition whatever to be cracked through twenty miles or more on a hot day. We should have marched only about ten miles the first day, with a halt of about ten minutes every hour, to let the men rest a little, and get their wind. Had that course been pursued, we would have reached our destination in good shape, with the ranks full, and the men would have been benefited by the march. As it was, it probably caused the death of some, and the permanent disabling of more. The trouble at that time was the total want of experience on the part of the most of our officers of all grades, combined with an amazing lack of common sense by some of high authority. I am not blaming any of our regimental officers for this foolish "forced march,"--for it amounted to that,--the responsibility rested higher up.

Our stay at Bethel was brief and uneventful. However, I shall always remember the place on account of a piece of news that came to me while we were there, and which for a time nearly broke me all up. It will be necessary to go back some years in order to explain it. I began attending the old Stone school house at Otter creek when I was about eight years old. One of my schoolmates was a remarkably pretty little girl, with blue eyes and auburn hair, nearly my own age. We kept about the same place in our studies, and were generally in the same classes. I always liked her, and by the time I was about fifteen years old was head over heels in love. She was far above me in the social scale of the neighborhood. Her folks lived in a frame house on "the other side of the creek," and were well-to-do, for that time and locality. My people lived in a log cabin, on a little farm in the broken country that extended from the south bank of Otter creek to the Mississippi and Illinois rivers. But notwithstanding the difference in our respective social and financial positions, I knew that she had a liking for me, and our mutual relations became quite "tender" and interesting. Then the war came along, I enlisted and went South. We had no correspondence after I left home; I was just too deplorably bashful to attempt it, and, on general principles, didn't have sense enough to properly carry on a proceeding of that nature. It may be that here was where I fell down. But I thought about her every day, and had many boyish day dreams of the future, in which she was the prominent figure. Soon after our arrival at Bethel I received a letter from home. I hurriedly opened it, anxious, as usual, to hear from the folks, and sitting down at the foot of a tree, began reading it. All went well to nearly the close, when I read these fatal words:

"Billy Crane and Lucy Archer got married last week."

The above names are fictitious, but the bride was my girl.

I can't explain my feelings,--if you ever have had such an experience, you will understand. I stole a hurried glance around to see if anybody was observing my demeanor, then thrust the letter into my jacket pocket, and walked away. Not far from our camp was a stretch of swampy land, thickly set with big cypress trees, and I bent my steps in that direction. Entering the forest, I sought a secluded spot, sat down on an old log, and read and re-read that heart-breaking piece of intelligence. There was no mistaking the words; they were plain, laconic, and nothing ambiguous about them. And, to intensify the bitterness of the draught, it may be set down here that the groom was a dudish young squirt, a clerk in a country store, who lacked the pluck to go for a soldier, but had stayed at home to count eggs and measure calico. In my opinion, he was not worthy of the girl, and I was amazed that she had taken him for a husband. I remember well some of my thoughts as I sat with bitterness in my heart, alone among those gloomy cypresses. I wanted a great big battle to come off at once, with the 61st Illinois right in front, that we might run out of cartridges, and the order would be given to fix bayonets and charge! Like Major Simon Suggs, in depicting the horrors of an apprehended Indian war, I wanted to see blood flow in a "great gulgin' torrent, like the Tallapoosa river." Well, it was simply a case of pure, intensely ardent boy-love, and I was hit, hard,--but survived. And I now heartily congratulate myself on the fact that this youthful shipwreck ultimately resulted in my obtaining for a wife the very best woman (excepting only my mother) that I ever knew in my life.

I never again met my youthful flame, to speak to her, and saw her only once, and then at a distance, some years after the close of the war when I was back in Illinois on a visit to my parents. Several years ago her husband died, and in course of time she married again, this time a man I never knew, and the last I heard of or concerning her, she and her second husband were living somewhere in one of the Rocky Mountain States.

For a short time after the evacuation of Corinth, Pittsburg Landing continued to be our base of supplies, and commissary stores were wagoned from there to the various places where our troops were stationed. And it happened, while the regiment was at Bethel, that I was one of a party of about a hundred men detailed to serve as guards for a wagon train destined for the Landing, and, return to Bethel with army rations. There was at the Landing at this time, serving as guards for the government stores, a regiment of infantry. There were only a few of them visible, and they looked pale and emaciated, and much like "dead men on their feet." I asked one of them what regiment was stationed there, and he told me it was the 14th Wisconsin Infantry. This was the one I had seen at Benton Barracks and admired so much on account of the splendid appearance of the men. I mentioned this to the soldier, and expressed to him my surprise to now see them in such bad shape. He went on to tell me that the men had suffered fearfully from the change of climate, the water, and their altered conditions in general; that they had nearly all been prostrated by camp diarrhea, and at that time there were not more than a hundred men in the regiment fit for duty, and even those were not much better than shadows of their former selves. And, judging from the few men that were visible, the soldier told the plain, unvarnished truth. Our regiment and the 14th Wisconsin soon drifted apart, and I never saw it again. But as a matter of history, I will say that it made an excellent and distinguished record during the war.

On June 16 our brigade left Bethel for Jackson, Tennessee, a town on the Mobile and Ohio railroad, and about thirty-five or forty miles, by the dirt road, northwest of Bethel. On this march, like the preceding one, I did not carry my knapsack. It was about this time that the most of the boys adopted the "blanket-roll" system. Our knapsacks were awkward, cumbersome things, with a combination of straps and buckles that chafed the shoulders and back, and greatly augmented heat and general discomfort. So we would fold in our blankets an extra shirt, with a few other light articles, roll the blanket tight, double it over and tie the two ends together, then throw the blanket over one shoulder, with the tied ends under the opposite arm--and the arrangement was complete. We had learned by this time the necessity of reducing our personal baggage to the lightest possible limit. We had left Camp Carrollton with great bulging knapsacks, stuffed with all sorts of plunder, much of which was utterly useless to soldiers in the field. But we soon got rid of all that. And my recollection is that after the Bethel march the great majority of the men would, in some way, when on a march, temporarily lay aside their knapsacks, and use the blanket roll. The exceptions to that method, in the main, were the soldiers of foreign birth, especially the Germans. They carried theirs to the last on all occasions, with everything in them the army regulations would permit, and usually something more.

Jackson, our objective point on this march, was the county seat of Madison county, and a portion of our line of march was through the south part of the county. This region had a singular interest for me, the nature of which I will now state. Among the few books we had at home was an old paper-covered copy, with horrible wood-cuts, of a production entitled, "The Life and Adventures of John A. Murrell, the Great Western Land Pirate," by Virgil A. Stewart. It was full of accounts of cold-blooded, depraved murders, and other vicious, unlawful doings. My father had known, in his younger days, a good deal of Murrell by reputation, which was probably the moving cause for his purchase of the book. When a little chap I frequently read it and it possessed for me a sort of weird, uncanny fascination. Murrell's home, and the theater of many of his evil deeds, during the year 1834, and for some time previously, was in this county of Madison, and as we trudged along the road on this march I scanned all the surroundings with deep interest and close attention. Much of the country was rough and broken, and densely wooded, with high ridges and deep ravines between them. With the aid of a lively imagination, many places I noticed seemed like fitting localities for acts of violence and crime.

I have in my possession now (bought many years ago) a duplicate of that old copy of Murrell we had at home. I sometimes look into it, but it no longer possesses for me the interest it did in my boyhood days. On this march I was a participant in an incident which was somewhat amusing, and also a little bit irritating. Shortly before noon of the first day, Jack Medford, of my company, and myself, concluded we would "straggle," and try to get a country dinner. Availing ourselves of the first favorable opportunity, we slipped from the ranks, and struck out. We followed an old country road that ran substantially parallel to the main road on which the column was marching, and soon came to a nice looking old log house standing in a grove of big native trees. The only people at the house were two middle-aged women and some children. We asked the women if we could have some dinner, saying that we would pay for it. They gave an affirmative answer, but their tone was not cordial and they looked "daggers." Dinner was just about prepared, and when all was ready, we were invited, with evident coolness, to take seats at the table. We had a splendid meal, consisting of corn bread, new Irish potatoes, boiled bacon and greens, butter and buttermilk. Compared with sow-belly and hardtack, it was a feast. Dinner over, we essayed to pay therefor. Their charge was something less than a dollar for both of us, but we had not the exact change. The smallest denomination of money either of us had was a dollar greenback, and the women said that they had no money at all to make change. Thereupon we proffered them the entire dollar. They looked at it askance, and asked if we had any "Southern" or Confederate money. We said we had not, that this was the only kind of money we had. They continued to look exceedingly sour, and finally remarked that they were unwilling to accept any kind of money except "Southern." We urged them to accept the bill, told them it was United States money, and that it would pass readily in any place in the South occupied by our soldiers; but no, they were obdurate, and declined the greenback with unmistakable scorn. Of course we kept our temper; it never would have done to be saucy or rude after getting such a good dinner, but, for my part, I felt considerably vexed. But there was nothing left to do except thank them heartily for their kindness and depart. From their standpoint their course in the matter was actuated by the highest and most unselfish patriotism, but naturally we couldn't look at it in that light. I will say here, "with malice towards none, and with charity for all," that in my entire sojourn in the South during the war, the women were found to be more intensely bitter and malignant against the old government of the United States, and the national cause in general, than were the men. Their attitude is probably another illustration of the truth of Kipling's saying, "The female of the species is more deadly than the male."

We arrived at Jackson on the evening of June 17, and went into camp in the outskirts of the town, in a beautiful grove of tall young oaks. The site was neither too shady nor too sunny, and, all things considered, I think it was about the nicest camping ground the regiment had during its entire service. We settled down here to a daily round of battalion drill, being the first of that character, as I now remember, we had so far had. A battalion drill is simply one where the various companies are handled as a regimental unit, and are put through regimental evolutions. Battalion drill at first was frequently very embarrassing to some commanding officers of companies. The regimental commander would give a command, indicating, in general terms, the movement desired, and it was then the duty of a company commander to see to the details of the movement that his company should make, and give the proper orders. Well, sometimes he would be badly stumped, and ludicrous "bobbles" would be the result. As for the men in the ranks, battalion drill was as simple as any other, for we only had to obey specific commands which indicated exactly what we were to do. To "form square," an antique disposition against cavalry, was a movement that was especially "trying" to some company officers. But so far as forming square was concerned, all our drill on that feature was time thrown away. In actual battle we never made that disposition a single time--and the same is true of several other labored and intricate movements prescribed in the tactics, and which we were industriously put through. But it was good exercise, and "all went in the day's work."

While thus amusing ourselves at battalion drill suddenly came marching orders, and which required immediate execution. Tents were forthwith struck, rolled and tied, and loaded in the wagons, with all other camp and garrison equipage. Our knapsacks were packed with all our effects, since special instructions had been given on that matter. Curiosity was on the qui vive to know where we were going, but apart from the fact that we were to be transported on the cars, apparently nobody knew whither we were bound. Col. Fry was absent, sick, and Major Ohr was then in command of the regiment. He was a fine officer, and, withal, a very sensible man, and I doubt if any one in the regiment except himself had reliable knowledge as to our ultimate destination. As soon as our marching preparations were complete, which did not take long, the bugle sounded "Fall in!" and the regiment formed in line on the parade ground. In my "mind's eye" I can now see Major Ohr in our front, on his horse, his blanket strapped behind his saddle, smoking his little briar root pipe, and looking as cool and unconcerned as if we were only going a few miles for a change of camp. Our entire brigade fell in, and so far as we could see, or learn, all of the division at Jackson, then under the command of Gen. John A. McClernand, was doing likewise. Well, we stood there in line, at ordered arms, and waited. We expected, every moment, to hear the orders which would put us in motion--but they were never given. Finally we were ordered to stack arms and break ranks, but were cautioned to hold ourselves in readiness to fall in at the tap of the drum. But the day wore on and nothing was done until late in the evening, when the summons came. We rushed to the gun stacks and took arms. The Major had a brief talk with the company officers, and then, to our great surprise, the companies were marched back to their dismantled camps, and after being instructed to stay close thereto, were dismissed. This state of affairs lasted for at least two days, and then collapsed. We were told that the orders had been countermanded; we unloaded our tents, pitched them again on the old sites, and resumed battalion drill. It was then gossiped around among the boys that we actually had been under marching orders for Virginia to reinforce the Army of the Potomac! Personally I looked on that as mere "camp talk," and put no confidence in it, and never found out, until about fifteen years later, that this rumor was a fact. I learned it in this wise: About nine years after the close of the war, Congress passed an act providing for the publication, in book form, of all the records, reports correspondence, and the like, of both the Union and Confederate armies. Under this law, about one hundred and thirty large volumes were published, containing the matter above stated. When the law was passed I managed to arrange to procure a set of these Records and they were sent to me from Washington as fast as printed. And from one of these volumes I ascertained that on June 28, 1862, E. M. Stanton, the Secretary of War, had telegraphed Gen. Halleck (who was then in command of the western armies) as follows:

"It is absolutely necessary for you immediately to detach 25,000 of your force, and send it by the nearest and quickest route by way of Baltimore and Washington to Richmond. [This] is rendered imperative by a serious reverse suffered by Gen. McClellan before Richmond yesterday, the full extent of which is not known."

In obedience to the above, General Halleck wired General McClernand on June 30 as follows:

"You will collect as rapidly as possible all the infantry regiments of your division, and take advantage of every train to transport them to Columbus [Ky.] and thence to Washington City."

But that same day (June 30) a telegram was sent by President Lincoln to Gen. Halleck, which operated to revoke the foregoing order of Stanton's--and so the 61st Illinois never became a part of the Army of the Potomac, and for which I am very thankful. That army was composed of brave men, and they fought long and well, but, in my opinion, and which I think is sustained by history, they never had a competent commander until they got U. S. Grant. So, up to the coming of Grant, their record, in the main, was a series of bloody disasters, and their few victories, like Antietam and Gettysburg, were not properly and energetically followed up as they should have been, and hence were largely barren of adequate results. Considering these things, I have always somehow "felt it in my bones" that if Mr. Lincoln had not sent the brief telegram above mentioned, I would now be sleeping in some (probably) unmarked and unknown grave away back in old Virginia.

While at Jackson an incident occurred while I was on picket in which Owen McGrath, the big Irishman I have previously mentioned, played an interesting part. As corporal I had three men under me, McGrath being one, and the others were a couple of big, burly young fellows belonging to Co. A. Our post was on the railroad a mile or two from the outskirts of Jackson, and where the picket line for some distance ran practically parallel with the railroad. The spot at this post where the picket stood when on guard was at the top of a bank on the summit of a slight elevation, just at the edge of a deep and narrow railroad cut. A bunch of guerrillas had recently been operating in that locality, and making mischief on a small scale, and our orders were to be vigilant and on the alert, especially at night. McGrath was on duty from 6 to 8 in the evening, and at the latter hour I notified one of the Co. A men that his turn had come. The weather was bad, a high wind was blowing, accompanied by a drizzling rain, and all signs portended a stormy night. The Co. A fellow buckled on his cartridge box, picked up his musket, and gave a scowling glance at the surroundings. Then, with much profanity, he declared that he wasn't going to stand up on that bank, he was going down into the cut, where he could have some shelter from the wind and rain. I told him that would never do, that there he could see nothing in our front, and might as well not be on guard at all. But he loudly announced his intention to stick to his purpose. The other Co. A man chimed in, and with many expletives declared that Bill was right, that he intended to stand in the cut too when his time came, that he didn't believe there was a Secesh within a hundred miles of us, anyway, and so on. I was sorely troubled, and didn't know what to do. They were big, hulking fellows, and either could have just smashed me, with one hand tied behind him. McGrath had been intently listening to the conversation, and saying nothing, but, as matters were evidently nearing a crisis, he now took a hand. Walking up to the man who was to relieve him, he laid the forefinger of his right hand on the fellow's breast, and looking him square in the eyes, spoke thus:

"It's the ar-r-dhers of the car-r-parral that the sintry stand here," (indicating,) "and the car-r-parral's ar-r-dhers will be obeyed. D'ye moind that, now?"

I had stepped to the side of McGrath while he was talking, to give him my moral support, at least, and fixed my eyes on the mutineer. He looked at us in silence a second or two, and then, with some muttering about the corporal being awful particular, finally said he could stand it if the rest could, assumed his post at the top of the bank, and the matter was ended. The storm blew over before midnight and the weather cleared up. In the morning we had a satisfying soldier breakfast, and when relieved at 9 o'clock marched back to camp with the others of the old guard, all in good humor, and with "peace and harmony prevailing." But I always felt profoundly grateful to grand old McGrath for his staunch support on the foregoing occasion; without it, I don't know what could have been done.

CHAPTER VII

BOLIVAR. JULY, AUGUST, and SEPTEMBER, 1862.

On July 17 our brigade, then under the command of Gen. L. F. Ross, left Jackson for Bolivar, Tennessee, a town about twenty-eight miles southwest of Jackson, on what was then called the Mississippi Central Railroad. (Here I will observe that the sketch of the regiment before mentioned in the Illinois Adjutant General's Reports is wrong as to the date of our departure from Jackson. It is inferable from the statement in the Reports that the time was June 17, which really was the date of our arrival there from Bethel.) We started from Jackson at about four o'clock in the morning, but marched only about eight miles when we were brought to an abrupt halt, caused by the breaking down, under the weight of a cannon and its carriage, of an ancient Tennessee bridge over a little stream. The nature of the crossing was such that the bridge simply had to be rebuilt, and made strong enough to sustain the artillery and army wagons, and it took the balance of the day to do it. We therefore bivouacked at the point where we stopped until the next morning. Soon after the halt a hard rain began falling, and lasted all afternoon. We had no shelter, and just had to take it, and "let it rain." But it was in the middle of the summer, the weather was hot, and the boys stood around, some crowing like chickens, and others quacking like ducks, and really seemed to rather enjoy the situation. About the only drawback resulting from our being caught out in the summer rains was the fact that the water would rust our muskets. In our time we were required to keep all their metal parts (except the butt-plate) as bright and shining as new silver dollars. I have put in many an hour working on my gun with an old rag and powdered dirt, and a corncob, or pine stick, polishing the barrel, the bands, lock-plate, and trigger-guard, until they were fit to pass inspection. The inside of the barrel we would keep clean by the use of a greased wiper and plenty of hot water. In doing this, we would ordinarily, with our screw-drivers, take the gun to pieces, and remove from the stock all metallic parts. I never had any head for machinery, of any kind, but, from sheer necessity, did acquire enough of the faculty to take apart, and put together, an army musket,--and that is about the full extent of my ability in that line. We soon learned to take care of our pieces in a rain by thoroughly greasing them with a piece of bacon, which would largely prevent rust from striking in.

We resumed our march to Bolivar early in the morning of the 18th. Our route was practically parallel with the railroad, crossing it occasionally. At one of these crossings, late in the afternoon, and when only five or six miles from Bolivar, I "straggled" again, and took to the railroad. I soon fell in with three Co. C boys, who had done likewise. We concluded we would endeavor to get a country supper, and with that in view, an hour or so before sundown went to a nice looking farm-house not far from the railroad, and made our wants known to the occupants. We had selected for our spokesman the oldest one of our bunch, a soldier perhaps twenty-five years old, named Aleck Cope. He was something over six feet tall, and about as gaunt as a sand-hill crane. He was bare-footed, and his feet, in color and general appearance, looked a good deal like the flappers of an alligator. His entire garb, on this occasion, consisted of an old wool hat and his government shirt and drawers. The latter garment, like the "cuttie sark" of witch Nannie in "Tam O'Shanter," "in longitude was sorely scanty," coming only a little below his knees, and both habiliments would have been much improved by a thorough washing. But in the duty assigned him he acquitted himself well with the people of the house, and they very cheerfully said they would prepare us a supper. They seemingly were well-to-do, as several colored men and women were about the premises, who, of course, were slaves. Soon were audible the death squawks of chickens in the barn-yard, which we heard with much satisfaction. In due time supper was announced, and we seated ourselves at the table. And what a banquet we had! Fried chicken, nice hot biscuits, butter, butter-milk, honey, (think of that!) preserved peaches, fresh cucumber pickles,--and so forth. And a colored house-girl moved back and forth behind us, keeping off the flies with a big peacock-feather brush. Aleck Cope sat opposite me, and when the girl was performing that office for him, the situation looked so intensely ludicrous that I wanted to scream. Supper over, we paid the bill, which was quite reasonable, and went on our way rejoicing, and reached Bolivar soon after dark, about the same time the regiment did. But it will now be set down that this was the last occasion when I "straggled" on a march. A day or so after arriving at Bolivar the word came to me in some way, I think from Enoch Wallace, that our first lieutenant, Dan Keeley, had spoken disapprovingly of my conduct in that regard. He was a young man, about twenty-five years old, of education and refinement, and all things considered, the best company officer we had. I was much attached to him, and I know that he liked me. Well, I learned that he had said, in substance, that a non-commissioned officer should set a good example to the men in all things, and that he hadn't expected of Stillwell that he would desert the ranks on a march. That settled the matter. My conduct had simply been thoughtless, without any shirking intentions, but I then realized that it was wrong, and, as already stated, straggled no more.

We went into camp at Bolivar a little south of the town, in a grove of scattered big oak trees. A few days after our arrival a good-sized body of Confederate cavalry, under the command of Gen. Frank C. Armstrong, moved up from the south, and began operating near Bolivar and vicinity. Our force there was comparatively small, and, according to history, we were, for a time, in considerable danger of being "gobbled up," but of that we common soldiers knew nothing. Large details were at once put to work throwing up breast-works, while the men not on that duty were kept in line of battle, or with their guns in stack on the line, and strictly cautioned to remain close at hand, and ready to fall in at the tap of a drum. This state of things continued for some days, then the trouble would seemingly blow over, and later would break out again. While we were thus on the ragged edge, and expecting a battle almost any hour, a little incident occurred which somehow made on me a deep and peculiar impression. To explain it fully, I must go back to our first days at Pittsburg Landing. A day or two after our arrival there, Lt. Keeley said to me that the regimental color guard, to consist of a sergeant and eight corporals, was being formed, that Co. D had been called on for a corporal for that duty, and that I should report to Maj. Ohr for instructions. Naturally I felt quite proud over this, and forthwith reported to the Major, at his tent, and stated my business. He looked at me in silence, and closely, for a few seconds, and then remarked, in substance, that I could go to my quarters, and if needed, would be notified later. This puzzled me somewhat, but I supposed it would come out all right in due time. There was a corporal in our company to whom I will give a fictitious name, and call him Sam Cobb. He was a big, fine looking fellow, and somewhere between twenty-five and thirty years old. And an hour or two after my dismissal by Maj. Ohr, I heard Sam loudly proclaiming, with many fierce oaths, to a little group of Co. D. boys, that he "had been promoted." That he was a "color corporal, by ----!" This announcement was accompanied by sundry vociferous statements in regard to Maj. Ohr knowing exactly the kind of men to get to guard the colors of the regiment in time of battle, and so on, and so on. I heard all this with mortification and bitterness of spirit. The reason now dawned on me why I had been rejected. I was only a boy, rather small for my age, and at this time feeble in appearance. Maj. Ohr, quite properly, wanted strong, stalwart, fine looking men for the color guard. A little reflection convinced me that he was right, and could not be blamed for his action. But he found out later, (in this particular case, at least) that something more than a fine appearance was required to make a soldier. Only two or three days after Sam's "promotion," came the battle of Shiloh, and at the very first volley the regiment received, he threw down his gun, and ran like a whipped cur. The straps and buckles of his cartridge box were new and stiff, so he didn't take the time to release them in the ordinary way, but whipped out his jack-knife and cut them as he ran. I did not see this personally, but was told it by boys who did. We saw no more of Sam until after the battle, when he sneaked into camp, with a fantastic story of getting separated from the regiment in a fall-back movement, that he then joined another, fought both days, and performed prodigies of valor.

But there were too many that saw the manner of his alleged "separation" for his story ever to be believed.

I will now return to the Bolivar incident. While the Confederates were operating in the vicinity of this place, as above mentioned, the "fall in" call was sounded one evening after dark, and the regiment promptly formed in line on the parade ground. We remained there an hour or so, when finally the command was given to stack arms, and the men were dismissed with orders to hold themselves in readiness to form in line, on the parade grounds, at a moment's warning. As I was walking back to our company quarters, Sam Cobb stepped up to me and took me to one side, under the shadow of a tall oak tree. It was a bright moonlight night, with some big, fleecy clouds in the sky. "Stillwell," asked Sam, "do you think we are going to have a fight?" "I don't know, Sam," I answered, "but it looks very much like it. I reckon Gen. Ross is not going out to hunt a fight; he prefers to stay here, protect the government stores, and fight on the defensive. If our cavalry can stand the Rebs off, then maybe they will let us alone,--but if our cavalry are driven in, then look out." Sam held his head down, and said nothing. As above stated, he was a grown man, and I was only a boy, but the thing that was troubling him was apparent from his demeanor, and I felt sorry for him. I laid a hand kindly on his shoulder, and said, "And Sam, if we should have a fight, now try, old fellow, and do better than you did before." He looked up quickly--at that instant the moon passed from behind a big cloud and shone through a rift in the branches of the tree, full in his face, which was as pale as death, and he said, in a broken voice: "Stillwell, I'll run; I just know I'll run,--by God, I can't help it!" I deeply pitied the poor fellow, and talked to him a few minutes, in the kindest manner possible, trying to reason him out of that sort of a feeling. But his case was hopeless. He was a genial, kind-hearted man, but simply a constitutional coward, and he doubtless told the truth when he said he "couldn't help it." In the very next fight we were in he verified his prediction. I may say something about that further on.

Since leaving Camp Carrollton, Co. D had lost two sergeants, one by death from sickness, the other by discharge for disability, so while we were at Bolivar these vacancies were filled by appointments made by Maj. Ohr, who was then commanding the regiment. In accordance with the custom in such matters, the appointments were announced in orders, which were read on dress parade. As I now write, it is a little over fifty-four years since this event took place, but even now my heart beats faster as the fact is recalled that as the adjutant read the list, there came the name "Corporal Leander Stillwell, Co. D, to be 4th Sergeant."

In the early part of August, 1862, while our regiment was at Bolivar, I cast my first vote, which was an illegal one, as then I was not quite nineteen years old. The circumstances connected with my voting are not lengthy, so the story will be told. In the fall of 1861 the voters of the state of Illinois elected delegates to a Constitutional Convention, to frame and submit to the people a new Constitution. A majority of the delegates so elected were Democrats, so they prepared a Constitution in accordance with their political views. It therefore became a party measure, the Democrats supporting and the Republicans opposing it. By virtue of some legal enactment all Illinois soldiers in the field, who were lawful voters, were authorized to vote on the question of the adoption of the proposed constitution, and so, on the day above indicated the election for this purpose was held in our regiment. An election board was duly appointed, consisting of commissioned officers of the regiment; they fixed up under a big tree some hardtack boxes to serve for a table, and the proceedings began. I had no intention of voting, as I knew I had not the legal right, but Enoch Wallace came to me and suggested that I go up and vote. When I said I was not old enough, he simply laughed, and took me by the arm and marched me to the voting place. The manner of voting was by word of mouth, the soldier gave his name, and stated that he was "For" or "Against" the constitution, as the case might be, and his vote was recorded. I voted "Against," and started away, no questions being asked me as to my age. But before getting out of hearing I heard one of the board say, somewhat sotto voce, "That's a mighty young looking voter." Capt. Ihrie, of Co. C, also on the board, responded carelessly in the same tone,

"Oh well, it's all right; he's a dam good soldier." That remark puffed me away up, and almost made me feel as if I had grown maybe three feet, or more, in as many seconds, and needed only a fierce mustache to be a match for one of Napoleon's Old Guard. And my vote was not the same as Ihrie's, either, as he was a Democrat, and supporting the new constitution. When the regiment was recruited it was Democratic by a large majority, but under the enlightening experiences of the war it had become Republican, and out of a total vote of about two hundred and fifty, it gave a majority against the new constitution of twenty-five. The final result was that the proposed constitution was beaten by the "home vote" alone, which gave something over 16,000 majority against it. Consequently the soldier vote (although heavily against the measure) cut no figure, as it was not needed, and my illegal exercise of the right of suffrage did neither good nor harm;--and the incident has long since been barred by the statute of limitations.

During the latter part of July, and throughout August and September, things were lively and exciting at Bolivar, and in that region generally. There was a sort of feeling of trouble in the air most of the time. Gen. Grant was in command in this military district, and he has stated in his Memoirs that the "most anxious" period of the war, to him, was, practically, during the time above stated. But we common soldiers were not troubled with any such feeling. We were devoid of all responsibility, except simply to look out for and take care of ourselves, and do our duty to the best of our ability. And, speaking for myself, I will say that this condition was one that was very "full of comfort." We had no planning nor thinking to do, and the world could just wag as it willed.

CHAPTER VIII

BOLIVAR. THE MOVEMENT to the VICINITY of IUKA, MISSISSIPPI. SEPTEMBER-DECEMBER, 1862.

On September 16 the regiment (with the rest of our brigade) left Bolivar, on the cars, went to Jackson, and thence to Corinth, Mississippi, where we arrived about sundown. From here, still on the cars, we started east on the Memphis and Charleston railroad. The train proceeded very slowly, and after getting about seven or eight miles from Corinth, it stopped, and we passed the rest of the night on the cars. Early next morning the train started, and we soon arrived at the little town of Burnsville, about fifteen miles southeast of Corinth, where we left the cars, and went into bivouac near the eastern outskirts of the town.

On the morning of the 19th, before daylight, we marched about two miles east of Burnsville, and formed in line of battle, facing the south, in thick woods, consisting mainly of tall pines. It was talked among us that the Confederate pickets were only a short distance from our front, and it certainly looked like a battle was impending. By this time the military situation was pretty well understood by all of us. A Confederate force of about eight thousand men under Gen. Sterling Price was at the town of Iuka, about two miles south of us, and Gen. Grant and Gen. Rosecrans had formulated a plan for attacking this force on two sides at once. Gen. Rosecrans was to attack from the south, while our column, under the immediate command of Gen. E. O. C. Ord, was to close in from the north. Gen. Grant was on the field, and was with the troops on the north. The plan was all right, and doubtless would have succeeded, if the wind, on September 19, 1862, in that locality had been blowing from the south instead of the north. It is on such seemingly little things that the fate of battles, and sometimes that of nations, depends. Gen. Rosecrans on the afternoon of the 19th encountered the enemy south of Iuka, had a severe battle, and was quite roughly handled. Only a few miles to the north was all of Ord's command, in line of battle, and expecting to go in every minute, but the order never came. So all day we just stood around in those pine woods, wondering what in the world was the matter. As already stated, the woods were dense, and the wind blowing from the north carried from us all sounds of the battle. I personally know that this was the case. There were a few cannon shots next morning, fired by a battery in Gen. Rosecrans' column, and those we distinctly heard from our position, and thought at the time they indicated a battle, but they were fired mainly as "feelers," and to ascertain if the enemy were present in force. But, as stated, all day on the 19th we heard not a sound to indicate that a desperate battle was in progress only a few miles from our front.

Early in the morning of the 19th I witnessed an incident that inspired in me my first deep-seated hatred of whisky, and which has abided with me ever since. We had formed in line of battle, but the command had been given, "In place, rest!" (which we were allowed to give a liberal construction), and we were scattered around, standing or sitting down, near the line. About this time two young assistant surgeons came from the rear, riding up the road on which the left of the regiment rested. They belonged to some infantry regiment of the division, but personally I didn't know them. They were both fool drunk. On reaching our line of battle they stopped, but kept in their saddles, pulling their horses about, playing "smarty," and grinning and chattering like a brace of young monkeys. I looked at these drunk young fools, and thought that maybe, in less than an hour, one of them might be standing over me, probing a bullet wound in one of my legs, and then and there promptly deciding the question whether the leg should be sawed off, or whether it could be saved. And what kind of intelligent judgment on this matter, on which my life or death might depend, could this whisky-crazed young gosling be capable of exercising? I felt so indignant at the condition and conduct of these men, right on the eve of what we supposed might be a severe battle and in which their care for the wounded would be required, that it almost seemed to me it would be doing the government good service to shoot both the galoots right on the spot. And there were other boys who felt the same way, who began making ominous remarks. The drunken young wretches seemed to have sense enough to catch the drift of something that was said, they put spurs to their horses and galloped off to the rear, and we saw them no more.

On the morning of the 20th some regiments of our division moved forward and occupied the town of Iuka, but Gen. Price had in the meantime skipped out, so there was no fighting. Our regiment, with some others, remained in the original position, so that I never got to see the old town of Iuka until several years after the war. Sometime during the afternoon of the 20th I went to Capt. Reddish and said to him that I had become so tired of just standing around, and asked him if I could take a short stroll in the woods. The old man gave his consent (as I felt satisfied he would) but cautioned me not to go too far away. The main thing in view, when I made the request, was the hope of finding some wild muscadine grapes. They were plentiful in this section of the country, and were now ripe, and I wanted a bait. I think a wild muscadine grape is just the finest fruit of that kind in existence. When ripe it has a strong and most agreeable fragrance, and when one is to the leeward of a vine loaded with grapes, and a gentle wind is blowing from the south, he is first made aware of their proximity by their grateful odor. I soon found some on this occasion, and they were simply delicious. Having fully satisfied my craving, I proceeded to make my way back to the regiment, when hearing the trampling sound of cavalry, I hurried through the woods to the side of the road, reaching there just as the head of the column appeared. It was only a small body, not more than a hundred or so, and there, riding at its head, was Grant! I had not seen him since the battle of Shiloh and I looked at him with intense interest. He had on an old "sugar-loaf" hat, with limp, drooping brim, and his outer coat was the ordinary uniform coat, with a long cape, of a private in the cavalry. His foot-gear was cavalry boots, splashed with mud, and the ends of his trousers' legs were tucked inside the boots. No shoulder-straps were visible, and the only evidence of rank about him that was perceptible consisted of a frayed and tarnished gold cord on his hat. He was looking downward as he rode by, and seemed immersed in thought. As the column passed along, I asked a soldier near the rear what troops they were, and he answered,

"Co. A, Fourth Illinois Cavalry--Gen. Grant's escort." This was the last time that I saw Grant during the war.

On the evening of the 20th the regiment was drawn back into Burnsville, and that night Co. D bivouacked in the "Harrison Hotel," which formerly had evidently been the principal hotel in the town. It was a rambling, roomy, old frame building, two stories and a half high, now vacant, stripped of all furniture, and with a thick layer of dust and dirt on the floors. We occupied a room on the second floor, that evidently had been the parlor. Being quartered in a hotel was a novel experience, and the boys got lots of fun out of it. One would call out, "Bill, ring the clerk to send up a pitcher of ice water, and to be quick about it;" while another would say, "And while you're at it, tell him to note a special order from me for quail on toast for breakfast;" and so on. But these pleasantries soon subsided, and it was not long before we were wrapped in slumber. It was a little after midnight, and I was sound asleep, when I heard someone calling, "Sergeant Stillwell! Where is Sergeant Stillwell?" I sprang to my feet, and answered, "Here! What's wanted?" The speaker came to me, and then I saw that it was Lt. Goodspeed, who was acting as adjutant of the regiment. He proceeded to inform me that I was to take charge of a detail of three corporals and twelve men and go to a point about a mile and a half east of Burnsville, to guard a party of section men while clearing and repairing the railroad from a recent wreck. He gave me full instructions, and then said, "Stillwell, a lieutenant should go in charge of this detail, but all that I could find made pretty good excuses and I think you'll do. It is a position of honor and responsibility, as there are some prowling bands of guerrillas in this vicinity, so be careful and vigilant." I was then acting as first sergeant, and really was exempt from this duty, but of course the idea of making that claim was not entertained for a moment. I took charge of my party, went to where the laborers were waiting for us with hand cars, and we soon arrived at the scene of the wreck. A day or two before our arrival at Burnsville a party of Confederate cavalry had torn up the track at this point, and wrecked and burnt a freight train. Some horses on the train had been killed in the wreck; their carcasses were lying around, and were rather offensive. The trucks and other ironwork of the cars were piled on the track, tangled up, and all out of shape, some rails removed and others warped by heat, and things generally in a badly torn-up condition. The main dirt road forked here, one fork going diagonally to the right of the track and the other to the left--both in an easterly direction. I posted three men and a corporal about a quarter of a mile to the front on the track, a similar squad at the same distance on each fork of the dirt road, and the others at intervals on each side of the railroad at the place of the wreck. The laborers went to work with a will, and about the time the owls were hooting for day the foreman reported to me that the track was clear, the rails replaced, and that they were ready to return to Burnsville. I then drew in my guards, we got on the hand cars, and were soon back in town. And thus ended my first, and only, personal supervision of the work of repairing a break in a railroad.

I barely had time to make my coffee and toast a piece of bacon when the bugle sounded "Fall in!" and soon (that being the morning of September 21st) we started on the back track, and that day marched to Corinth. It so happened that on this march our regiment was at the head of the column. The proper place of my company, according to army regulations, was the third from the right or head of the line, but from some cause--I never knew what--on that day we were placed at the head. And, as I was then acting as first sergeant of our company, that put me the head man on foot. These details are mentioned for the reason that all that day I marched pretty close to the tail of the horse that Gen. Ord was riding, and with boyish curiosity, I scanned the old general closely. He was a graduate of West Point, and an old regular. He had served in the Florida and the Mexican wars, and he also had been in much scrapping with hostile Indians in the vicinity of the Pacific Coast. He looked old to me, but really he was, at this time, only about forty-four years of age. He certainly was indifferent to his personal appearance, as his garb was even plainer, and more careless, than Grant's. He wore an old battered felt hat, with a flapping brim, and his coat was one of the old-fashioned, long-tailed oil-cloth "wrap-rascals" then in vogue. It was all splattered with mud, with several big torn places in it. There was not a thing about him, that I could see, to indicate his rank. Later he was transferred to the eastern armies, eventually was assigned to the command of the Army of the James, and took an active and prominent part in the operations that culminated in the surrender of Lee at Appomattox.

We reached Corinth that evening, went into bivouac, and remained there a couple of days. On the morning of September 24th we fell in, marched down to the depot, climbed on cars, and were soon being whirled north to Jackson, on the Mobile and Ohio railroad. We arrived there about noon, and at once transferred to a train on the Mississippi Central track and which forthwith started for Bolivar. I think the train we came on to Jackson went right back to Corinth to bring up more troops. We common soldiers could not imagine what this hurried rushing around meant, and it was some time before we found out. But history shows that Grant was much troubled about this time as to whether a threatened Confederate attack would be delivered at Corinth or at Bolivar. However, about the 22nd, the indications were that Bolivar would be assailed, and troops were at once brought from Corinth to resist this apprehended movement of the Confederates.

This probably is a fitting place for something to be said about our method of traveling by rail during the Civil war, as compared with the conditions of the present day in that regard. At the time I am now writing, about fifteen thousand United States soldiers have recently been transported on the cars from different places in the interior of the country, to various points adjacent to the Mexican border, for the purpose of protecting American interests. And it seems that in some cases the soldiers were carried in ordinary passenger coaches. Thereupon bitter complaints were made on behalf of such soldiers because Pullman sleepers were not used! And these complaints were effective, too, for, according to the press reports of the time, the use of passenger coaches for such purposes was summarily stopped and Pullmans were hurriedly concentrated at the places needed, and the soldiers went to war in them. Well, in our time, the old regiment was hauled over the country many times on trains, the extent of our travels in that manner aggregating hundreds and hundreds of miles. And such a thing as even ordinary passenger coaches for the use of the enlisted men was never heard of. And I have no recollection now that (during the war) any were provided for the use of the commissioned officers, either, unless they were of pretty high rank. The cars that we rode in were the box or freight cars in use in those days. Among them were cattle cars, flat or platform cars, and in general every other kind of freight car that could be procured. We would fill the box cars, and in addition clamber upon the roofs thereof and avail ourselves of every foot of space. And usually there was a bunch on the cow-catchers. The engines used wood for fuel; the screens of the smoke-stacks must have been very coarse, or maybe they had none at all, and the big cinders would patter down on us like hail. So, when we came to the journey's end, by reason of the cinders and soot we were about as dirty and black as any regiment of sure-enough colored troops that fought under the Union flag in the last years of the war. When the regiment was sent home in September, 1865, some months after the war was over, the enlisted men made even that trip in our old friends, the box cars. It is true that on this occasion there was a passenger coach for the use of the commissioned officers, and that is the only time that I ever saw such a coach attached to a train on which the regiment was taken anywhere. Now, don't misunderstand me. I am not kicking because, more than half a century after the close of the Civil War, Uncle Sam sent his soldier boys to the front in Pullmans. The force so sent was small and the government could well afford to do it, and it was right. I just want you to know that in my time, when we rode, it was in any kind of an old freight car, and we were awful glad to get that. And now on this matter, "The words of Job are ended."

The only railroad accident I ever happened to be in was one that befell our train as we were in the act of leaving Jackson on the afternoon of the 24th. There was a good deal of hurry and confusion when we got on the cars, and it looked like it was every fellow for himself. Jack Medford (my chum) and I were running along the side of the track looking for a favorable situation, when we came to a flat car about the middle of the train, as yet unoccupied. "Jack," said I, "let's get on this!" He was a little slow of speech; he stopped, looked and commenced to say something, but his hesitation lost us the place,--and was fraught with other consequences. Right at that moment a bunch of the 12th Michigan on the other side of the track piled on the car quicker than a flash, and took up all available room. Jack and I then ran forward and climbed on top of a box car, next to the tender of the engine, and soon after the train started. It had not yet got under full head-way, and was going only about as fast as a man could walk, when, from some cause, the rails spread, and the first car to leave the rails was the flat above mentioned. But its trucks went bouncing along on the ties, and doubtless nobody would have been hurt, had it not been for the fact that the car plunged into a cattle guard, of the kind then in use. This guard was just a hole dug in the track, probably four or five feet deep, the same in length, and in width extending from rail to rail. Well, the front end of the car went down into that hole, and then the killing began. They stopped the train very quickly, the entire event couldn't have lasted more than half a minute, but that flat car was torn to splinters, three soldiers on it were killed dead, being frightfully crushed and mangled, and several more were badly injured. The men on the car jumped in every direction when the car began breaking up, and so the most of them escaped unhurt. If the train had been going at full speed, other cars would have been involved, and there is simply no telling how many would then have been killed and wounded.

On what little things does the fate of man sometimes depend! If in response to my suggestion Jack Medford had promptly said, "All right," we would have jumped on that flat car, and then would have been caught in the smash-up. But he took a mere fraction of time to look and think, and that brief delay was, perhaps, our temporal salvation.

We arrived at Bolivar during the afternoon of the 24th and re-occupied our old camp. The work of fortifying that place was pushed with renewed vigor, and strong lines of breastworks, with earthen forts at intervals, were constructed which practically inclosed the entire town. But we never had occasion to use them. Not long after our return to Bolivar, Gen. Grant became satisfied that the point the enemy would assail was Corinth, so the most of the troops at Bolivar were again started to Corinth, to aid in repelling the impending attack, but this time they marched overland. Our regiment and two others, with some artillery, were left to garrison Bolivar. And so it came to pass that the battle of Corinth was fought, on our part, by the command of Gen. Rosecrans on October 4th, and the battle of Hatchie Bridge the next day by the column from Bolivar, under the command of Gen. Ord,--and we missed both battles. For my part, I then felt somewhat chagrined that we didn't get to take part in either off those battles. Here we had been rushed around the country from pillar to post, hunting for trouble, and then to miss both these fights was just a little mortifying. However, the common soldier can only obey orders, and stay where he is put, and doubtless it was all for the best.

Early on the morning of October 9th, a force of about four thousand men, including our regiment, started from Bolivar, marching southwest on the dirt road. We arrived at Grand Junction at dark, after a march of about twenty miles. Grand Junction was the point where the Memphis & Charleston and the Mississippi Central railroads crossed. We had not much more than stacked arms, and of course before I had time to cook my supper, when I was detailed for picket, and was on duty all night. But I didn't go supperless by any means, as I made coffee and fried some bacon at the picket post. Early next morning the command fell in line, and we all marched back to Bolivar again. We had hardly got started before it began to rain, and just poured down all day long. But the weather was pleasant, we took off our shoes and socks and rolled up our breeches, after the manner heretofore described, and just "socked on" through the yellow mud, whooping and singing, and as wet as drowned rats. We reached Bolivar some time after dark. The boys left there in camp in some way had got word that we were on the return, and had prepared for us some camp-kettles full of hot, strong coffee, with plenty of fried sow-belly,--so we had a good supper. What the object of the expedition was, and what caused us to turn back, I have never learned, or if I did, have now forgotten.

On returning to Bolivar we settled down to the usual routine of battalion drill and standing picket. The particular guard duty the regiment performed nearly all the time we were at Bolivar (with some casual exceptions) was guarding the railroad from the bridge over Hatchie river, north to Toone's Station, a distance of about seven miles. Toone's Station, as its name indicates, was nothing but a stopping point, with a little rusty looking old frame depot and a switch. The usual tour of guard duty was twenty-four hours all the while I was in the service, except during this period of railroad guarding, and for it the time was two days and nights. Every foot of the railroad had to be vigilantly watched to prevent its being torn up by bands of guerrillas or disaffected citizens. One man with a crow-bar, or even an old ax, could remove a rail at a culvert, or some point on a high grade, and cause a disastrous wreck.

I liked this railroad guard duty. Between Bolivar and Toone's the road ran through dense woods, with only an occasional little farm on either side of the road, and it was pleasant to be out in those fine old woods, and far away from the noise and smells of the camps. And there are so many things that are strange and attractive, to be seen and heard, when one is standing alone on picket, away out in some lonesome place, in the middle of the night. I think that a man who has never spent some wakeful hours in the night, by himself, out in the woods, has simply missed one of the most interesting parts of life. The night is the time when most of the wild things are astir, and some of the tame ones, too. There was some kind of a very small frog in the swamps and marshes near Bolivar that gave forth about the most plaintive little cry that I ever heard. It was very much like the bleating of a young lamb, and, on hearing it the first time, I thought sure it was from some little lamb that was lost, or in distress of some kind. I never looked the matter up to ascertain of what particular species those frogs were. They may be common throughout the South, but I never heard this particular call except around and near Bolivar. And the woods between Bolivar and Toone's were full of owls, from great big fellows with a thunderous scream, down to the little screech owls, who made only a sort of chattering noise. One never failing habit of the big owls was to assemble in some grove of tall trees just about daybreak, and have a morning concert, that could be heard half a mile away. And there were also whippoorwills, and mocking birds, and, during the pleasant season of the year, myriads of insects that would keep sounding their shrill little notes the greater part of the night. And the only time one sees a flying squirrel, (unless you happen to cut down the tree in whose hollow he is sleeping,) is in the night time. They are then abroad in full force.

When on picket in my army days I found out that dogs are great nocturnal ramblers. I have been on guard at a big tree, on some grass-grown country road, when something would be heard coming down the road towards me; pat, pat, pitty-pat,--then it would stop short. The night might be too dark for me to see it, but I knew it must be a dog. It would stand silent for a few seconds, evidently closely scrutinizing that man alone under the tree, with something like a long shining stick in his hands; then it would stealthily leave the road, and would be heard rustling through the leaves as it made a half circle through the woods to get by me. On reaching the road below me, its noise would cease for a little while,--it was then looking back over its shoulder to see if that man was still there. Having satisfied itself on that point, then--pat, pat, pitty-pat, and it went off in a trot down the road. When you see an old farm dog asleep in the sun on the porch in the day time, with his head between his paws, it is, as a general rule, safe to assume that he was up and on a scout all the previous night, and maybe traveled ten or fifteen miles. Cats are also confirmed night prowlers, but I don't think they wander as far as dogs. Later, when we were in Arkansas, sometimes a full grown bear would walk up to some drowsy picket, and give him the surprise of his life.

One quiet, star-lit summer night, while on picket between Bolivar and Toone's, I had the good fortune to witness the flight of the largest and most brilliant meteor I ever have seen. It was a little after midnight, and I was standing alone at my post, looking, listening, and thinking. Suddenly there came a loud, rushing, roaring sound, like a passenger train close by, going at full speed, and there in the west was a meteor! Its flight was from the southwest to the northeast, parallel with the horizon, and low down. Its head, or body, looked like a huge ball of fire, and it left behind a long, immense tail of brilliant white, that lighted up all the western heavens. While yet in full view, it exploded with a crash like a near-by clap of thunder, there was a wide, glittering shower of sparks,--and then silence and darkness. The length of time it was visible could not have been more than a few seconds, but it was a most extraordinary spectacle.

On October 19th the regiment (except those on guard duty) went as escort of a foraging expedition to a big plantation about twelve miles from Bolivar down the Hatchie river. We rode there and back in the big government wagons, each wagon being drawn by a team of six mules. Like Joseph's brethren when they went down into Egypt, we were after corn. The plantation we foraged was an extensive one on the fertile bottom land of the Hatchie river, and the owner that year had grown several hundred acres of corn, which had all been gathered, or shocked, and we just took it as we found it. The people evidently were wealthy for that time and locality, many slaves were on the place, and it was abounding in live stock and poultry of all kinds. The plantation in general presented a scene of rural plenty and abundance that reminded me of the home of old Baltus Van Tassel, as described by Washington Irving in the story of "The Legend of Sleepy Hollow,"--with this difference: Everything about the Tennessee plantation was dirty, out of order, and in general higgledy-piggledy condition. And the method of farming was slovenly in the extreme. The cultivated land had been cleared by cutting away the underbrush and small trees, while the big ones had merely been "deadened," by girdling them near the ground. These dead trees were all standing in ghastly nakedness, and so thick in many places that it must have been difficult to plow through them, while flocks of crows and buzzards were sailing around them or perched in their tops, cawing and croaking, and thereby augmenting the woe-begone looks of things. The planter himself was of a type then common in the South. He was a large, coarse looking man, with an immense paunch, wore a broad-brimmed, home-made straw hat and butter nut jeans clothes. His trousers were of the old-fashioned, "broad-fall" pattern. His hair was long, he had a scraggy, sandy beard, and chewed "long green" tobacco continually and viciously. But he was shrewd enough to know that ugly talk on his part wouldn't mend matters, but only make them worse, so he stood around in silence while we took his corn, but he looked as malignant as a rattlesnake. His wife was directly his opposite in appearance and demeanor. She was tall, thin, and bony, with reddish hair and a sharp nose and chin. And goodness, but she had a temper! She stood in the door of the dwelling house, and just tongue-lashed us "Yankees," as she called us, to the full extent of her ability. The boys took it all good naturedly, and didn't jaw back. We couldn't afford to quarrel with a woman. A year later, the result of her abuse would have been the stripping of the farm of every hog and head of poultry on it, but at this time the orders were strict against indiscriminate, individual foraging, and except one or two bee-stands full of honey, nothing was taken but the corn. And I have no doubt that long ere this the Government has paid that planter, or his heirs, a top-notch price for everything we took. It seems to be easy, now-a-days, to get a special Act through Congress, making "full compensation" in cases of that kind.

Not long after the foregoing expedition, I witnessed a somewhat amusing incident one night on the picket line. One day, for some reason, the regiment was required, in addition to the railroad guards, to furnish a number of men for picket duty. First Lieut. Sam T. Carrico, of Co. B, was the officer, and it fell to my lot to be the sergeant of the guard. We picketed a section of the line a mile or so southwest of Bolivar, and the headquarters post, where the lieutenant and the sergeant of the guard stayed, was at a point on a main traveled road running southwest from the town. It was in the latter part of October, and the night was a bad and cold one. Lieut. Carrico and I had "doubled up," spread one of our blankets on the ground, and with the other drawn over us, were lying down and trying to doze a little, when about ten o'clock we heard a horseman coming at full speed from the direction of Bolivar. We thereupon rose to a sitting posture, and awaited developments. The horseman, on nearing our post and being challenged, responded, "Friend, without the countersign!" and in a peremptory manner told the sentinel on duty that he wanted to see the officer of the guard. Lieut. Carrico and I walked up to the horseman, and, on getting close to him, saw that he was a Union officer of the rank of

Captain. Addressing himself to the lieutenant, in a loud and hasty manner he told him his story, which, in substance, was that he was Captain ---- (giving his name), on Gen. Grant's staff, that he had just arrived in Bolivar on the train from Memphis, that he had important business a few miles outside of the lines, and being in a great hurry, he had not gone to post headquarters to get the countersign, as he felt satisfied that the statement of his rank and business would be sufficient to insure his being passed through the picket line, and so on. Lieut. Carrico listened in silence until the fellow finished, and then said, quietly but very firmly, "Captain, if you claimed to be Gen. Grant himself, you shouldn't pass through my line without the countersign." At this the alleged "staff officer" blew up, and thundered and bullied at a great rate. Carrico was not much more than a boy, being only about twenty-two years old, and of slight build, but he kept perfectly cool and remained firm as a rock. Finally the officer wheeled his horse around and started back to town at a furious gallop. Carrico then walked up to the sentinel on duty and said to him, "Now, if that fellow comes back, you challenge him, and make him conform to every item of the army regulations;" and to make sure about it, he gave the guard specific instructions as to his duties in such cases. We stood around and waited, and it was not long before we heard the horseman returning at his usual rate of speed. He never checked his gait until the challenge of the sentinel rang out, "Halt! Who comes there?" "Friend, with the countersign!" was the answer. "Dismount, friend, advance, and give the countersign!" cried the sentinel. Kuh-sock, went the fine, high-top boots of the rider in the mud, and leading his horse, he walked up, gave the talismanic word, to which the response was made, "Countersign's correct! Pass, friend." The officer then sprang into the saddle, and rode up to the lieutenant and me. Taking a memorandum book and pencil from one of his pockets, he said to Carrico, "Give me your name, company, and regiment, sir." "Samuel T. Carrico, first lieutenant Co. B, 61st Illinois Infantry." The officer scribbled in his note-book, then turned to me, "And yours?" "Leander Stillwell, sergeant Co. D, 61st Illinois Infantry;" and that answer was also duly recorded. "Good night, gentlemen; you'll render an account for this outrage later;" and with this parting salutation, the officer galloped away. "All right!" Carrico called after him, "you know where to find us." The victim of the "outrage" had not returned when we were relieved at 9 o'clock the next morning, and we never saw or heard of him any more. Of course his threat on leaving us was pure bluff, for Lieut. Carrico had only done his plain and simple duty. The fellow was probably all right; his returning with the countersign would indicate it. But his "important business" was doubtless simply to keep a date with some lady-love out in the country, and he wanted to meet her under the friendly cover of the night.

A few words will here be said in the nature of a deserved tribute to Lieut. Carrico. Later he rose to the rank of Captain of his company, and was one among the very best and bravest of the line officers of the regiment. He had nerves like hammered steel, and was as cool a man in action as I ever have known. Of all the officers of the regiment who were mustered in at its organization, he is now the only survivor. He is living at Alva, Oklahoma, and is a hale, hearty old man.

CHAPTER IX

THE AFFAIR at SALEM CEMETERY. JACKSON, CARROLL STATION. DECEMBER, 1862, JANUARY, 1863. BOLIVAR. FEBRUARY-MAY, 1863.

On the afternoon of December 18th, suddenly, without any previous warning or notification, the bugle sounded "Fall in!" and all the regiment fit for duty and not on guard at once formed on the regimental parade ground. From there we marched to the depot, and with the 43rd Illinois of our brigade got on the cars, and were soon being whirled over the road in a northerly direction. It was a warm, sunshiny day, and we common soldiers supposed we were going on just some little temporary scout, so we encumbered ourselves with nothing but our arms, and haversacks, and canteens. Neglecting to take our blankets was a grievous mistake, as later we found out to our sorrow. We arrived at Jackson a little before sundown, there left the cars, and, with the 43rd, forthwith marched out about two miles east of town. A little after dark we halted in an old field on the left of the road, in front of a little old country graveyard called Salem Cemetery, and there bivouacked for the night. Along in the evening the weather turned intensely cold. It was a clear, star-lit night, and the stars glittered in the heavens like little icicles. We were strictly forbidden to build any fires, for the reason, as our officers truly said, the Confederates were not more than half a mile away, right in our front. As before stated, we had no blankets, and how we suffered with the cold! I shall never forget that night of December 18th, 1862. We would form little columns of twenty or thirty men, in two ranks, and would just trot round and round in the tall weeds and broom sedge to keep from chilling to death. Sometimes we would pile down on the ground in great bunches, and curl up close together like hogs, in our efforts to keep warm. But some part of our bodies would be exposed, which soon would be stinging with cold, then up we would get and renew the trotting process. At one time in the night some of the boys, rendered almost desperate by their suffering started to build a fire with some fence rails. The red flames began to curl around the wood, and I started for the fire, intending to absorb some of that glowing heat, if, as Uncle Remus says, "it wuz de las' ack." But right then a mounted officer dashed up to the spot, and sprang from his horse. He was wearing big cavalry boots, and jumped on that fire with both feet and stamped it out in less time than I am taking to tell about it. I heard afterwards that he was Col. Engelmann, of the 43rd Illinois, then the commander of our brigade. Having put out the fire, he turned on the men standing around, and swore at them furiously. He said that the rebels were right out in our front, and in less than five minutes after we had betrayed our presence by fires, they would open on us with artillery, and "shell hell out of us;"--and more to the same effect. The boys listened in silence, meek as lambs, and no more fires were started by us that night. But the hours seemed interminably long, and it looked like the night would never come to an end. At last some little woods birds were heard, faintly chirping in the weeds and underbrush near by, then some owls set up a hooting in the woods behind us, and I knew that dawn was approaching. When it became light enough to distinguish one another, we saw that we presented a doleful appearance--all hollow-eyed, with blue noses, pinched faces, and shivering as if we would shake to pieces. Permission was then given to build small fires to cook our breakfast, and we didn't wait for the order to be repeated. I made a quart canful of strong, hot coffee, toasted some bacon on a stick, and then, with some hardtack, had a good breakfast and felt better. Breakfast over (which didn't take long), the regiment was drawn back into the cemetery, and placed in line behind the section of inclosing fence that faced to the front. The fence was of post and plank, the planks arranged lengthwise, with spaces between. We were ordered to lie flat on the ground, and keep the barrels of our guns out of sight, as much as possible. Our position in general may be described about as follows: The right of the regiment rested near the dirt road, and at right angles to it. The ground before us was open for more than half a mile. It sloped down gently, then it rose gradually to a long, bare ridge, or slight elevation of ground, which extended parallel to our front. The road was enclosed by an old-time staked and ridered fence, of the "worm" pattern. On our right, and on the other side of the road, was a thick forest of tall trees, in which the 43rd Illinois was posted. The cemetery was thickly studded with tall, native trees, and a few ornamental ones, such as cedar and pine. Soon after we had been put in position, as above stated, Col. Engelmann, the brigade commander, came galloping up, and stopped about opposite the front of the regiment. Maj. Ohr, our regimental commander, who was in the rear of the regiment on foot, walked out to meet him. Engelmann was a German, and a splendid officer.

"Goot morning, Major," he said, in a loud voice we all heard. "How are de poys?" "All right," answered the Major; "we had rather a chilly night, but are feeling first rate now." "Dat iss goot," responded the Colonel; and continued in his loud tone, "our friends are right out here in de bush; I reckon dey'll show up presently. Maybe so dey will give us a touch of deir artillery practice,--but dat hurts nobody. Shoost have de poys keep cool."

Then he approached the Major closer, said something in a low tone we did not hear, waved his hand to us, and then galloped off to the right. He was hardly out of sight, when sure enough, two or three cannon shots were heard out in front, followed by a scattering fire of small arms. We had a small force of our cavalry in the woods beyond the ridge I have mentioned, and they soon appeared, slowly falling back. They were spread out in a wide, extended skirmish line, and acted fine. They would trot a little ways to the rear, then face about, and fire their carbines at the advancing foe, who, as yet, was unseen by us. Finally they galloped off to the left and disappeared in the woods, and all was still for a short time. Suddenly, without a note of warning, and not preceded by even a skirmish line, there appeared coming over the ridge in front, and down the road, a long column of Confederate cavalry! They were, when first seen, at a walk, and marching by the flank, with a front of four men. How deep the column was we could not tell. The word was immediately passed down our line not to fire until at the word of command, and that we were to fire by file, beginning on the right. That is, only two men, front and rear rank, would fire together, and so on, down the line. The object of this was apparent: by the time the left of the regiment had emptied their guns, the right would have reloaded, and thus a continuous firing would be maintained. With guns cocked and fingers on the triggers, we waited in tense anxiety for the word to fire. Maj. Ohr was standing a few paces in the rear of the center of the regiment, watching the advance of the enemy. Finally, when they were in fair musket range, came the order, cool and deliberate, without a trace of excitement: "At-ten-shun, bat-tal-yun! Fire by file! Ready!--Commence firing!" and down the line crackled the musketry. Concurrently with us, the old 43rd Illinois on the right joined in the serenade. In the front file of the Confederate column was one of the usual fellows with more daring than discretion, who was mounted on a tall, white horse. Of course, as long as that horse was on its feet, everybody shot at him, or the rider. But that luckless steed soon went down in a cloud of dust, and that was the end of old Whitey. The effect of our fire on the enemy was marked and instantaneous. The head of their column crumpled up instanter, the road was full of dead and wounded horses, while several that were riderless went galloping down the road by us, with bridle reins and stirrups flapping on their necks and flanks. I think there is no doubt that the Confederates were taken completely by surprise. They stopped short when we opened on them, wheeled around, and went back much faster than they came, except a little bunch who had been dismounted. They hoisted a white rag, came in, and surrendered. The whole affair was exceedingly "short and sweet;" in duration it could not have exceeded more than a few minutes, but it was highly interesting as long as it lasted. But now the turn of the other fellows was to come. Soon after their charging column disappeared behind the ridge in our front, they put in position on the crest of the ridge two black, snaky looking pieces of artillery, and began giving us the benefit of the "artillery practice" Col. Engelmann had alluded to. They were beyond the range of our muskets; we had no artillery with our little force, and just had to lie there and take it. I know nothing about the technicalities of cannon firing, so I can only describe in my own language how it appeared to us. The enemy now knew just where we were, there were no obstructions between them and us, and they concentrated their fire on our regiment. Sometimes they threw a solid shot at us, but mostly they fired shells. They were in plain sight, and we could see every movement connected with the firing of the guns. After a piece was fired, the first thing done was to "swab" it. Two men would rush to the muzzle with the swabber, give it a few quick turns in the bore, then throw down the swabber and grab up the rammer. Another man would then run forward with the projectile and insert it in the muzzle of the piece, the rammers would ram it home, and then stand clear. The man at the breech would then pull the lanyard,--and now look out! A tongue of red flame would leap from the mouth of the cannon, followed by a billow of white smoke; then would come the scream of the missile as it passed over our heads (if a solid shot), or exploded near our front or rear (if a shell), and lastly we would hear the report of the gun. Then we all drew a long breath. When they threw shells at us their method was to elevate the muzzle of the gun, and discharge the missile in such a manner that it would describe what I suppose would be called the parabola of a curve. As it would be nearing the zenith of its flight we could follow it distinctly with the naked eye. It looked like a big, black bug. You may rest assured that we watched the downward course of this messenger of mischief with the keenest interest. Sometimes it looked as if it would hit our line, sure, but it never did. And, as stated, we could only lie there and watch all this, without the power on our part to do a thing in return. Such a situation is trying on the nerves. But firing at our line was much like shooting at the edge of a knife-blade, and their practice on us, which lasted at least two hours, for all practical results, to quote Col. Engelmann, "shoost hurt nobody." A private of Co. G had his head carried away by a fragment of a shell, and a few others were slightly injured, and that was the extent of our casualties. After enduring this cannonading for the time above stated, Col. Engelmann became apprehensive that the Confederate cavalry were flanking us, and trying to get between us and Jackson, so he ordered our force to retire. We fell back, in good order, for about a mile, then halted, and faced to the front again. Reinforcements soon came out from Jackson, and then the whole command advanced, but the enemy had disappeared. Our regiment marched in column by the flank up the road down which the Confederates had made their charge. They had removed their killed and wounded, but at the point reached by their head of column, the road was full of dead horses. Old Whitey was sprawled out in the middle of the lane, "with his nostrils all wide," and more than a dozen bullet holes in his body. Near his carcass I saw a bloody yarn sock, with a bullet hole square through the instep. I made up my mind then and there, that if ever I happened to get into the cavalry I would, if possible, avoid riding a white horse.

I will now say something about poor Sam Cobb, heretofore mentioned, and then he will disappear from this history. Sam was with us at the beginning of this affair on December 19th, but the very instant that the enemy came in sight he broke from the ranks and ran, and never showed up until we returned to Jackson some days later. He then had one of his hands tied up, and claimed that he had been wounded in the fight. The nature of his wound was simply a neat little puncture, evidently made by a pointed instrument, in the ball of the forefinger of one of his hands. Not a shot had been fired at us up to the time when he fled, so it was impossible for his hurt to have been inflicted by the enemy. It was the belief of all of us that he had put his forefinger against a tree, and then jabbed the point of his bayonet through the ball thereof. I heard Capt. Reddish in bitter language charge him with this afterwards, and poor Sam just hung his head and said nothing. When the regiment veteranized in 1864, Sam didn't re-enlist, and was mustered out in February, 1865, at the end of his term of service. On returning to his old home, he found that his reputation in the army had preceded him, and it is likely that the surroundings were not agreeable. At any rate, he soon left there, emigrated to a southwestern State, and died there several years ago. In my opinion, he really was to be sincerely pitied, for I think, as he had told me at Bolivar, he just "couldn't help it."

We advanced this day (December 19) only two or three miles beyond Salem Cemetery, and bivouacked for the night in an old field. The weather had changed, and was now quite pleasant;

besides, the embargo on fires was lifted, so the discomfort of the previous night was only something to be laughed about. The next day we were afoot early, and marched east in the direction of Lexington about fifteen miles. But we encountered no enemy, and on December 21 turned square around and marched back to Jackson. Gen. Forrest was in command of the Confederate cavalry operating in this region, and he completely fooled Gen. J. C. Sullivan, the Union commander of the district of Jackson. While we were on this wild-goose chase towards Lexington, Forrest simply whirled around our flanks at Jackson, and swept north on the railroad, scooping in almost everything to the Kentucky line, and burning bridges and destroying culverts on the railroad in great shape.

During our short stay that ensued at Jackson, an event occurred that I have always remembered with pleasure. In 1916 I wrote a brief preliminary statement touching this Salem Cemetery affair, followed by one of my army letters, the two making a connected article, and the same was published in the Erie (Kansas) "Record." It may result in some repetition, but I have concluded to here reproduce this published article, which I have called, "A Soldier's Christmas Dinner."

A SOLDIER'S CHRISTMAS DINNER.

By Judge Leander Stillwell.

Christmas Day in the year eighteen hundred and sixty-two was a gloomy one, in every respect, for the soldiers of the Union army in West Tennessee. Five days before, the Confederate General Van Dorn had captured Grant's depot of supplies at Holly Springs, and government stores of the value of a million and a half of dollars had gone up in smoke and flame. About the same time Forrest had struck the Mobile and Ohio railroad, on which we depended to bring us from the north our supplies of hardtack and bacon, and had made a wreck of the road from about Jackson, Tennessee, nearly to Columbus, Kentucky. For some months previous to these disasters the regiment to which I belonged, the 61st Illinois Infantry, had been stationed at Bolivar, Tennessee, engaged in guarding the railroad from that place to Toone's Station, a few miles north of Bolivar. On December 18, with another regiment of our brigade, we were sent by rail to Jackson to assist in repelling Forrest, who was threatening that place. On the following day the two regiments, numbering in the aggregate about 500 men, in connection with a small detachment of our cavalry, had a lively and spirited little brush with the Confederate forces about two miles east of Jackson, near a country burying ground called Salem Cemetery, which resulted in our having the good fortune to give them a salutary check.

Reinforcements were sent out from Jackson, and Forrest disappeared. The next day our entire command marched about fifteen miles eastwardly in the direction of the Tennessee river. It was doubtless supposed by our commanding general that the Confederates had retreated in that direction, but he was mistaken. Forrest had simply whipped around Jackson, struck the railroad a few miles north thereof, and then had continued north up the road, capturing and destroying as he went. On the succeeding day, December 21st, we all marched back to Jackson, and my regiment went into camp on a bleak, muddy hillside in the suburbs of the town, and there we remained until December 29th, when we were sent to Carroll Station, about eight miles north of Jackson.

I well remember how gloomy I felt on the morning of that Christmas Day at Jackson, Tennessee. I was then only a little over nineteen years of age. I had been in the army nearly a year, lacking just a few days, and every day of that time, except a furlough of two days granted at our camp of instruction before we left Illinois for the front, had been passed with the regiment in camp and field.

Christmas morning my thoughts naturally turned to the little old log cabin in the backwoods of western Illinois, and I couldn't help thinking about the nice Christmas dinner that I knew the folks at home would sit down to on that day.

There would be a great chicken pot pie, with its savory crust and a superabundance of light, puffy dumplings; delicious light, hot biscuits; a big ball of our own home-made butter, yellow as gold; broad slices of juicy ham, the product of hogs of our own fattening, and home cured with hickory-wood smoke; fresh eggs from the barn in reckless profusion, fried in the ham gravy; mealy Irish potatoes, baked in their jackets; coffee with cream about half an inch thick; apple butter and crab apple preserves; a big plate of wild honey in the comb; and winding up with a thick wedge of mince pie that mother knew so well how to make--such mince pie, in fact, as was made only in those days, and is now as extinct as the dodo. And when I turned from these musings upon the bill of fare they would have at home to contemplate the dreary realities of my own possible dinner for the day--my oyster can full of coffee and a quarter ration of hardtack and sow-belly comprised the menu. If the eyes of some old soldier should light upon these lines, and he should thereupon feel disposed to curl his lip with unutterable scorn and say: "This fellow was a milksop and ought to have been fed on Christian Commission and Sanitary goods, and put to sleep at night with a warm rock at his feet;"--I can only say in extenuation that the soldier whose feelings I have been trying to describe was only a boy--and, boys, you probably know how it was yourselves during the first year of your army life. But, after all, the soldier had a Christmas dinner that day, and it is of that I have started out to speak.

Several years ago my old army letters, which had been so carefully kept and cherished for all these many years, passed from the keeping of those to whom they had been addressed, back into the possession of him who penned them, and now, after the lapse of fifty-four years, one of these old letters, written to my father, shall re-tell the story of this Christmas dinner.

> "Jackson, Tennessee,
> December 27, 1862.
> "Mr. J. O. Stillwell,
> "Otter Creek, Illinois.
>
> "I wrote you a short and hasty letter the fore part of this week to let you know that I was all right, and giving you a brief account of our late ups and downs,

but I doubt if you have received it. The cars have not been running since we came back to Jackson from our march after Forrest. The talk in camp is that the rebs have utterly destroyed the railroad north of here clean to the Mississippi river, and that they have also broken it in various places and damaged it badly south of here between Bolivar and Grand Junction. I have no idea when this letter will reach you, but will write it anyhow, and trust to luck and Uncle Sam to get it through in course of time.

"We are now in camp on a muddy hillside in the outskirts of Jackson. I think the spot where we are must have been a cavalry camp last summer. Lots of corn cobs are scattered on the ground, old scraps of harness leather, and such other truck as accumulates where horses are kept standing around. When we left Bolivar we were in considerable of a hurry, with no time to primp or comb our hair, and neither did we bring our tents along, so we are just living out of doors now, and "boarding at Sprawl's." There is plenty of wood, though, to make fires, and we have jayhawked enough planks and boards to lie on to keep us out of the mud, so we just curl up at night in our blankets with all our clothes on, and manage to get along fairly well. Our worst trouble now is the lack of grub. The destruction of the railroad has cut off our supplies, and there is no telling just exactly how long it may be before it will be fixed and in running order again, so they have been compelled, I suppose, to cut down our rations. We get half rations of coffee, and quarter rations of hardtack and bacon. What we call small rations, such as Yankee beans, rice, and split peas, are played out; at least, we don't get any. The hardtack is so precious now that the orderly sergeant no longer knocks a box open and lets every man help himself, but he stands right over the box and counts the number of tacks he gives to every man. I never thought I'd see the day when army hardtack would be in such demand that they'd have to be counted out to the soldiers as if they were money, but that's what's the matter now. And that ain't all. The boys will stand around until the box is emptied, and then they will pick up the fragments that have fallen to the ground in the divide, and scrape off the mud with their knives, and eat the little pieces, and glad to get them. Now and then, to help out the sow-belly, we get quarter rations of fresh beef from the carcass of a Tennessee steer that the quartermaster manages to lay hands on somehow. But it's awful poor beef, lean, slimy, skinny and stringy. The boys say that one can throw a piece up against a tree, and it will just stick there and quiver and twitch for all the world like one of those blue-bellied lizards at home will do when you knock him off a fence rail with a stick.

"I just wish that old Forrest, who is the cause of about all this trouble, had to go without anything to eat until he was so weak that he would have to be fed with a spoon. Maybe after he had been hungry real good for a while he'd know how it feels himself, and would let our railroads alone.

"But I want to tell you that I had a real bully Christmas dinner, in spite of old Forrest and the whole caboodle. It was just a piece of the greatest good luck I've had for many a day.

"When Christmas morning came I was feeling awful blue. In spite of all I could do, I couldn't help but think about the good dinner you folks at home would have that day, and I pictured it all out in my imagination. Then about every one of the boys had something to say about what he would have for Christmas dinner if he was home, and they'd run over the list of good things till it was almost enough to make one go crazy. To make matters worse, just the day before in an old camp I had found some tattered fragments of a New York illustrated newspaper with a whole lot of pictures about Thanksgiving Day in the Army of the Potomac. They were shown as sitting around piles of roast turkeys, pumpkin pies, pound cake, and goodness knows what else, and I took it for granted that they would have the same kind of fodder today. You see, the men in that army, by means of their railroads, are only a few hours from home, and old Forrest is not in their neighborhood, so it is an easy thing for them to have good times. And here we were, away down in Tennessee, in the mud and the cold, no tents, on quarter rations, and picking scraps of hardtack out of the mud and eating them--it was enough to make a preacher swear. But along about noon John Richey came to me and proposed that inasmuch as it was Christmas Day, we should strike out and forage for a square meal. It didn't take much persuasion, and straightway we sallied forth. I wanted to hunt up the old colored woman who gave me the mess of boiled roasting ears when we were here last summer, but John said he thought he had a better thing than that, and as he is ten years older than I am, I knocked under and let him take the lead.

"About half a mile from our camp, in the outskirts of the town, we came to a large, handsome, two-story and a half frame house, with a whole lot of nigger cabins in the rear. John took a survey of the premises and said, 'Lee, right here's our meat.' We went into the yard at a little side gate between the big house and the nigger quarters, and were steering for one of the cabins, when out steps from the back porch of the big house the lady of the place herself. That spoiled the whole game; John whirled in his tracks and commenced to sidle away. But the lady walked towards us and said in a very kind and friendly manner: 'Do you men want anything?' 'Oh, no, ma'am,' replied John; 'we just came here to see if we could get some of the colored women to do some washing for us, but I guess we'll not bother about it today;' still backing away as he spoke. But the lady was not satisfied. Looking at us very sharply, she asked: 'Don't you men want something to eat?' My heart gave a great thump at that, but, to my inexpressible disgust, John, with his head thrown back and nose pointed skyward, answered, speaking very fast, 'Oh, no, ma'am, not at all, ma'am, a thousand times obleeged, ma'am,' and continued his sneaking retreat. By this time I had hold of the cape of his overcoat and was plucking it in utter desperation. 'John,' I said, speaking low, 'what in thunder do you mean? This is the best chance we'll ever have.' I was looking at the lady meanwhile in the most imploring manner, and she was regarding me with a kind of a pleasant, amused smile on her face. She saw, I guess, a mighty dirty looking boy, whose nose and face were pinched and blue with hunger, cold, loss of sleep, and hard knocks generally, and she brought the business to a head at once. 'You men come right in,' she said, as if she was the major-general commanding the department. 'We have just finished our dinner, but in a few minutes the servants can have something prepared for you,--and I think you are hungry.' John, with the most aggravating mock modesty that I ever saw in my life, began saying: 'We are very much obleeged, ma'am, but we haven't the slightest occasion in the world to eat, ma'am, and----' when I couldn't stand it any longer for fear he would ruin everything after all. 'Madam,' I said, 'please don't pay any attention to what my partner says, for we are most desperately hungry.' The lady laughed right out at that, and said, 'I thought so; come in.'

"She led the way into the basement story of the house, where the dining room was, (all the rich people in the South have their dining rooms in the basement,) and there was a nice warm room, a dining table in the center, with the cloth and dishes yet on it, and a big fireplace at one end of the room, where a crackling wood fire was burning. I tell you, it was different from our muddy camp on the bleak hillside, where the wind blows the smoke from our fires of green logs in every direction about every minute of the day. I sat down by the fire to warm my hands and feet, which were cold. A colored girl came in and commenced to arrange the table, passing back and forth from the dining room to the kitchen, and in a short time the lady told us that our dinner was ready, to sit up to the table, and eat heartily. We didn't wait for a second invitation that time. And, oh, what a dinner we had! There was a great pile of juicy, fried beefsteak, cooked to perfection and tender as chicken; nice, warm light bread, a big cake of butter, stewed dried apples, cucumber pickles, two or three kinds of preserves, coffee with sugar and cream, and some of the best molasses I ever tasted,--none of this sour, scorched old sorghum stuff, but regular gilt-edge first class New Orleans golden syrup, almost as sweet as honey. Then, to top off with, there was a nice stewed dried apple pie, and some kind of a custard in little dishes, something different from anything in that line that I had ever seen before, but mighty good. And then, in addition to all that, we were seated on chairs, at a table with a white cloth on it, and eating out of china plates and with knives and forks, a colored girl waiting on us, and the lady of the house sitting there and talking to us as pleasantly as if we were Grant and Halleck in person. Under the influence of the good grub, John thawed out considerably, and made a full confession to the lady about his queer actions at the beginning. He told her that we were going to the nigger quarters to try to get something to eat, and that when she came out and gave us such a kind invitation to come in the house, he was too much ashamed of our appearance to accept. That we had come up from Bolivar about a week before, riding on top of the box cars, where we got all covered with smoke, dust, and cinders; then ordered out to the front that night, then the fight with Forrest the next day, then the march towards the Tennessee river and back of about forty miles, and since then in camp with no shelter, tramping around in the mud, and sleeping on the ground; that on account of all these things we looked so rough and so dirty that he just felt ashamed to go into a nice house where handsome, well-dressed ladies were. Oh! I tell you, old John is no slouch; he patched up matters remarkably well. The lady listened attentively, said she knew we were hungry the moment she saw us, that she had heard the soldiers were on short rations in consequence of the destruction of the railroad, and turning towards me she went on to say: 'There was such a pitiful, hungry look on this boy's face that it would have haunted me for a long time if I had let you go away without giving you a dinner. Many a hungry soldier,' she continued, 'both of the Northern and Southern army, has had something to eat at this table, and I expect many more will in the future, before this terrible and distressing war shall have come to an end.' She didn't say a word, though, by which we could tell whether her sympathies were on the Union side or against us, and of course we didn't try to find out. She was just the sweetest looking woman I have yet seen in the whole Southern Confederacy. If they have any angels anywhere that look kinder, or sweeter, or purer than she did, I would just like to see them trotted out. I guess she was about thirty-five years old. She was of medium height, a little on the plump order, with blue eyes, brown hair, a clear, ruddy complexion, and the whitest, softest looking little hands I ever saw in my life.

"When we had finished our dinner, John and I thanked her ever so many times for her kindness, and then bade her a most respectful good-by. He and I both agreed on our way back to camp to say nothing about the lady and the nice dinner she gave us, because if we blowed about it, the result would probably be more hungry callers than her generosity could well afford.

"But these close times I guess are not going to last much longer. The talk in camp this evening is that we are going to have full rations once more in a day or two, that the railroad will soon be in running order again, and then we can just snap our fingers at old Forrest and his whole outfit.

"Well, I will bring my letter to a close. Don't worry if you fail to get a letter from me now as regularly as before. Things are a trifle unsettled down here yet, and we may not be able to count on the usual regularity of the mails for some time to come.

"So good-by for this time.

"LEANDER STILLWELL."

Soon after we returned to Jackson a detail of some from each company was sent to Bolivar and brought up our knapsacks and blankets, and we were then more comfortable. On December 29th, my company and two others of our regiment were sent by rail to Carroll Station, about eight miles north of Jackson. There had been a detachment of about a hundred men of the 106th Illinois Infantry previously stationed here, guarding the railroad, but Forrest captured them about December 20th, so on our arrival we found nothing but a crude sort of stockade, and the usual rubbish of an old camp. There was no town there, it consisted only of a platform and a switch. Our life here was somewhat uneventful, and I recall now only two incidents which, possibly, are worth noticing. It has heretofore been mentioned how I happened to learn when on picket at night something about the nocturnal habits of different animals and birds. I had a somewhat comical experience in this respect while on guard one night near Carroll Station. But it should be preceded by a brief explanation. It was no part of the duty of a non-commissioned officer to stand a regular tour of guard duty, with his musket in his hands. It was his province simply to exercise a general supervisory control over the men at his post, and especially to see that they relieved each other at the proper time. But it frequently happened in our regiment that our numbers present for duty were so diminished, and the guard details were so heavy, that the sergeants and corporals had to stand as sentries just the same as the privates, and this was especially so at Carroll Station.

On the occasion of the incident about to be mentioned, the picket post was on the crest of a low ridge, or slight elevation, and under some big oak trees by an old tumble-down deserted building which had at one time been a blacksmith shop. There were three of us on this post, and one of my turns came at midnight. I was standing by one of the trees, listening, looking, and meditating. The night was calm, with a full moon. The space in our front, sloping down to a little hollow, was bare, but the ascending ground beyond was covered with a dense growth of young oaks which had not yet shed their leaves. We had orders to be extremely watchful and vigilant, as parties of the enemy were supposed to be in our vicinity. Suddenly I heard in front, and seemingly in the farther edge of the oak forest, a rustling sound that soon increased in volume. Whatever was making the noise was coming my way, through the trees, and down the slope of the opposite ridge. The noise grew louder, and louder, until it sounded just like the steady tramp, over the leaves and dead twigs, of a line of marching men, with a front a hundred yards in width. I just knew there must be trouble ahead, and that the Philistines were upon me. But a sentinel who made a false alarm while on duty was liable to severe punishment, and, at any rate, would be laughed at all over the regiment, and never hear the last of it. So I didn't wake up my comrades, but got in the shadow of the trunk of a tree, cocked my gun, and awaited developments. And soon they came. The advancing line emerged from the forest into the moonlight, and it was nothing but a big drove of hogs out on a midnight foraging expedition for acorns and the like! Well, I let down the hammer of my gun, and felt relieved,--and was mighty glad I hadn't waked the other boys. But I still insist that this crackling, crashing uproar, made by the advance of the "hog battalion" through the underbrush and woods, under the circumstances mentioned, would have deceived "the very elect."

A few days later I was again on picket at the old blacksmith shop. Our orders were that at least once during the day one of the guard should make a scout out in front for at least half a mile, carefully observing all existing conditions, for the purpose of ascertaining if any parties of the enemy were hovering around in our vicinity. On this day, after dinner, I started out alone, on this little reconnoitering expedition. I had gone something more than half a mile from the post, and was walking along a dirt road with a cornfield on the left, and big woods on the right. About a hundred yards in front, the road turned square to the left, with a cornfield on each side. The corn had been gathered from the stalk, and the stalks were still standing. Glancing to the left, I happened to notice a white cloth fluttering above the cornstalks, at the end of a pole, and slowly moving my way. And peering through the tops of the stalks I saw coming down the road behind the white flag about a dozen Confederate cavalry! I broke into a run, and soon reached the turn in the road, cocked my gun, leveled it at the party, and shouted, "Halt!" They stopped, mighty quick, and the bearer of the flag called to me that they were a flag of truce party. I then said, "Advance, One." Whereupon they all started forward. I again shouted "Halt!" and repeated the command, "Advance, One!" The leader then rode up alone, I keeping my gun cocked, and at a ready, and he proceeded to tell me a sort of rambling, disjointed story about their being a flag of truce party, on business connected with an exchange of some wounded prisoners. I told the fellow that I would conduct him and his squad to my picket post, and then send word to our commanding officer, and he would take such action as he thought fit and proper. On reaching the post, I sent in one of the guards to the station to report to Lieut. Armstrong, in command of our detachment, that there was a flag of truce party at my post who desired an interview with the officer in command at Carroll Station. The Lieutenant soon arrived with an armed party of our men, and he and the Confederate leader drew apart and talked awhile. This bunch of Confederates were all young men, armed with double-barreled shot-guns, and a decidedly tough-looking outfit. They finally left my post, escorted by Lieut. Armstrong and his guard, and I understood in a general way that he passed them on to someone higher in authority at some other point in our vicinity, possibly at Jackson. They may have been acting in good faith, but from the manner of their leader, and the story he told me, I have always believed that their use of a flag of truce was principally a device to obtain some military intelligence,--but, of course, I do not know. My responsibility ended when Lieut. Armstrong reached my picket post in response to the message sent him.

We remained at Carroll Station until January 27, 1863, were then relieved by a detachment of the 62nd Illinois Infantry, and were sent by rail back to Bolivar, where we rejoined the balance of the regiment. We then resumed our former duty of guarding the railroad north to Toone's Station, and continued at this until the last of May, 1863. But before taking up what happened then, it will be in order to speak of some of the changes that in the meantime had occurred among the commissioned officers of my company and of the regiment. Capt. Reddish resigned April 3rd, 1863, First Lieutenant Daniel S. Keeley was promoted Captain in his place, and Thomas J. Warren, the sergeant-major of the regiment, was commissioned as First Lieutenant in Keeley's stead. Lieut. Col. Fry resigned May 14, 1863. His place was taken by Major Simon P. Ohr, and Daniel Grass, Captain of Co. H, was made Major. The resignations of both Fry and Reddish, as I always have understood, were because of ill-health. They were good and brave men, and their hearts were in the cause, but they simply were too old to endure the fatigue and hardships of a soldier's life. But they each lived to a good old age. Col. Fry died in Greene county, Illinois, January 27th, 1881, aged nearly 82 years; and Capt. Reddish passed away in Dallas county, Texas, December 30th, 1881, having attained the Psalmist's limit of three score and ten.

CHAPTER X

THE SIEGE OF VICKSBURG. JUNE AND JULY, 1863.

General Grant closed up against Vicksburg on May 19, and on that day assaulted the Confederate defenses of the place, but without success. On the 22nd a more extensive assault was made, but it also failed, and it was then evident to Grant that Vicksburg would have to be taken by a siege. To do this he would need strong reinforcements, and they were forthwith sent him from various quarters. So it came to pass that we went also. On May 31st we climbed on the cars, headed for Memphis, and steamed away from old Bolivar--and I have never seen the place since. For my part, I was glad to leave. We had been outside of the main track of the war for several months, guarding an old railroad, while the bulk of the western army had been actively engaged in the stirring and brilliant campaign against Vicksburg, and we were all becoming more or less restless and dissatisfied. From my standpoint, one of the most mortifying things that can happen to a soldier in time of war is for his regiment to be left somewhere as a "guard," while his comrades of the main army are in the field of active operations, seeing and doing "big things," that will live in history. But, as before remarked, the common soldier can only obey orders, and while some form the moving column, others necessarily have stationary duties. But at last the old 61st Illinois was on the wing,--and the Mississippi Central Railroad could "go hang."

The regiment at this time was part of Gen. Nathan Kimball's division of the 16th Corps, and the entire division left Tennessee to reinforce Grant at Vicksburg. We arrived at Memphis in the afternoon of the same day we left Bolivar, the distance between the two places being only about 72 miles. The regiment bivouacked that night on a sandbar on the water front of Memphis, which said bar extended from the water's edge back to a high, steep sand-and-clay bank. And that, by the way, is the only night I have ever spent within the limits of the city of

Memphis. While we were there on this occasion, I witnessed a pathetic incident, which is yet as fresh and vivid in my memory as if it had happened only yesterday. Soon after our arrival I procured a pass for a few hours, and took a stroll through the city. While thus engaged I met two hospital attendants carrying on a stretcher a wounded Union soldier. They halted as I approached, and rested the stretcher on the sidewalk. An old man was with them, apparently about sixty years old, of small stature and slight frame, and wearing the garb of a civilian. I stopped, and had a brief conversation with one of the stretcher-bearers. He told me that the soldier had been wounded in one of the recent assaults by the Union troops on the defenses of Vicksburg, and, with others of our wounded, had just arrived at Memphis on a hospital boat. That the old gentleman present was the father of the wounded boy, and having learned at his home in some northern State of his son being wounded, had started to Vicksburg to care for him; that the boat on which he was journeying had rounded in at the Memphis wharf next to the above mentioned hospital boat, and that he happened to see his son in the act of being carried ashore, and thereupon at once went to him, and was going with him to a hospital in the city. But the boy was dying, and that was the cause of the halt made by the stretcher-bearers. The soldier was quite young, seemingly not more than eighteen years old. He had an orange, which his father had given him, tightly gripped in his right hand, which was lying across his breast. But, poor boy! it was manifest that that orange would never be tasted by him, as the glaze of death was then gathering on his eyes, and he was in a semi-unconscious condition. And the poor old father was fluttering around the stretcher, in an aimless, distracted manner, wanting to do something to help his boy--but the time had come when nothing could be done. While thus occupied I heard him say in a low, broken voice, "He is--the only boy--I have." This was on one of the principal streets of the city, and the sidewalks were thronged with people, soldiers and civilians, rushing to and fro on their various errands,--and what was happening at this stretcher excited no attention beyond careless, passing glances. A common soldier was dying,--that was all, nothing but "a leaf in the storm." But for some reason or other the incident impressed me most sadly and painfully. I didn't wait for the end, but hurried away,--tried to forget the scene, but couldn't.

On the evening of June 1st we filed on board the big, side-wheel steamer "Luminary," which soon cast off from the wharf, and in company with other transports crowded with soldiers, went steaming down the Mississippi. Co. D, as usual, was assigned to a place on the hurricane deck of the boat. After we had stacked arms, and hung our belts on the muzzles of the guns, I hunted up a corner on the forward part of the deck, sat down, looked at the river and the scenery along the banks,--and thought. There came vividly to my mind the recollection of the time, about fourteen months previous, when we started out from St. Louis, down the "Father of Waters," bound for the "seat of war." The old regiment, in every respect, had greatly changed since that time. Then we were loud, confident, and boastful. Now we had become altogether more quiet and grave in our demeanor. We had gradually realized that it was not a Sunday school picnic excursion we were engaged in, but a desperate and bloody war, and what the individual fate of each of us might be before it was over, no one could tell. There is nothing which, in my opinion, will so soon make a man out of a boy as actual service in time of war. Our faces had insensibly taken on a stern and determined look, and soldiers who a little over a year ago were mere laughing, foolish boys, were now sober, steady, self-relying men. We had been taking lessons in what was, in many important respects, the best school in the world.

Our voyage down the river was uneventful. We arrived at the mouth of the Yazoo river on the evening of June 3rd. There our fleet turned square to the left, and proceeded up that stream. Near the mouth of the Chickasaw Bayou, the fleet landed on the left bank of the stream, the boats tied up for the night, we went on the shore and bivouacked there that night. It was quite a relief to get on solid ground, and where we could stretch our legs and stroll around a little. Next morning we re-embarked at an early hour, and continued up the Yazoo. During the forenoon we learned from one of the boat's crew that we were approaching a point called "Alligator Bend," and if we would be on the lookout we would see some alligators. None of us, so far as I know, had ever seen any of those creatures, and, of course, we were all agog to have a view of them. A few of the best shots obtained permission from the officers to try their muskets on the reptiles, in case any showed up. On reaching the bend indicated, there were the alligators, sure enough, lazily swimming about, and splashing in the water. They were sluggish, ugly looking things, and apparently from six to eight feet long. Our marksmen opened fire at once. I had read in books at home that the skin of an alligator was so hard and tough that it was impervious to an ordinary rifle bullet. That may have been true as regards the round balls of the old small-bore rifle, but it was not the case with the conical bullets of our hard-hitting muskets. The boys would aim at a point just behind the fore-shoulder, the ball would strike the mark with a loud "whack," a jet of blood would spurt high in the air, the alligator would give a convulsive flounce,--and disappear. It had doubtless got its medicine. But this "alligator practice" didn't last long. Gen. Kimball, on learning the cause, sent word mighty quick from the headquarters boat to "Stop that firing!"--and we stopped.

About noon on the 4th we arrived at the little town of Satartia on the left bank of the Yazoo, and about 40 miles above its mouth; there the fleet halted, tied up, and the troops debarked, and marched out to the highlands back of the town. We were now in a region that was new to us, and we soon saw several novel and strange things. There was a remarkable natural growth, called "Spanish moss," that was very plentiful, and a most fantastic looking thing. It grew on nearly all the trees, was of a grayish-white color, with long, pendulous stems. The lightest puff of air would set it in motion, and on a starlight night, or when the moon was on the wane and there was a slight breeze, it presented a most ghostly and uncanny appearance. And the woods were full of an unusual sort of squirrels, being just as black as crows. They were in size, as I now remember, of a grade intermediate the fox-and gray-squirrels we had at home. But all their actions and habits appeared to be just the same as those of their northern cousins. And there was a most singular bird of the night that was quite numerous here, called the "chuck-will's widow," on account of the resemblance its note bore to those words. It belonged to the whippoorwill family, but was some larger. It would sound its monotonous call in the night for hours at a stretch, and I think its mournful cry, heard when alone, on picket at night out in dense, gloomy woods, is just the most lonesome, depressing strain I ever heard.

On the afternoon of the 4th all our force advanced in the direction of the little town of Mechanicsburg, which lay a few miles back of the river. Those in the front encountered Confederate cavalry, and a lively little skirmish ensued, in which our regiment was not engaged. Our troops burnt Mechanicsburg, and captured about forty of the Confederates. I was standing by the side of the road when these prisoners were being taken to the rear. They were all young chaps, fine, hearty looking fellows, and were the best looking little bunch of Confederates I saw during the war. Early in the morning of June 6th we fell into line and marched southwest, in the direction of Vicksburg. Our route, in the main, was down the valley of the Yazoo river. And it will be said here that this was the hottest, most exhausting march I was on during my entire service. In the first place, the weather was intensely hot. Then the road down the valley on which we marched mostly ran through immense fields of corn higher than our heads. The fields next the road were not fenced, and the corn grew close to the beaten track. Not the faintest breeze was stirring, and the hot, stifling dust enveloped us like a blanket. Every now and then we would pass a soldier lying by the side of the road, overcome by the heat and unconscious, while one or two of his comrades would be standing by him, bathing his face and chest with water, and trying to revive him. I put green hickory leaves in my cap, and kept them well saturated with water from my canteen. The leaves would retain the moisture and keep my head cool, and when they became stale and withered, would be thrown away, and fresh ones procured. Several men died on this march from sun-stroke; none, however, from our regiment, but we all suffered fearfully. And pure drinking water was very scarce too. It was pitiful to see the men struggling for water at the farm house wells we occasionally passed. In their frenzied desperation they would spill much more than they saved, and ere long would have the well drawn dry. But one redeeming feature about this march was--we were not hurried. There were frequent halts, to give the men time to breathe, and on such occasions, if we were fortunate enough to find a pool of stagnant swamp-water, we would wash the dirt and dust from our faces and out of our eyes.

As we trudged down the Yazoo valley, we continued to see things that were new and strange. We passed by fields of growing rice, and I saw many fig trees, loaded with fruit, but which was yet green. And in the yards of the most of the farm houses was a profusion of domestic flowers, such as did not bloom in the north, of wonderful color and beauty. But, on the other hand, on the afternoon of the second day's march, I happened to notice by the side of the road an enormous rattlesnake, which evidently had been killed by some soldier only a short time before we passed. It seemingly was between five and six feet long, and the middle of its body appeared to be as thick as a man's thigh. Its rattles had been removed, presumably as a trophy. It was certainly a giant among rattlesnakes, and doubtless was an "old-timer."

On the evening of June 7th, about sundown, we arrived at Haines' Bluff on the Yazoo river, and there went into camp. This point was about twelve miles north of Vicksburg, and had been strongly fortified by the Confederates, but Grant's movements had compelled them to abandon their works without a battle. There had been a large number of the Confederates camped there, and the ground was littered with the trash and rubbish that accumulates in quarters. And our friends in gray had left some things in these old camps which ere long we all fervently wished they had taken with them, namely, a most plentiful quantity of the insect known as "Pediculus vestimenti," which forthwith assailed us as voraciously as if they had been on quarter rations, or less, ever since the beginning of the war.

On June 16th we left Haines' Bluff, and marched about two miles down the Yazoo river to Snyder's Bluff, where we went into camp. Our duties here, as they had been at Haines', were standing picket, and constructing fortifications. We had the usual dress parade at sunset, but the drills were abandoned;

we had more important work to do. General Joe Johnston, the Confederate commander outside of Vicksburg, was at Jackson, Mississippi, or in that immediate vicinity, and was collecting a force to move on Grant's rear, in order to compel him to raise the siege. Grant thought that if Johnston attacked, it would be from the northeast, so he established a line of defense extending southeast, from Haines' Bluff on the north to Black river on the south, and placed Gen. Sherman in command of this line. As Grant has said somewhere in his Memoirs, the country in this part of Mississippi "stands on edge." That is to say, it consists largely of a succession of high ridges with sharp, narrow summits. Along this line of defense, the general course of these ridges was such that they were admirably adapted for defensive purposes. We went to work on the ridges with spades and mattocks, and constructed the strongest field fortifications that I ever saw during the war. We dug away the crests, throwing the dirt to the front, and made long lines of breastworks along our entire front, facing, of course, the northeast. Then, at various places, on commanding points, were erected strong redoubts for artillery, floored, and revetted on the inner walls with thick and strong green lumber and timbers. On the exterior slopes of the ridges were dug three lines of trenches, or rifle pits, extending in a parallel form from near the base of the ridges almost to the summit, with intervals between the lines. All the trees and bushes in our front on the slopes of the ridges were cut down, with their tops outwards, thus forming a tangled abattis which looked as if a rabbit could hardly get through. And finally, on the inner slope of the ridges, a little below their summits, was constructed a "covered way;" that is, a road dug along the sides of the ridges, and over which an army, with batteries of artillery, could have marched with perfect safety. The purpose of these covered ways was to have a safe and sheltered road right along our rear by which any position on the line could be promptly reinforced, if necessary.

Sometimes I would walk along the parapet of our works, looking off to the northeast where the Confederates were supposed to be, and I ardently wished that they would attack us. Our defenses were so strong that in my opinion it would have been a physical impossibility for flesh and blood to have carried them. Had Johnston tried, he simply would have sacrificed thousands of his men without accomplishing anything to his own advantage.

It will be said here that I have no recollection of having personally taken part in the construction of the fortifications above mentioned. In fact, I never did an hour's work in the trenches, with spade and mattock, during all my time. I never "took" willingly to that kind of soldiering. But there were plenty of the boys who preferred it to standing picket, because when on fatigue duty, as it was called, they would quit about sundown, and then get an unbroken night's sleep. So, when it fell to my lot to be detailed for fatigue, I would swap with someone who had been assigned to picket,--he would do my duty, and I would perform his; we were both satisfied, and the fair inference is that no harm was thereby done to the cause. And it was intensely interesting to me, when on picket at night on the crest of some high ridge, to stand and listen to the roar of our cannon pounding at Vicksburg, and watch the flight of the shells from Grant's siege guns and from the heavy guns of our gunboats on the Mississippi. The shells they threw seemed principally to be of the "fuse" variety, and the burning fuse, as the shell flew through the air, left a stream of bright red light behind it like a rocket. I would lean on my gun and contemplate the spectacle with far more complacency and satisfaction than was felt when anxiously watching the practice on us by the other fellows at Salem Cemetery about six months before.

There was another thing I was wont to observe with peculiar attention, when on picket at night during the siege; namely, the operations of the Signal Corps. In the night time they used lighted lanterns in the transmission of intelligence, and they had a code by which the signals could be read with practically the same accuracy as if they had been printed words. The movements of the lights looked curious and strange, something elf-like, with a suspicion of witchcraft, or deviltry of some kind, about them. They would make all sorts of gyrations, up, down, a circle, a half circle to the right, then one to the left, and so on. Sometimes they would be unusually active. Haines' Bluff would talk to

Snyder's; Snyder's to Sherman's headquarters; Sherman's to Grant's, and back and forth, all along the line. Occasionally at some station the lights would act almost like some nervous man talking at his highest speed in a perfect splutter of excitement,--and then they would seem as if drunk, or crazy. Of course, I knew nothing of the code of interpretation, and so understood nothing,--could only look and speculate. In modern warfare the telephone has probably superseded the Signal Service, but the latter certainly played an important part in our Civil War.

During the siege we lived high on some comestibles not included in the regular army rations. Corn was in the roasting ear state, and there were plenty of big fields of it beyond and near the picket lines, and we helped ourselves liberally. Our favorite method of cooking the corn was to roast it in the "shuck." We would "snap" the ears from the stalk, leaving the shuck intact, daub over the outside a thin plaster of mud (or sometimes just saturate the ears in water), then cover them with hot ashes and live coals. By the time the fire had consumed the shuck down to the last or inner layer, the corn was done, and it made most delicious eating. We had no butter to spread on it, but it was good enough without. And then the blackberries! I have never seen them so numerous and so large as they were there on those ridges in the rear of Vicksburg. I liked them best raw, taken right from the vine, but sometimes, for a change, would stew them in my coffee can, adding a little sugar, and prepared in this manner they were fine. But, like the darkey's rabbit,--they were good any way. The only serious drawback that we had on our part of the line was the unusual amount of fatal sickness that prevailed among the men. The principal types of disease were camp diarrhea and malarial fevers, resulting, in all probability, largely from the impure water we drank. At first we procured water from shallow and improvised wells that we dug in the hollows and ravines. Wild cane grew luxuriantly in this locality, attaining a height of fifteen or twenty feet, and all other wild vegetation was rank in proportion. The annual growth of all this plant life had been dying and rotting on the ground for ages, and the water would filter through this decomposing mass, and become well-nigh poisonous. An order was soon issued that we should get all water for drinking and cooking purposes from the Yazoo river, and boil it before using, but it was impossible to compel complete obedience to such an order. When men got thirsty, they would drink whatever was handy,--orders to the contrary notwithstanding. And the water of the river was about as bad as the swamp water. I have read somewhere that "Yazoo" is an Indian word, signifying "The River of Death," and if so, it surely was correctly named. It is just my opinion, as a common soldier, that the epidemic of camp diarrhea could have been substantially prevented if all the men had eaten freely of blackberries. I didn't have a touch of that disorder during all the time we were in that locality, and I attribute my immunity to the fact that I ate liberally of blackberries about every day. But camp diarrhea is something that gets in its work quick, and after the men got down with it, they possibly had no chance to get the berries. And all the time we were at Snyder, nearly every hour of the day, could be heard the doleful, mournful notes of the "Dead March," played by the military bands, as some poor fellow was being taken to his long home. It seemed to me at the time, and seems so yet, that they should have left out that piece of music. It did no good, and its effect was very depressing, especially on the sick. Under such circumstances, it would seem that common sense, if exercised, would have dictated the keeping dumb of such saddening funeral strains.

Sometime during the latter part of June the regiment was paid two months' pay by Major C. L. Bernay, a Paymaster of the U.S. Army. He was a fine old German, of remarkably kind and benevolent appearance, and looked more like a venerable Catholic priest than a military man. After he had paid off the regiment, his escort loaded his money chest and his personal stuff into an ambulance, and he was soon ready to go to some other regiment. Several of our officers had assembled to bid him good-by, and I happened to be passing along, and witnessed what transpired. The few farewell remarks of the old man were punctuated by the roar of the big guns of our army and navy pounding away at Vicksburg, and the incident impressed me as somewhat pathetic. "Goot-by, Colonel," said Major Bernay, extending his hand; (Boom!) "Goot-by Major;"

(Boom!) "Goot-by, Captain;" (Boom!) and so on, to the others. Then, with a wave of his hand to all the little group, "Goot-by, shentlemens, all." (Boom!) "Maybe so (Boom!) we meet not again." (Boom, boom, boom!) It was quite apparent that he was thinking of the so-called "fortunes of war." Then he sprang into his ambulance, and drove away. His prediction proved true--we never met again.

The morning of the Fourth of July opened serene and peaceful, more so, in fact, than in old times at home, for with us not even the popping of a fire-cracker was heard. And the stillness south of us continued as the day wore on,--the big guns of the army and navy remained absolutely quiet. Our first thought was that because the day was a national holiday, Grant had ordered a cessation of the firing in order to give his soldiers a day of needed rest. It was not until some time in the afternoon that a rumor began to circulate among the common soldiers that Vicksburg had surrendered, and about sundown we learned that such was the fact. So far as I saw or heard, we indulged in no whooping or yelling over the event. We had been confident, all the time, that the thing would finally happen, so we were not taken by surprise. There was a feeling of satisfaction and relief that the end had come, but we took it coolly and as a matter of course.

On the same day that Vicksburg surrendered Grant started the greater part of his army, under the command of Gen. Sherman, in the direction of Jackson for the purpose of attacking Gen. Johnston. Our division, however, remained at Snyder's until July 12th, when we left there, marching southeast. I remember this march especially, from the fact that the greater part of it was made during the night. This was done in order to avoid the excessive heat that prevailed in the daytime. As we plodded along after sunset, at route step, and arms at will, a low hum of conversation could be heard, and occasionally a loud laugh, "that spoke the vacant mind." By ten o'clock we were tired (we had been on the road since noon), and moreover, getting very sleepy. Profound silence now prevailed in the ranks, broken only by the rattle of canteens against the shanks of the bayonets, and the heavy, monotonous tramp of the men. As Walter Scott has said somewhere in one of his poetical works:

"No cymbal clashed, no clarion rang,
Still were the pipe and drum;
Save heavy tread and armor's clang,
The sullen march was dumb."

The column halted about midnight, we bivouacked in the woods by the side of the road, and I was asleep about as soon as I struck the ground.

We resumed the march early in the morning, and during the forenoon arrived at Messinger's ford, on Black river, where we went into camp. We remained here only until July 17, and on that day marched a few miles south to the railroad crossing on Black river, and bivouacked on the west bank of the stream. The Confederates during the campaign had thrown up breastworks of cotton bales, which evidently had extended for quite a distance above and below the railroad crossing. When our fellows came along they tore open the bales and used the cotton to sleep on, and when we arrived at the place the fleecy stuff was scattered over the ground, in some places half-knee deep, all over that portion of the river bottom. It looked like a big snowfall. Cotton, at that very time, was worth one dollar a pound in the New York market, and scarce at that. A big fortune was there in the dirt, going to waste, but we were not in the cotton business just then, so it made no difference to us. At the beginning of the war, it was confidently asserted by the advocates of the secession movement that "Cotton was king;" that the civilized world couldn't do without it, and as the South had a virtual monopoly of the stuff, the need of it would compel the European nations to recognize the independence of the Southern Confederacy, and which would thereby result in the speedy and complete triumph of the Confederate cause. But in thus reasoning they ignored a law of human nature. Men, under the pressure of necessity, can get along without many things which they have previously regarded as indispensable. At this day, in my opinion, many of the alleged wants of mankind are purely artificial, and we would be better off if they were cut out altogether. Aside from various matters of food and drink and absurdities in garb and ornaments, numbers of our rich women in eastern cities regard life as a failure unless they each possess a thousand dollar pet dog, decorated with ribbons and diamond ornaments and honored at dog-functions with a seat at the table, where, on such occasions, pictures of the dogs, with their female owners sitting by them, are taken and reproduced in quarter-page cuts in the Sunday editions of the daily papers. If these women would knock the dogs in the head and bring into the world legitimate babies, (or even illegitimate, for their husbands are probably of the capon breed,) then they might be of some use to the human race; as it is they are a worthless, unnatural burlesque on the species. But this has nothing to do with the war, or the 61st Illinois, so I will pass on.

While we were at the Black river railroad bridge thousands of paroled Confederate soldiers captured at Vicksburg passed us, walking on the railroad track, going eastward. We had strict orders to abstain from making to them any insulting or taunting remarks, and so far as I saw, these orders were faithfully obeyed. The Confederates looked hard. They were ragged, sallow, emaciated, and seemed depressed and disconsolate. They went by us with downcast looks and in silence. I heard only one of them make any remark whatever, and he was a little drummer boy, apparently not more than fifteen years old. He tried to say something funny,--but it was a dismal failure.

While in camp at the railroad crossing on Black river, a most agreeable incident occurred, the pleasure of which has not been lessened by the flight of time, but rather augmented. But to comprehend it fully, some preliminary explanation might be advisable. Before the war there lived a few miles from our home, near the Jersey Landing settlement, a quaint and most interesting character, of the name of Benjamin F. Slaten. He owned and lived on a farm, but had been admitted to the bar, and practiced law to some extent, as a sort of a side-line. But I think that until after the war his practice, in the main, was confined to the courts of justices of the peace. He was a shrewd, sensible old man, of a remarkably kind and genial disposition, but just about the homeliest looking individual I ever saw. And he had a most singular, squeaky sort of a voice, with a kind of a nasal twang to it, which if heard once could never be forgotten. He was an old friend of my father's, and had been his legal adviser (so far as his few and trifling necessities in that line required) from time immemorial. And for a year or so prior to the outbreak of the war my thoughts had been running much on the science of law, and I had a strong desire, if the thing could be accomplished, to sometime be a lawyer myself. So, during the period aforesaid, whenever I would meet "Uncle Ben" (as we frequently called him), I would have a lot of questions to fire at him about some law points, which it always seemed to give him much pleasure to answer. I remember yet one statement he made to me that later, (and sometimes to my great chagrin,) I found out was undeniably true. "Leander," said he, "if ever you get into the practice of law, you'll find that it is just plum full of little in-trick-ate pints." (But things are not as bad now in that respect as they were then.) The war ensued, and in September, 1862, he entered the service as Captain of Co. K of the 97th Illinois Infantry. He was about forty-two years old at this time. In due course of events the regiment was sent south, and became a part of the Army of the Tennessee, but the paths of the 61st and the 97th were on different lines, and I never met Capt. Slaten in the field until the happening of the incident now to be mentioned.

When we were at Black river I was on picket one night about a mile or so from camp, at a point on an old country road. Some time shortly after midnight, while I was curled up asleep in a corner of the old worm fence by the side of the road, I was suddenly awakened by an energetic shake, accompanied by the loud calling of my name. I sprang to my feet at once, thinking maybe some trouble was afoot, and, to my surprise, saw Capt. Keeley standing in front of me, with some other gentleman. "Stillwell," said Keeley, "here's an old friend of yours. He wanted to see you, and being pressed for time, his only chance for a little visit was to come to you on the picket line." My caller stood still, and said nothing. I saw that he was an officer, for his shoulder straps were plainly visible, but I could not be sure of his rank, for there was no moon, and the night was dark. He was wearing an old "sugar-loaf" hat, seemingly much decayed, his blouse was covered with dust, and, in general, he looked tough.

His face was covered with a thick, scraggy beard, and under all these circumstances it was impossible for me to recognize him. I was very anxious to do so in view of the trouble the officer had taken to come away out on the picket line, in the middle of the night, to see me, but I just couldn't, and began to stammer a sort of apology about the darkness of the night hindering a prompt recognition, when the "unknown" gave his head a slant to one side, and, in his never forgettable voice, spoke thus to Keeley: "I told you he wouldn't know me." "I know you now," said I; "I'd recognize that voice if I heard it in Richmond! This is Capt. Ben Slaten, of the 97th Illinois;" and springing forward I seized his right hand with both of mine, while he threw his left arm about my neck and fairly hugged me. It soon came out in the conversation that ensued that his regiment had been with Sherman in the recent move on Jackson; that it was now returning with that army to the vicinity of Vicksburg, and had arrived at Black river that night; that he had at once hunted up the 61st Illinois to have a visit with me, and ascertaining that I was on picket, had persuaded Capt. Keeley to come with him to the picket line, as his regiment would leave early in the morning on the march, hence this would be his only opportunity for a brief meeting. And we all certainly had a most delightful visit with the old Captain. From the time of his arrival until his departure there was no sleeping, by anybody, on that picket post. We sat on the ground in a little circle around him, and listened to his comical and side-splitting stories of army life, and incidents in camp and field generally. He was an inimitable story teller, and his peculiar tone and manner added immensely to the comicality of his anecdotes. And somehow he had the happy faculty of extracting something humorous, or absurd, from what the generality of men would have regarded as a very serious affair. He did the most of the talking that night, while the rest of us sat there and fairly screamed with laughter. It was well known and understood that there were no armed Confederates in our vicinity, so we ran no risk in being a little careless. Finally, when the owls began tuning up for day, the old Captain bade us good-by, and trudged away, accompanied by Capt. Keeley.

To fully comprehend this little episode, it is, perhaps,

necessary to have some understanding and appreciation of how a soldier away down south, far from home and the friends he had left behind, enjoyed meeting some dear old friend of the loved neighborhood of home. It was almost equal to having a short furlough.

I never again met Capt. Slaten during the war. He came out of it alive, with an excellent record,--and about thirty-seven years after the close died at his old home in Jersey county, Illinois, sincerely regretted and mourned by a large circle of acquaintances and friends.

CHAPTER XI

HELENA, ARKANSAS. LIFE in a HOSPITAL. AUGUST, 1863.

General Sherman soon drove General Johnston out of Jackson, and beyond Pearl river, and then his column returned to the vicinity of Vicksburg. On July 22nd our division marched back to Snyder's Bluff, and resumed our old camp. But we had not been here long before it was rumored that we were under marching orders, and would soon leave for some point in Arkansas. Sure enough, on July 29th we marched to the Yazoo river and filed on board the side-wheel steamer "Sultana," steamed down the river to its mouth, and there turned up the Mississippi, headed north. I will remark here that one of the most tragical and distressing incidents of the war was directly connected with a frightful disaster that later befell the above named steamboat. It left Vicksburg for the north on or about April 25, 1865, having on board nearly 1900 Union soldiers, all of whom (with few exceptions) were paroled prisoners. On the morning of April 27th, while near Memphis, the boilers of the boat exploded, and it was burnt to the water's edge. Over 1100 of these unfortunate men perished in the wreck, in different ways; some scalded to death by escaping steam, some by fire, others (and the greatest number) by drowning. Besides the soldiers, cabin passengers and members of the boat's crew, to the number of about 140, also perished. It was the greatest disaster, of that kind, that ever occurred on the Mississippi.

It may, perhaps, be noticed that the regiment is leaving the vicinity of Vicksburg without my saying a word about the appearance, at that time, of that celebrated stronghold. There is good reason for it; namely, it so happened that we never were in the place. We were close to it, on the north and on the east, but that was all. And I never yet have seen Vicksburg, and it is not probable now that I ever shall.

We arrived at Helena, Arkansas, on July 31st, debarked and

went into camp near the bank of the river, about two miles below the town. There were no trees in our camp except a few cottonwoods; the ground on which we walked, sat, and slept was, in the main, just a mass of hot sand, and we got water for drinking and cooking purposes from the Mississippi river. The country back of the town, and in that immediate vicinity generally, was wild and thinly settled, and had already been well-foraged, so we were restricted to the ordinary army diet, of which one of the principal items, as usual, was fat sow-belly. I never understood why we were not allowed to camp in the woods west of the town. There was plenty of high, well-shaded space there, and we soon could have sunk wells that would have furnished cool, palatable water. But this was not done, and the regiment remained for about two weeks camped on the river bank, in the conditions above described. A natural result was that numbers of the men were prostrated by malarial fever, and this time I happened to be one of them. I now approach a painful period of my army career. I just lay there, in a hot tent, on the sand,--oh, so sick! But I fought off going to the hospital as long as possible. I had a superstitious dread of an army hospital. I had seen so many of the boys loaded into ambulances, and hauled off to such a place, who never returned, that I was determined never to go to one if it could be avoided in any honorable way. But the time came when it was a military necessity that I should go, and there was no alternative. The campaign that was in contemplation was a movement westward against the Confederates under Gen. Sterling Price at Little Rock, with the intention of capturing that place and driving the Confederates from the State. The officer in command of the Union forces was Gen. Frederick Steele. Marching orders were issued, fixing the 13th of August as the day our regiment would start. All the sick who were unable to march (and I was among that number) were to be sent to the Division Hospital. So, on the morning before the regiment moved, an ambulance drove up to my tent, and some of the boys carried me out and put me in the vehicle. Capt. Keeley was standing by; he pressed my hand and said, "Good-by, Stillwell; brace up! You'll be all right soon." I was feeling too wretched to talk much; I only said, "Good-by, Captain," and let it go at that. Later, when I rejoined the regiment, Keeley told me that when he bade me good-by that morning he never expected to see me again.

Our Division Hospital, to which I was taken, consisted of a little village of wall tents in the outskirts of Helena. The tents were arranged in rows, with perhaps from fifteen to twenty in a row, with their ends pinned back against the sides, thus making an open space down an entire row. The sick men lay on cots, of which there was a line on each side of the interior of the tents, with a narrow aisle between. I remained at the hospital eight days, and was very sick the most of the time, and retain a distinct recollection of only a few things. But, aside from men dying all around me, both day and night, nothing important happened. All the accounts that I have read of this movement of Gen. Steele's on Little Rock agree in stating that the number of men he left sick at Helena and other places between there and Little Rock was extraordinary and beyond all usual proportions. And from what I saw myself, I think these statements must be true. And a necessary consequence of this heavy sick list was the fact that it must have been impossible to give the invalids the care and attention they should have received. We had but few attendants, and they were soldiers detailed for that purpose who were too feeble to march, but were supposed to be capable of rendering hospital service. And the medical force left with us was so scanty that it was totally inadequate for the duties they were called on to perform. Oh, those nights were so long! At intervals in the aisle a bayonet would be stuck in the ground with a lighted candle in its socket, and when a light went out, say after midnight, it stayed out, and we would toss around on those hard cots in a state of semi-darkness until daylight. If any attendants moved around among us in the later hours of the night I never saw them. We had well-water to drink, which, of course, was better than that from the river, but it would soon become insipid and warm, and sometimes, especially during the night, we didn't have enough of that. On one occasion, about midnight, soon after I was taken to the hospital, I was burning with fever, and became intolerably thirsty for a drink of water. No attendants were in sight, and the candles had all gone out but one or two, which emitted only a sort of flickering light that barely served to "render darkness visible." My suffering became well-nigh unendurable, and I could stand it no longer. I got up and staggered to the door of the tent and looking about me saw not far away a light gleaming through a tent that stood apart from the others. I made my way to it as best I could, and went in. A young fellow, maybe an assistant surgeon, was seated at the further end cf a little desk, writing. My entrance was so quiet that he did not hear me, and walking up to him, I said, in a sort of a hollow voice: "I want--a drink--of water." The fellow dropped his pen, and nearly fell off his stool. The only garment I had on was a white, sleazy sort of cotton bed-gown, which they garbed us all in when we were taken to the hospital; and this chap's eyes, as he stared at me, looked as if they would pop out of his head. Perhaps he thought I was a "gliding ghost." But he got me some water, and I drank copiously. I don't clearly remember what followed. It seems to me that this man helped me back to my tent, but I am not sure. However, I was in the same old cot next morning.

The fare at the hospital was not of a nature liable to generate an attack of the gout, but I reckon those in charge did the best they could. The main thing seemed to be a kind of thin soup, with some grains of rice, or barley, in it. What the basis of it was I don't know. I munched a hardtack occasionally, which was far better than the soup. But my appetite was quite scanty, anyhow. One day we each had at dinner, served in our tin plates, about two or three tablespoonfuls of preserved currants, for which it was said we were indebted to the U.S. Sanitary Commission. It seemed that a boat load of such goods came down the river, in charge of a committee of ladies, destined for our hospitals at Vicksburg. The boat happened to make a temporary stop at Helena, and the ladies ascertained that there was at the hospitals there great need of sanitary supplies, so they donated us the bulk of their cargo. I will remark here that that little dab of currants was all the U.S. Sanitary stuff I consumed during my army service. I am not kicking; merely stating the fact. Those goods very properly went to the hospitals, and as my stay therein was brief, my share of the delicacies was consequently correspondingly slight.

As regards the medicine given us in the hospital at Helena, my recollection is that it was almost entirely quinine, and the doses were frequent and copious, which I suppose was all right.

There was a boy in my company of about my age; a tall, lanky chap, named John Barton. He had lived in our neighborhood at home, and we were well acquainted prior to our enlistment. He was a kind hearted, good sort of a fellow, but he had, while in the army, one unfortunate weakness,--the same being a voracious appetite for intoxicating liquor. And he had a remarkable faculty for getting the stuff, under any and all circumstances. He could nose it out, in some way, as surely and readily as a bear could find a bee-tree. But to keep the record straight, I will further say that after his discharge he turned over a new leaf, quit the use of whisky, and lived a strictly temperate life. He was "under the weather" when the regiment left Helena, and so was detailed to serve as a nurse at the hospital, and was thus engaged in my tent. Since making that bad break at Owl Creek I had avoided whisky as if it were a rattlesnake, but somehow, while here in the hospital, I began to feel an intense craving for some "spiritus frumenti," as the surgeons called it. So one day I asked John Barton if he couldn't get me a canteenful of whisky. He said he didn't know, was afraid it would be a difficult job,--but to give him my canteen, and he would try. That night, as late maybe as one or two o'clock, and when the lights were nearly all out, as usual, I heard some one stealthily walking up the aisle, and stopping occasionally at different cots, and presently I heard a hoarse whisper, "Stillwell! Stillwell!" "Here!" I answered, in the same tone. The speaker then came to me,--it was old John, and stooping down, he whispered, "By God, I've got it!" "Bully for you, John!" said I. He raised me to a sitting posture, removed the cork, and put the mouth of the canteen to my lips,--and I drank about as long as I could hold my breath. John took a moderate swig himself, then carefully put the canteen in my knapsack, which was serving as my pillow, cautioned me to keep it concealed to avoid its being stolen, and went away. I was asleep in about five minutes after my head struck my knapsack, and slept all the balance of the night just like a baby. On waking up, I felt better, too, and wanted something to eat.

However, let no one think, who may read these lines, that I favor the use of whisky as a medicine, for I don't. But the situation in those Helena hospitals was unusual and abnormal. The water was bad, our food was no good and very unsatisfactory, and the conditions generally were simply wretched. I am not blaming the military authorities. They doubtless did the best they could. It seemed to me that I was getting weaker every day. It looked as if something had to be done, and acting on the maxim that "desperate cases require desperate remedies," I resorted for the time being to the whisky treatment. I made one unsuccessful attempt afterwards to get some to serve as a tonic, which perhaps may be mentioned later, and then forever abandoned the use of the stuff for any purpose.

Immediately succeeding the above mentioned incident, the fever let up on me, and I began to get better, though still very weak. My great concern, right now, was to rejoin the regiment just as soon as possible. It was taking part in an active campaign, in which fighting was expected, and the idea was intolerable that the other boys should be at the front, marching and fighting, while I was in the rear, playing the part of a "hospital pimp." It was reported that a steamboat was going to leave soon, via Mississippi and White rivers, with convalescents for Steele's army, and I made up my mind to go on that boat, at all hazards. But to accomplish that it was necessary, as I was informed, to get a written permit from the Division Surgeon, Maj. Shuball York, of the 54th Illinois Infantry. So one morning, bright and early, I blacked my shoes and brushed up my old cap and clothing generally, and started to Maj. York's headquarters to get the desired permission. He was occupying a large two-story house, with shade trees in the yard, in the residence part of town, and his office was in the parlor, in the first story of the building. I walked in, and found an officer of the rank of Major seated at a table, engaged in writing. I removed my cap and, standing at attention, saluted him, and asked if this was Maj. York, and was answered in the affirmative. I had my little speech carefully prepared, and proceeded at once to deliver it, as follows:

"My name is Leander Stillwell; I am a sergeant of Co. D, of the 61st Illinois Infantry, which is now with Gen. Steele's army.

The regiment marched about a week ago, and, as I was then sick with a fever, I could not go, but was sent to the Division Hospital, here in Helena. I am now well, and have come to you to request a permit to enable me to rejoin my regiment."

The Major looked at me closely while I was speaking, and after I had concluded he remained silent for a few seconds, still scrutinizing me intently. Then he said, in a low and very kind tone: "Why, sergeant, you are not able for duty, and won't be for some time. Stay here till you get a little stronger."

His statement was a bitter disappointment to me. I stood there in silence a little while, twisting and turning, with trembling hands, my old faded and battered cap. I finally managed to say, "I want--to go--to--my regiment;"--and here my lips began to tremble, and I got no further. Now don't laugh at this. It was simply the case of a boy, weak and broken down by illness, who was homesick to be with his comrades. The Major did not immediately respond to my last remark, but continued to look at me intently. Presently he picked up his pen, and said: "I am inclined to think that the best medical treatment for you is to let you go to your regiment;" and he thereupon wrote and handed me the permit, which was quite brief, consisting only of a few lines. I thanked him, and departed with a light heart.

I will digress here for a moment to chronicle, with deep sorrow, the sad fate that ultimately befell the kind and noble surgeon, Maj. York. While he, with his regiment, was home on veteran furlough, in March, 1864, an organized gang of Copperheads made a dastardly attack on some of the soldiers of the regiment at Charleston, Illinois, and murdered Maj. York and five privates, and also severely wounded the Colonel, Greenville M. Mitchell, and three privates.

The war ended over half a century ago, and the feelings and passions engendered thereby, as between the people of the Nation and those of the late Confederate States, have well-nigh wholly subsided, which is right. But nevertheless I will set it down here that in my opinion the most "undesirable citizens" that ever have afflicted our country were the traitorous, malignant breed that infested some portions of the loyal States during the war, and were known as "Copperheads." The rattlesnake gives warning before it strikes, but the copperhead snake, of equally deadly venom, gives none, and the two-legged copperheads invariably pursued the same course. They deserved the name.

On leaving Maj. York's office I returned to the hospital and gathered up my stuff, which included my gun, cartridge box, knapsack, haversack, and canteen,--and said good-by to Barton and the other boys I knew. Then to the commissary tent, and exhibiting my permit, was furnished with five days' rations of hardtack, bacon, coffee, and sugar. Thence to the river landing, and on to the steamboat "Pike," which was to take the present batch of convalescents to Steele's army.

CHAPTER XII

DEVALL'S BLUFF. LITTLE ROCK.
AUGUST-OCTOBER, 1863.

On the morning of August 21st, the "Pike" cast off, and started down the Mississippi river. On reaching the mouth of White river, we turned up that stream, and on August 26th arrived at Devall's Bluff, on the west bank, where we debarked. Our trip from Helena was slow and uneventful. The country along White river from its mouth to Devall's Bluff was wild, very thinly settled, and practically in a state of nature. We passed only two towns on the stream--St. Charles and Clarendon, both small places. On different occasions I saw several bears and deer on the river bank, they having come there for water. Of course they ran back into the woods when the boat got near them. All of Steele's infantry was temporarily in camp at Devall's Bluff, while his cavalry was some miles further out. I soon found the old regiment, and received a warm welcome from all of Co. D. They were much surprised to see me, as they had no idea that I would be able to leave the hospital so soon. They had had no fighting on this campaign, so far, and they said that their march across the country from Helena had been monotonous and devoid of any special interest.

During my first night at Devall's Bluff there came a heavy and protracted rain storm, and on waking up the following morning I found myself about half hip-deep in a puddle of water. And this was the beginning of more trouble. My system was full of quinine taken to break the fever while in the hospital, and the quinine and this soaking in the water did not agree. In a short time I began to feel acute rheumatic twinges in the small of my back, and in a day or two was practically helpless, and could not get up, or walk around, without assistance.

The regiment left Devall's Bluff, with the balance of the army, on September 1st, advancing towards Little Rock. I was totally unable to march, but was determined to go along some way, and with Capt. Keeley's permission, the boys put me into one of the regimental wagons. This wagon happened to be loaded with barrels of pickled pork, standing on end, and my seat was on top of one of the barrels, and it was just the hardest, most painful day's ride in a wagon I ever endured. I was suffering intensely from acute rheumatism in the "coupling region," and in this condition trying to keep steady on the top of a barrel, and being occasionally violently pitched against the ends of the barrel staves when the wagon gave a lurch into a deep rut,--which would give me well-nigh intolerable pain. To make matters worse, the day was very hot, so, when evening came and the column halted, I was mighty near "all in." But some of the boys helped me out and laid me on my blanket in the shade, and later brought me some supper of hardtack, bacon, and coffee. Except the rheumatism, I was all right, and had a good appetite, and after a hearty supper, felt better. Next morning, in consequence of the active exertions of Capt. Keeley in the matter, an ambulance drove up where I was lying, and I was loaded into it, and oh, it was a luxury! Poor Enoch Wallace had been taken down with a malarial fever, and he was also a passenger, likewise two other soldiers whose names I have forgotten. Enoch had been promoted to second lieutenant and had been acting as such for some months, but his commission was not issued until September 3rd,--a day when he was a very sick man. From this on, until September 10th, the day our forces captured Little Rock, my days were spent in the ambulance. At night, the sick of each division (of whom there were hundreds) would bivouac by the side of some lagoon, or small water course, the attendants would prepare us some supper, and the surgeons would make their rounds, administering such medicine as the respective cases required. The prevailing type of sickness was malarial fever, for which, the sovereign specific seemed to be quinine. As for me, I was exempt from the taking of medicine, for which I was thankful. The surgeon, after inquiry into my case, would sententiously remark, "Ah! acute rheumatism," and pass on. I was at a loss to understand this seeming neglect, but a sort of explanation was given me later, which will be mentioned in its order. The food that was given the sick was meager and very unsatisfactory, but it was probably the best that could be furnished, under the circumstances. Each man was given an oyster-can full of what seemed to be beef-soup, with some rice or barley grains in it. By the time it got around to us there was usually a thin crust of cold tallow on the top, and the mere looks of the mess was enough to spoil one's appetite,--if he had any. One evening, Wallace and I were sitting side by side with our backs against a tree, when an attendant came to us and gave each one his can of the decoction above mentioned. It was comical to see the look of disgust that came over the face of poor Enoch. He turned towards me, and tilting his can slightly to enable me to see the contents, spoke thus: "Now, ain't this nice stuff to give a sick man? I've a good notion to throw the whole business in that fellow's face;" (referring to the attendant). "The trouble with you, Enoch," I said, "is that you are losing your patriotism, and I shouldn't be surprised if you'd turn Secesh yet. Kicking on this rich, delicious soup! Next thing you'll be ordering turtle-soup and clamoring for napkins and finger-bowls. You remind me of a piece of poetry I have read somewhere, something like this:

'Jeshurun waxed fat,
And down his belly hung,
Against the government he kicked,
And high his buttocks flung'."

The poor old fellow leaned back against the tree, and indulged in a long, silent laugh that really seemed to do him good. I would joke with him, after this fashion, a good deal, and long afterwards he told me that he believed he would have died on that march if I hadn't kept his spirits up by making ridiculous remarks. (In speaking of Wallace as "old," the word is used in a comparative sense, for the fact is he was only about thirty-four years of age at this time.)

On the evening of September 9th, the sick of our division bivouacked by the side of a small bayou, in a dense growth of forest trees. Next morning the rumor spread among us that on that day a battle was impending, that our advance was close to the Confederates, and that a determined effort would be made for the capture of Little Rock. Sure enough, during the forenoon, the cannon began to boom a few miles west of us, and our infantry was seen rapidly moving in that direction. As I lay there helpless on the ground, I could not avoid worrying somewhat about the outcome of the battle. If our forces should be defeated, we sick fellows would certainly be in a bad predicament. I could see, in my mind's eye, our ambulance starting on a gallop for Devall's Bluff, while every jolt of the conveyance would inflict on me excruciating pain. But this suspense did not last long. The artillery practice soon began moving further towards the west, and was only of short duration anyhow. And we saw no stragglers, which was an encouraging sign, and some time during the afternoon we learned that all was going in our favor. From the standpoint of a common soldier, I have always thought that General Steele effected the capture of Little Rock with commendable skill and in a manner that displayed sound military judgment. The town was on the west side of the Arkansas river, and our army approached it from the east. Gen. Price, the Confederate commander, had constructed strong breastworks a short distance east of the town, and on the east side of the river, commanding the road on which we were approaching. The right of these works rested on the river, and the left on an impassable swamp. But Gen. Steele did not choose to further Price's plans by butting his infantry up against the Confederate works. He entertained him at that point by ostentatious demonstrations, and attacked elsewhere. The Arkansas was very low, in many places not much more than a wide sandbar, and was easily fordable at numerous points. So Steele had his cavalry and some of his infantry ford the river to the west side, below the town, and advance along the west bank, which was not fortified. Gen. Price, seeing that his position was turned and that his line of retreat was in danger of being cut off, withdrew his troops from the east side and evacuated Little Rock about five o'clock in the afternoon, retreating southwest. Our troops followed close on his heels, and marched in and took possession of the capital city of the State of Arkansas. Our loss, in the entire campaign, was insignificant, being only a little over a hundred, in killed, wounded, and missing. The 61st was with the troops that operated on the east side of the river, and sustained no loss whatever. A few cannon balls, poorly aimed and flying high, passed over the regiment, but did no mischief,--beyond shaking the nerves of some recruits who never before had been under fire.

About sundown on the evening of the 10th, the ambulance drivers hitched up, and the sick were taken to a division hospital located near the east bank of the river. Capt. Keeley came over the next day to see Wallace and myself, and, at my urgent request, he arranged for me to be sent to the regiment. As heretofore stated, I just loathed the idea of being in a hospital. There were so many disagreeable and depressing things occurring there every day, and which could not be helped, that they inspired in me a sort of desperate determination to get right out of such a place,--and stay out, if possible. Early next morning an ambulance drove up, I was put in it, and taken to the camp of the old regiment. Some of the boys carried me into a tent, and laid me down on a cot, and I was once more in the society of men who were not groaning with sickness, but were cheerful and happy. But it was my fate to lie on that cot for more than a month, and unable even to turn over without help. And I shall never forget the kindness of Frank Gates during that time. He would come every day, when not on duty, and bathe and rub my rheumatic part with a rag soaked in vinegar, almost scalding hot, which seemed to give me temporary relief. There was an old doctor, of the name of Thomas D. Washburn, an assistant surgeon of the 126th Illinois Infantry, who, for some reason, had been detailed to serve temporarily with our regiment, and he would sometimes drop in to see me. He was a tall old man, something over six feet high, and gaunt in proportion. I don't remember that he ever gave me any medicine, or treatment of any kind, for the reason, doubtless, that will now be stated. One day I said to him, "Doctor, is there nothing that can be done for me? Must I just lie here and suffer indefinitely?" He looked down at me sort of sympathetically, and slowly said: "I will answer your question by telling you a little story. Once upon a time a young doctor asked an old one substantially the same question you have just asked me, which the old doctor answered by saying: 'Yes, there is just one remedy:--six weeks'." And, patting me lightly on the shoulder, he further remarked, "That's all;" and left. The sequel in my case confirmed Dr. Washburn's story.

The spot where the regiment went into camp on the day of the capture of Little Rock was opposite the town, on the east bank of the Arkansas, not far from the river, and in a scattered grove of trees. The locality was supposed to be a sort of suburb of the town, and was designated at the time in army orders as "Huntersville." But the only house that I now remember of being near our camp was a little, old, ramshackle building that served as a railroad depot. Speaking of the railroad, it extended only from here to Devall's Bluff, a distance of about fifty miles, and was the only railroad at that time in the State of Arkansas. The original project of the road contemplated a line from Little Rock to a point on the Mississippi opposite Memphis. Work was begun on the western terminus, and the road was completed and in operation as far as Devall's Bluff before the war, and then the war came along and the work stopped. Since then the road has been completed as originally planned. This little old sawed-off railroad was quite a convenience to our army at the Rock, as it obviated what otherwise would have been the necessity of hauling our supplies in wagons across the country from Devall's Bluff. It also frequently came handy for transporting the troops, and several times saved our regiment, and, of course, others, from a hot and tiresome march.

For some weeks while in camp at Huntersville, we lived high on several articles of food not included in the army rations. There were a good many sheep in the country round about that the military authorities confiscated, and so we had many a feast on fine, fresh mutton. Corn was plentiful also, and corn meal was issued to us liberally. Last, but not least, the rich Arkansas river bottom lands abounded in great big yellow sweet potatoes that the country people called "yams," and we just reveled in them to our entire satisfaction.

There was a boy in my company named William Banfield, about the same age as myself. We had been near neighbors at home, and intimate friends. Bill was a splendid soldier, seldom sick, and always performed his soldier duties cheerfully and without grumbling. And Bill was blessed with a good digestion, and apparently was always hungry. The place where he would build his cook-fire in this camp was near the front of my tent, where I had a good view of his operations. I was lying helpless on my cot, and, like others so situated from time immemorial, had nothing to do, and scarcely did anything else but watch the neighbors. Among the cherished possessions of our company was an old-fashioned cast-iron Dutch oven, of generous proportions, which was just the dandy for baking mutton. Well, Bill would, in the first place, get his chunk of mutton, a fine big piece of the saddle, or of a ham, and put it on to cook in the oven. Then we had another oven, a smaller affair of the skillet order, in which Bill would set to cooking a corn meal cake. At the right stage of the proceedings he would slice up some yams, and put them in with the mutton. Next, and last, he would make at least a quart of strong, black coffee. Both from long experience and critical observation, Bill knew to the fraction of a minute how long it would take for all his converging columns of table comforts to reach the done point on time and all together, and the resulting harmony was perfection itself, and (to use an overworked phrase) "left nothing to be desired." Dinner now being ready, the first thing Bill did was to bring me an ample allowance of the entire bill of fare, and which, by the way, I had to dispose of as best I could lying down, as it was impossible for me to sit up. Having seen to the needs of a disabled comrade, Bill next proceeded to clear his own decks for action. He seated himself at the foot of a big tree, on the shady side, with his back against the trunk; then spreading his legs apart in the shape of a pair of carpenter's compasses, he placed between them the oven containing the mutton and yams, at his left hand the skillet with the cornbread, and on his right his can of coffee--and then the services began. And how Bill would enjoy his dinner! There was no indecent haste about it, no bolting of the delicacies, or anything of the sort. He proceeded slowly and with dignity, while occasionally he would survey the landscape with a placid, contented air. But everything was devoured,--the last crumb of cornbread did duty in sopping up the final drop of grease. The banquet over, Bill would sit there a while in silence, gazing, perchance, at the shimmering waters of the Arkansas, and its sandbars, glittering in the sun. But ere long his head would begin to droop, he would throw one leg over the Dutch oven, swinging the limb clear of that utensil, settle himself snugly against the tree, and in about five minutes would be asleep.

At the time I am now writing, (October, 1916,) Bill is yet alive, and residing at Grafton, Illinois. He is a good old fellow, and "long may he wave."

CHAPTER XIII

LITTLE ROCK, OCTOBER, 1863.
GRANTED a FURLOUGH. CHAPLAIN B. B. HAMILTON.
THE JOURNEY on FURLOUGH from LITTLE ROCK to JERSEY COUNTY, ILLINOIS. RETURN to REGIMENT, NOVEMBER, 1863.

About the middle of October the regiment shifted its camp ground from Huntersville to an open space on the west side of the river, near the State penitentiary, where we remained all the ensuing winter. Soon after this change of camp it was reported among us that one man from each company would soon be granted a thirty day furlough. Prior to this, while in Tennessee, there had been a very few furloughs granted in exceptional cases, which were all the indulgencies of that kind the regiment had so far received. I made no request to be the favored man of our company in this matter, but one day Capt. Keeley told me that he had decided that I should be the furloughed man from Co. D, and could make my arrangements accordingly. By this time I had so far recovered from my rheumatism that I could walk around with the aid of a cane, but was very "shaky" on foot, and any sudden shock or jar would make me flinch with pain. I wondered how I should be able to get from the camp to the railroad depot on the other side of the river, with my knapsack, haversack and canteen, and their necessary contents, for I was utterly unable to carry them. I happened to mention this problem to the chaplain of the regiment, B. B. Hamilton. He was an old and valued friend of my parents, and, as he had lived only a few miles from our home, I knew him quite well before the war, and had heard him preach many a time. He was of the Baptist denomination, and my parents were of the same religious faith. At this time he was still what I would now call a young man, being only about forty years old. My father's given name was Jeremiah, and the Chaplain almost invariably, when speaking to me, would, in a grave, deliberate manner, address me as "Son of Jeremiah." When I mentioned to him my perplexity above indicated, he responded: "Son of Jeremiah, let not your heart be troubled. The Lord will provide." Knowing that what he said could be depended upon, I asked no questions. The precious document giving me thirty-days leave of absence was delivered to me in due time, and our little squad arranged to start on the next train, and which would leave Little Rock for Devall's Bluff early the following day. I had my breakfast betimes the next morning, and was sitting on the ground in front of my tent, with my traps by me, when Chaplain Hamilton came riding up on his horse. He dismounted, and saying to me, "Son of Jeremiah, the Lord has provided," thereupon helped me on his horse, and we started for the depot, the Chaplain walking by my side. We crossed the Arkansas on a sort of improvised army bridge, and were approaching the depot, when a locomotive on the track near-by began to let off steam. The horse evidently was not accustomed to that, he gave a frantic snort, and began to prance and rear. For a second or so I was in an agony of apprehension. I was incumbered with my knapsack and other things, was weak and feeble, and no horseman anyhow, and knew that if I should be violently thrown to the ground, it would just about break me all to pieces, and my furlough would end then and there. But it is likely that the Chaplain may have apprehended the horse's conduct; at any rate, he was on the alert. With one bound he was in front of the frightened animal, holding him firmly by the bridle bits, and had him under control at once. And about the same time the engine stopped its noise, and the trouble was over. The cars destined for Devall's Bluff were on the track, and the Chaplain, and some of our furlough party who had already arrived, helped me on the train. Of course there were no passenger coaches,--just box and gravel cars, and I seated myself on the floor of one of the latter. I gratefully thanked the Chaplain for his kindness, he said a few pleasant words, gave me a kind message for the folks at home, wished me a safe and pleasant trip, and then rode away.

This is probably a fitting place to pay a brief tribute to the memory of Chaplain Hamilton, so I will proceed to do so. The first chaplain of the regiment was a minister named Edward

Rutledge. He was appointed May 16, 1862, and resigned September 3rd, of the same year. I do not remember of his ever officiating often in the capacity of chaplain. I recall just one occasion when he preached to us, and that was under somewhat peculiar circumstances. He came to the regiment when we were in camp at Owl Creek, Tennessee, and, soon after his arrival, there was read one Saturday evening at dress parade an order in substance and effect as follows: That at a designated time on the following morning the men would assemble on their respective company parade grounds, wearing their "side-arms," (which included waist- and shoulder-belts, cartridge-box, cap-pouch and bayonet,) and under the command of a commissioned officer each company would march to the grove where the chaplain would hold religious services. Well, I didn't like that order one bit, and the great majority of the boys felt the same way. The idea of having to attend church under compulsion seemed to me to infringe on our constitutional rights as free-born American citizens, that while it might have been a thing to be endured in the days described in Fox's "Book of Martyrs," nevertheless, it wasn't exactly fair right now. But orders must be obeyed, so we all turned out with the prescribed "side-arms," and, like the young oysters that were inveigled by the Walrus and the Carpenter,--

"Our clothes were brushed, our faces washed,
Our shoes were clean and neat."

But it is much to be feared that the chaplain's discourse didn't do anybody a bit of good. For my part, I don't now remember a word, not even the text. The order aforesaid gave so much dissatisfaction to the rank and file, and perhaps to some of the line officers also, that it was never repeated, and thereafter attendance on the chaplain's preaching was a matter left to each man's pleasure and discretion. Judging only from what came under my personal notice, I don't think that much good was ever accomplished by chaplains in the Western army, as regards matters of a purely theological nature. As some one has said somewhere: "Army service in time of war is d--d hard on religion." But in practical, everyday matters, chaplains had ample opportunities for doing, and did, a great deal of good. They held the rank and wore the uniform of a captain,--and, while they had no military command over the men, they were, nevertheless, so far as I ever saw, always treated by the soldiers with the most kind and respectful consideration. To fill the vacancy caused by the resignation of Rutledge, B. B. Hamilton was commissioned chaplain on October 30, 1862, and came to us about that date. He had been active in the ministry at home for many years, and during that time had preached in Jersey, Greene, and the adjoining counties, so he was personally known to many of the officers and men. He was a man of good, sound common sense, an excellent judge of human nature, and endowed with a dry, quaint sort of humor that was delightful. When talking with intimate friends, he was prone, at times, to drop into an Oriental style of conversation, well garnished with sayings and illustrations from the Bible. I don't remember now of his preaching to us very often, and when he did he was tactful in selecting a time when the conditions were all favorable. In his discourses he ignored all questions of theology, such as faith, free-will, foreordination, the final perseverance of the saints, and such like, and got right down to matters involved in our every-day life. He would admonish us to be careful about our health, to avoid excesses of any kind that might be injurious to us in that respect, and above all things, to be faithful and brave soldiers, and conduct ourselves in such a manner that our army record would be an honor to us, and a source of pride and satisfaction to our parents and friends at home. In camp or on the march, he was a most useful and industrious man. He would visit the sick, write letters for them, and in general look after their needs in countless ways. He wrote a fine, neat, legible hand, and rendered much assistance to many of the line officers in making out the muster and pay rolls of their respective companies, and in attending to other matters connected with the company records, or official correspondence. And when the regiment had fighting to do, or a prospect of any, Chaplain Hamilton was always at the front. In the affair at Salem Cemetery, Hez. Giberson of Co. G was knocked down and rendered insensible for a short time by the near-by explosion of a shell. Hamilton ran to him, picked him up, and taking him by the arm, marched him to the rear, while shells were bursting all around us. I saw them as they walked by,--Giberson white as a sheet, staggering, and evidently deathly sick, but the chaplain clung to him, kept him on his feet, and ultimately turned him over to the surgeon.

The spring of 1865 found the regiment at Franklin, Tennessee. The war was then practically over in that region, and any organized armies of the Confederates were hundreds of miles away. Hamilton's health had become greatly impaired, and in view of all those conditions, he concluded to resign, and did so, on March 3rd, 1865, and thereupon returned to his old home in Illinois. The vacancy caused by his resignation was never filled, and thereafter we had no religious services in the regiment except on two or three occasions, rendered by volunteers, whose names I have forgotten. After leaving the army, Chaplain Hamilton led a life of activity and usefulness until incapacitated by his final illness. He died at Upper Alton, Illinois, on November 11th, 1894, at the age of nearly seventy-three years, respected and loved by all who knew him. He was a good, patriotic, brave man. I never saw him but once after he left the army, but we kept up a fraternal correspondence with each other as long as he lived.

I will now return to the little squad of furloughed Sixty-onesters that was left a while ago on the freight cars at Little Rock. The train pulled out early in the day for Devall's Bluff, where we arrived about noon. We at once made our way to the boat-landing,--and I simply am unable to describe our disappointment when we found no steamboats there. After making careful inquiry, we were unable to get any reliable information in regard to the time of the arrival of any from below,--it might be the next hour, or maybe not for several days. There was nothing to do but just bivouac there by the river bank, and wait. And there we waited for two long days of our precious thirty, and were getting fairly desperate, when one afternoon the scream of a whistle was heard, and soon the leading boat of a small fleet poked its nose around the bend about half a mile below,--and we sprang to our feet, waved our caps and yelled!

We ascertained that the boats would start on the return trip to the mouth of White river as soon as they unloaded their army freight. This was accomplished by the next morning, we boarded the first one ready to start, a small stern-wheeler, and some time on the second day thereafter arrived at the mouth of White river. There we landed, on the right bank of the Mississippi, and later boarded a big side-wheeler destined for Cairo, which stopped to take us on. When it rounded in for that purpose, the members of our little squad were quite nervous, and there was a rush on the principle of every fellow for himself. I was hobbling along with my traps, as best I could, when in going down the river bank, which was high and steep, in some way I stumbled and fell, and rolled clear to the bottom, and just lay there helpless. There was one of our party of the name of John Powell, of Co. G, a young fellow about twenty-two or -three years old. He was not tall, only about five feet and eight or nine inches, but was remarkably broad across the shoulders and chest, and had the reputation of being the strongest man in the regiment. He happened to see the accident that had befallen me, and ran to me, picked me up in his arms, with my stuff, the same as if I had been a baby, and "toted" me on the boat. He hunted up a cozy corner on the leeward side, set me down carefully, and then said, "Now, you d--d little cuss, I guess you won't fall down here." And all the balance of the trip, until our respective routes diverged, he looked after me the same as if I had been his brother. He was a splendid, big-hearted fellow. While ascending the Mississippi, the weather was cloudy and foggy, the boat tied up at nights, and our progress generally was tantalizingly slow. We arrived at Cairo on the afternoon of October 26th. It was a raw, chilly, autumn day, a drizzling rain was falling, and everything looked uncomfortable and wretched. We went to the depot of the Illinois Central railroad, and on inquiry learned that our train would not leave until about nine o'clock that night, so apparently there was nothing to do but sit down and wait. My thoughts were soon dwelling on the first time I saw Cairo,--that bright sunny afternoon in the latter part of March, 1862. I was then in superb health and buoyant spirits, and inspired by radiant hopes and glowing anticipations. Only a little over a year and a half had elapsed, and I was now at the old town again, but this time in broken health, and hobbling about on a stick. But it soon occurred to me that many of my comrades had met a still more unfortunate fate, and by this comparison method I presently got in a more cheerful frame of mind. And something happened to come to pass that materially aided that consummation. Some of our party who had been scouting around the town returned with the intelligence that they had found a place called "The Soldiers' Home," where all transient soldiers were furnished food and shelter "without money and without price." This was most welcome news, for our rations were practically exhausted, and our money supply was so meager that economy was a necessity. It was nearing supper time, so we started at once for the Home, in hopes of getting a square meal. On reaching the place we found already formed a long "queue" of hungry soldiers, in two ranks, extending from the door away out into the street. We took our stand at the end of the line, and waited patiently. The building was a long, low, frame structure, of a barrack-like style, and of very unpretentious appearance,--but, as we found out soon, the inside was better. In due time, the door was opened, and we all filed in. The room was well-lighted, and warm, and long rows of rough tables extended clear across, with benches for seats. And oh, what a splendid supper we had! Strong, hot coffee, soft bread, cold boiled beef, molasses, stewed dried apples,--and even cucumber pickles! Supper over, we went back to the depot, all feeling better, and I've had a warm spot in my heart for the old town of Cairo ever since. But it certainly did look hard at this time. Its population, at the beginning of the war, was only a little over two thousand, the houses were small and dilapidated, and everything was dirty, muddy, slushy, and disagreeable in general. In October, 1914, I happened to be in Cairo again, and spent several hours there, roaming around, and looking at the town. The lapse of half a century had wrought a wonderful change. Its population was now something over fifteen thousand, the streets were well paved and brilliantly lighted, and long blocks of tall, substantial buildings had superseded the unsightly shacks of the days of the Civil War. But on this occasion I found no vestige of our "Soldiers' Home," nor was any person of whom inquiry was made able to give me the slightest information as to where it had stood. The only thing I saw in the town, or that vicinity, that looked natural, was the Ohio river, and even its placid appearance was greatly marred by a stupendous railroad bridge, over which trains of cars were thundering every hour in the day. But the river itself was flowing on in serene majesty, as it had been from the time "the morning stars sang together," and as it will continue to flow until this planet goes out of business.

We left Cairo on the cars on the night of October 26th, and for the first time in our military service, we rode in passenger coaches, which was another piece of evidence that once more we were in that part of the world that we uniformly spoke of as "God's Country." I remember an incident that occurred during our ride that night that gave us all the benefit of a hearty laugh. There was (and is yet) a station on the Illinois Central, in Jackson county, Illinois, by the name of "Makanda." It was some time after midnight when we neared this station, the boys were sprawled out on their seats, and trying to doze. The engine gave the usual loud whistle to announce a stop, the front door of our coach was thrown open, and a brakeman with a strong Hibernian accent called out in thunder tones what sounded exactly like "My-candy!" as here written,--and with the accent on the first syllable. There were several soldiers in the coach who were not of our party, also going home on furlough, and one of these, a big fellow with a heavy black beard, reared up and yelled back at the brakeman,--"Well, who the hell said it wasn't your candy?" and the boys all roared. Many years later I passed through that town on the cars, and the brakeman said "My-candy," as of yore. I felt a devilish impulse to make the same response the soldier did on that October night in 1863, but the war was over, no comrades were on hand to back me,--so I prudently refrained. At Sandoval the most of our party transferred to the Ohio and Mississippi railroad, (as it was called then,) and went to St. Louis, reaching there on the afternoon of October 27th. Here all except myself left on the Chicago, Alton and St. Louis railroad, for different points thereon, and from which they would make their way to their respective homes. There was no railroad running through Jersey county at this time, (except a bit of the last named road about a mile in length across the southeast corner of the county,) and the railroad station nearest my home was twenty miles away, so I had to resort to some other mode of travel. I went down to the wharf and boarded a little Illinois river steamboat,--the Post-Boy, which would start north that night, paid my fare to Grafton, at the mouth of the Illinois river, arranged with the clerk to wake me at that place, and then turned in. But the clerk did not have to bother on my account; I was restless, slept but little, kept a close lookout, and when the whistle blew for Grafton, I was up and on deck in about a minute. The boat rounded in at the landing, and threw out a plank for my benefit,--the lone passenger for Grafton. Two big, burly deck-hands, rough looking, bearded men, took me by the arm, one on each side, and carefully and kindly helped me ashore. I have often thought of that little incident. In those days a river deck-hand was not a saint, by any means. As a rule, he was a coarse, turbulent, and very profane man, but these two fellows saw that I was a little, broken-down boy-soldier, painfully hobbling along on a stick, and they took hold of me with their strong, brawny hands, and helped me off the boat with as much kindness and gentleness as if I had been the finest lady in the land.

I was now only five miles from home, and proposed to make the balance of my journey on foot. I climbed up to the top of the river bank, and thence made my way to the main and only street the little town then possessed, and took "the middle of the road." It was perhaps four or five o'clock in the morning, a quiet, starlight night, and the people of the village were all apparently yet wrapped in slumber. No signs of life were visible, except occasionally a dog would run out in a front yard and bark at me. The main road from Grafton, at that time, and which passed near my home, wound along the river bottom a short distance, and then, for a mile or more, ascended some high hills or bluffs north of the town. The ascent of these bluffs was steep, and hence the walking was fatiguing, and several times before reaching the summit where the road stretched away over a long, high ridge, I had to sit down and rest. The quails were now calling all around me, and the chickens were crowing for day at the farm houses, and their notes sounded so much like home! After attaining the crest, the walking was easier, and I slowly plodded on, rejoicing in the sight of the many familiar objects that appeared on every hand. About a mile or so from home, I left the main highway, and followed a country road that led to our house, where I at last arrived about nine o'clock. I had not written to my parents to advise them of my coming, for it would not have been judicious, in mere expectation of a furlough, to excite hopes that might be disappointed, and after it was issued and delivered to me, there was no use in writing, for I would reach home as soon as a letter. So my father and mother, and the rest of the family, were all taken completely by surprise when I quietly walked into the yard of the old home. I pass over any detailed account of our meeting. We, like others of that time and locality, were a simple, backwoods people, with nothing in the nature of gush or effervescence in our dispositions. I know that I was glad to see my parents, and the rest, and they were all unmistakably glad to see me, and we manifested our feelings in a natural, homely way, and without any display whatever of extravagant emotions. Greetings being over, about the first inquiry was whether I had yet had any breakfast, and my answer being in the negative, a splendid old-time breakfast was promptly prepared. But my mother was keenly disappointed at my utter lack of appetite. I just couldn't eat hardly a bit, and invented some sort of an excuse, and said I'd do better in the future, but, somehow, right then, I wasn't hungry, which was true. However, this instance of involuntary abstinence was fully made up for later.

While on my furlough I went with my father in the farm wagon occasionally to Grafton, and Jerseyville, and even once to Alton, twenty miles away, but the greater part of the time was spent at the farm, and around the old home, and in the society of the family. I reckon I rambled over every acre of the farm, and besides, took long walks in the woods of the adjacent country, for miles around. The big, gushing Sansom Spring, about half a mile from home, was a spot associated with many happy recollections. I would go there, lie flat on the ground, and take a copious drink of the pure, delicious water, then stroll through the woods down Sansom branch to its confluence with Otter creek, thence down the creek to the Twin Springs that burst out at the base of a ridge on our farm, just a few feet below a big sugar maple, from here on to the ruins of the old grist mill my father operated in the latter '40s, and then still farther down the creek to the ancient grist mill (then still standing) of the old pioneer, Hiram White. Here I would cross to the south bank of the creek and make my way home up through Limestone, or the Sugar Hollow. From my earliest youth I always loved to ramble in the woods, and somehow these around the old home now looked dearer and more beautiful to me than they ever had before.

The last time I ever saw my boyhood home was in August, 1894. It had passed into the hands of strangers, and didn't look natural. And all the old-time natural conditions in that locality were greatly changed. The flow of water from Sansom Spring was much smaller than what it had been in the old days, and only a few rods below the spring it sunk into the ground and disappeared. The big, shady pools along Sansom branch where I had gone swimming when a boy, and from which I had caught many a string of perch and silversides, were now dry, rocky holes in the ground, and the branch in general was dry as a bone. And Otter Creek, which at different places where it ran through our farm had once contained long reaches of water six feet deep and over, had now shrunk to a sickly rivulet that one could step across almost anywhere in that vicinity. And the grand primeval forest which up to about the close of the war, at least, had practically covered the country for many miles in the vicinity of my old home, had now all been cut down and destroyed, and the naked surface of the earth was baking in the rays of the sun. It is my opinion, and is stated for whatever it may be worth, that the wholesale destruction of the forests of that region had much to do with the drying up of the streams.

But it is time to return to the boy on furlough.

Shortly before leaving Little Rock for home, Capt. Keeley had confidentially informed me that if the military situation in Arkansas continued quiet, it would be all right for me before my furlough expired to procure what would effect a short extension thereof, and he explained to me the _modus operandi_. Including the unavoidable delays, over a third of my thirty days had been consumed in making the trip home, and the return journey would doubtless require about the same time. I therefore thought it would be justifiable to obtain an extension, if possible. My health was rapidly growing better, the rheumatism was nearly gone--but there was still room for improvement. I had closely read the newspapers in order to keep posted on the military status in the vicinity of Little Rock, and had learned from them that the troops were building winter quarters, and that in general, "All was quiet along the Arkansas." So, on November 9th, I went to Dr. J. H. Hesser, a respectable physician of Otterville, told him my business, and said that if his judgment would warrant it, I would be glad to obtain from him a certificate that would operate to extend my furlough for twenty days. He looked at me, asked a few questions, and then wrote and gave me a brief paper which set forth in substance that, in his opinion as a physician, I would not be able for duty sooner than December 5th, 1863, that being a date twenty days subsequent to the expiration of my furlough. I paid Dr. Hesser nothing for the certificate, for he did not ask it, but said that he gave it to me as a warranted act of kindness to a deserving soldier. (In September of the following year Dr. Hesser enlisted in Co. C of our regiment as a recruit, and about all the time he was with us acted as hospital steward of the regiment, which position he filled ably and satisfactorily.) But I did not avail myself of all my aforesaid extension. I knew it would be better to report at company headquarters before its expiration than after, so my arrangements were made to start back on November 16th. Some hours before sunrise that morning, I bade good-by to mother and the children, and father and I pulled out in the farm wagon for our nearest railroad station, which was Alton, and, as heretofore stated, twenty miles away, where we arrived in ample time for my train. We drove into a back street and unhitched the team--the faithful old mules, Bill and Tom, tied them to the wagon and fed them, and then walked to the depot. The train came in due season, and stopped opposite the depot platform, where father and I were standing. We faced each other, and I said, "Good-bye, father;" he responded, "Good-bye, Leander, take care of yourself." We shook hands, then he instantly turned and walked away, and I boarded the train. That was all there was to it. And yet we both knew more in regard to the dangers and perils that environ the life of a soldier in time of war than we did on the occasion of the parting at Jerseyville nearly two years ago--hence we fully realized that this farewell might be the last. Nor did this manner spring from indifference, or lack of sensibility; it was simply the way of the plain unlettered backwoods people of those days. Nearly thirty-five years later the "whirligig of time" evolved an incident which clearly brought home to me a vivid idea of what must have been my father's feelings on this occasion. The Spanish-American war began in the latter part of April, 1898, and on the 30th of that month, Hubert, my oldest son, then a lad not quite nineteen years old, enlisted in Co. A of the 22nd Kansas Infantry, a regiment raised for service in that war. On May 28th the regiment was sent to Washington, D. C., and was stationed at Camp Alger, near the city. In the early part of August it appeared that there was a strong probability that the regiment, with others at Washington, would soon be sent to Cuba or Porto Rico. I knew that meant fighting, to say nothing of the camp diseases liable to prevail in that latitude at that season of the year. So my wife and I concluded to go to Washington and have a little visit with Hubert before he left for the seat of war. We arrived at the capital on August 5th, and found the regiment then in camp near the little village of Clifton, Virginia, about twenty-six miles southwest of Washington. We had a brief but very enjoyable visit with Hubert, who was given a pass, and stayed a few days with us in the city. But the time soon came for us to separate, and on the day of our departure for home Hubert went with us to the depot of the Baltimore and Ohio railroad, where his mother and I bade him good-by. Then there came to me, so forcibly, the recollection of the parting with my father at the Alton depot in November, 1863, and for the first time I think I fully appreciated what must have been his feelings on that occasion.

But, (referring to the Washington incident,) it so happened that on the day my wife and I left that city for home, or quite soon thereafter, it was officially announced that a suspension of hostilities had been agreed on between Spain and the United States. This ended the war, and consequently Hubert's regiment was not sent to the Spanish islands. I will now resume my own story.

My route from Alton, and method of conveyance, on returning to the regiment, were the same, with one or two slight variations, as those in going home, and the return trip was uneventful. But there were no delays, the boat ran day and night, and the journey was made in remarkably quick time. I arrived at Little Rock on the evening of November 20th, only five days over my furlough,--and with a twenty-day extension to show for that, reported promptly to Capt. Keeley, and delivered to him the certificate given me by Dr. Hesser. Keeley pronounced the paper satisfactory, and further said it would have been all right if I had taken the benefit of the entire twenty days. However, it somehow seemed to me that he really was pleased to see that I had not done so, but hurried back fifteen days ahead of time. After a brief conversation with him about the folks at home, and matters and things there in general, he treated me to a most agreeable surprise. He stepped to the company office desk, and took therefrom a folded paper which he handed to me with the remark: "There, Stillwell, is something I think will please you." I unfolded and glanced at it, and saw that it was a non-commissioned officer's warrant, signed by Major Grass as commanding officer of the regiment, and countersigned by Lieut. A. C. Haskins as adjutant, appointing me First Sergeant of Co. D. The warrant was dated November 4th, but recited that the appointment took effect from September 1st, preceding. As before stated, Enoch Wallace was our original first sergeant, and as he was promoted to second lieutenant on September 3, 1863, his advancement left his old position vacant, and his mantle had now fallen on me. I was deeply gratified with this appointment, and really was not expecting it, as there were two other duty sergeants who outranked me, and in appointing me I was promoted over their heads. However, they took it in good part, and remained my friends, as they always had been. And the plain truth is, too, which may have reconciled these sergeants somewhat, the position of first or orderly sergeant, as we usually called it, was not an enviable one, by any means. His duties were incessant, involving responsibility, and frequently were very trying. He had to be right with his company every hour in the day, and it was not prudent for him to absent himself from camp for even ten minutes without the consent of his company commander, and temporarily appointing a duty sergeant to act in his place while away. Among his multifarious duties may be mentioned the following: Calling the roll of the company morning and evening, and at such other hours as might be required; attending sick calls with the sick, and carefully making a note of those excused from duty by the surgeon; making out and signing the company morning report; procuring the signature of the company commander thereto, and then delivering it to the adjutant; forming the company on its parade ground for dress parade, drills, marches, and the like; making the details of the men required from his company for the various kinds of guard and fatigue duty; drawing rations for the company, and distributing them among the various messes; seeing to it that the company grounds (when in camp) were properly policed every morning;--and just scores of little matters of detail that were occurring all the time. It was a very embarrassing incident when sometimes a boy who was a good soldier was, without permission, absent at roll call. He might have strolled up town, or to a neighboring camp to see an old-time friend, and stayed too long. On such occurrences I would, as a general rule, pass rapidly from his name to the next--and just report the boy present, and later talk to him privately and tell him not to let it happen again. It is true, sometimes an aggravated case occurred when, in order to maintain discipline, a different course had to be pursued, but not often. Speaking generally, I will say that it was bad policy for the orderly to be running to the captain about every little trouble or grievance. The thing for him to do was to take the responsibility and act on his own judgment, and depend on the captain to back him (as he almost invariably would) if the affair came to a "show-down." Beginning as far back as the summer of 1862, I had frequently temporarily acted as orderly sergeant, for weeks at a time, and so possessed a fair amount of experience when I entered on the duties of the position under a permanent appointment. But my long, solitary rambles out in the woods, beyond the lines, were at an end, and that was a matter of more regret to me than anything else connected with the office of orderly sergeant. While on this topic I will remark that it always seemed to me that the men who had the "softest snaps" of any in a regiment of infantry were the lieutenants of the respective companies. The first lieutenant had no company cares or responsibilities whatever, unless the captain was absent, or sick in quarters, and the second lieutenant was likewise exempt, unless the captain and first lieutenant were both absent, or sick. Of course there were duties that devolved on the lieutenants from time to time, such as drilling the men, serving as officer of the guard, and other matters, but when those jobs were done, they could just "go and play," without a particle of care or anxiety about the services of the morrow.

CHAPTER XIV

LITTLE ROCK. WINTER of 1863-4. RE-ENLIST for THREE YEARS MORE.

When I returned to Little Rock from my absence on furlough, the regiment was found installed in cosy, comfortable quarters of pine log cabins. There were extensive pine forests near Little Rock, the boys were furnished teams and axes to facilitate the work, and cut and shaped the logs for the cabin walls, and roofed them with lumber, boards or shingles, which they procured in various ways. The walls were chinked and daubed with mud, and each cabin was provided with an ample, old-fashioned fire-place, with a rock or stick chimney. As wood was close at hand, and in abundance, there was no difficulty whatever in keeping the cabins warm. But I will remark here that of all the mean wood to burn, a green pine log is about the worst. It is fully as bad as green elm, or sycamore. But there was no lack of dry wood to mix with the green, and the green logs had this virtue: that after the fire had once taken hold of them they would last a whole night. The winter of 1863-4 was remarkably cold, and to this day is remembered by the old soldiers as "the cold winter." On the last day of 1863 a heavy fall of snow occurred at Little Rock, and the first day of the new year, and several days thereafter, were bitterly cold. But the weather did not cause the troops in our immediate locality any special suffering, so far as I know, or ever heard. All of us not on picket were just as comfortable as heart could wish in our tight, well-warmed cabins, and those on guard duty were permitted to build rousing fires and so got along fairly well. Big fires on the picket line would not have been allowed if any enemy had been in our vicinity, but there were none; hence it was only common sense to let the pickets have fires and keep as comfortable as circumstances would permit. It was probably on account of the severe weather that active military operations in our locality were that winter practically suspended. There were a few cavalry affairs at outlying posts, but none of any material importance.

The most painful sight that I saw during the war was here at Little Rock this winter. It was the execution, by hanging, on January 8, 1864, of a Confederate spy, by the name of David O. Dodds. He was a mere boy, seemingly not more than nineteen or twenty years old. There was no question as to his guilt. When arrested there was found on his person a memorandum book containing information, written in telegraphic characters, in regard to all troops, batteries, and other military matters at Little Rock. He was tried by a court martial, and sentenced to the mode of death always inflicted on a spy, namely, by hanging. I suppose that the military authorities desired to render his death as impressive as possible, in order to deter others from engaging in a business so fraught with danger to our armies; therefore, on the day fixed for carrying out the sentence of the court, all our troops in Little Rock turned out under arms and marched to the place of execution. It was in a large field near the town; a gallows had been erected in the center of this open space, and the troops formed around it in the form of an extensive hollow square, and stood at parade rest. The spy rode through the lines to the gallows in an open ambulance, sitting on his coffin. I happened to be not far from the point where he passed through, and saw him plainly. For one so young, he displayed remarkable coolness and courage when in the immediate presence of death. The manner of his execution was wretchedly bungled, in some way, and the whole thing was to me indescribably repulsive. In the crisis of the affair there was a sudden clang of military arms and accouterments in the line not far from me, and looking in that direction I saw that a soldier in the front rank had fainted and fallen headlong to the ground. I didn't faint, but the spectacle, for the time being, well-nigh made me sick. It is true that from time immemorial the punishment of a convicted spy has been death by hanging. The safety of whole armies, even the fate of a nation, may perhaps depend on the prompt and summary extinction of the life of a spy. As long as he is alive he may possibly escape, or, even if closely guarded, may succeed in imparting his dangerous intelligence to others who will transmit it in his stead; hence no mercy can be shown. But in spite of all that, this event impressed me as somehow being unspeakably cruel and cold-blooded. On one side were thousands of men with weapons in their hands, coolly looking on; on the other was one lone, unfortunate boy. My conscience has never troubled me for anything I may have done on the firing line, in time of battle. There were the other fellows in plain sight, shooting, and doing all in their power to kill us. It was my duty to shoot at them, aim low, and kill some of them, if possible, and I did the best I could, and have no remorse whatever. But whenever my memory recalls the choking to death of that boy, (for that is what was done), I feel bad, and don't like to write or think about it. But, for fear of being misunderstood, it will be repeated that the fate of a spy, when caught, is death. It is a military necessity. The other side hanged our spies, with relentless severity, and were justified in so doing by laws and usages of war. Even the great and good Washington approved of the hanging of the British spy, Maj. Andre, and refused to commute the manner of his execution to being shot, although Andre made a personal appeal to him to grant him that favor, in order that he might die the death of a soldier. The point with me is simply this: I don't want personally to have anything to do, in any capacity, with hanging a man, and don't desire even to be in eye-sight of such a gruesome thing, and voluntarily never have. However, it fell to my lot to be an involuntary witness of two more military executions while in the service. I will speak of them now, and then be through with this disagreeable subject. On March 18th, 1864, two guerrillas were hanged in the yard of the penitentiary at Little Rock, by virtue of the sentence of a court martial, and my regiment acted as guard at the execution. We marched into the penitentiary inclosure, and formed around the scaffold in hollow square. As soon as this had been done, a door on the ground floor of the penitentiary was swung open, and the two condemned men marched out, pinioned side by side, and surrounded by a small guard. The culprits were apparently somewhere between forty and fifty years of age. They ascended the scaffold, were placed with their feet on the trap, the nooses were adjusted, the trap was sprung,--and it was all over. The crimes of which these men had been convicted were peculiarly atrocious. They were not members of any organized body of the Confederate army, but guerrillas pure and simple. It was conclusively established on their trial that they, with some associates, had, in cold blood, murdered by hanging several men of that vicinity, private citizens of the State of Arkansas, for no other cause or reason than the fact that the victims were Union men. In some cases the murdered men had been torn from their beds at night, and hanged in their own door-yards, in the presence of their well-nigh distracted wives and children. There can be no question that these two unprincipled assassins richly merited their fate, and hence it was impossible to entertain for them any feeling of sympathy. Nevertheless, I stand by my original proposition, that to see any man strung up like a dog, and hanged in cold blood, is a nauseating and debasing spectacle.

In January, 1864, while we were at Little Rock, the "veteranizing" project, as it was called, was submitted to the men. That is to say, we were asked to enlist for "three years more, or endurin' the war." Sundry inducements for this were held out to the men, but the one which, at the time, had the most weight, was the promise of a thirty-days furlough for each man who re-enlisted. The men in general responded favorably to the proposition, and enough of the 61st re-enlisted to enable the regiment to retain its organization to the end of the war. On the evening of February 1st, with several others of Co. D, I walked down to the adjutant's tent, and "went in" for three years more. I think that no better account of this re-enlistment business can now be given by me than by here inserting a letter I wrote on December 22nd, 1894, as a slight tribute to the memory of our acting regimental commander in February, 1864, Maj. Daniel Grass. He was later promoted to lieutenant-colonel, and after the war, came to Kansas, where, for many years, he was a prominent lawyer and politician. On the evening of December 18th, 1894, while he was crossing a railroad track in the town where he lived, (Coffeyville, Kansas,) he was struck by a railroad engine, and sustained injuries from which he died on December 21st, at the age of a little over seventy years. A few days thereafter the members of the bar of the county held a memorial meeting in his honor, which I was invited to attend. I was then judge of the Kansas 7th Judicial District, and my judicial duties at the time were such that I could not go, and hence was compelled to content myself by writing a letter, which was later published in the local papers of the county, and which reads as follows:

"Erie, Kansas,
"December 22, 1894.
"Hon. J. D. McCue,
"Independence, Kansas.
"My Dear Judge:

"I received this evening yours of the 20th informing me of the death of my old comrade and regimental commander during the war for the Union, Col. Dan Grass. I was deeply moved by this sad intelligence, and regret that I did not learn of his death in time to attend his funeral. I wish I could be present at the memorial meeting of the bar next Monday that you mention, but I have other engagements for that day that cannot be deferred. It affords me, however, a mournful pleasure to comply with your request suggesting that I write a few words in the nature of a tribute to our departed friend and comrade, to be read at this meeting of the bar. But I am fearful that I shall perform this duty very unsatisfactorily. There are so many kind and good things that I would like to say about him that throng my memory at this moment that I hardly know where to begin.

"I served in the same regiment with Col. Grass from January 7th, 1862, to December 15th, 1864. On the last named day he was taken prisoner by the rebels in an engagement near Murfreesboro, Tenn. He was subsequently exchanged, but by that time the war was drawing to a close, and he did not rejoin us again in the field. In May, 1865, he was mustered out of the service. During his term of service with us, (nearly three years,) I became very well acquainted with him, and learned to admire and love him as a man and a soldier. He was temperate in his habits, courteous and kind to the common soldiers, and as brave a man in action as I ever saw. He was, moreover, imbued with the most fervid and intense patriotism. The war with him was one to preserve the Republic from destruction, and his creed was that the government should draft, if necessary, every available man in the North, and spend every dollar of the wealth of the country, sooner than suffer the rebellion to succeed, and the Nation to be destroyed. I think the most eloquent speech I ever heard in my life was one delivered by Col. Grass to his regiment at Little Rock, Arkansas, in February, 1864. The plan was then in progress to induce the veteran troops in the field to re-enlist for three years more. We boys called it 'veteranizing.' For various reasons it did not take well in our regiment. Nearly all of us had been at the front without a glimpse of our homes and friends for over two years. We had undergone a fair share of severe fighting and toilsome marching and the other hardships of a soldier's life, and we believed we were entitled to a little rest when our present term should expire. Hence, re-enlisting progressed slowly, and it looked as if, so far as the 61st Illinois was concerned, that the undertaking was going to be a failure. While matters were in this shape, one day Col. Grass caused the word to be circulated throughout the regiment that he would make us a speech that evening at dress parade on the subject of 'veteranizing.' At the appointed time we assembled on the parade ground with fuller ranks than usual, everybody being anxious to hear what 'Old Dan,' as the boys called him, would say. After the customary movements of the parade had been performed, the Colonel commanded, 'Parade, Rest!' and without further ceremony commenced his talk. Of course I cannot pretend, after this lapse of time, to recall all that he said. I remember best his manner and some principal statements, and the effect they produced on us.

He began talking to us like a father would talk to a lot of dissatisfied sons. He told us that he knew we wanted to go home; that we were tired of war and its hardships; that we wanted to see our fathers and mothers, and 'the girls we left behind'; that he sympathized with us, and appreciated our feelings. 'But, boys,' said he, 'this great Nation is your father, and has a greater claim on you than anybody else in the world. This great father of yours is fighting for his life, and the question for you to determine now is whether you are going to stay and help the old man out, or whether you are going to sneak home and sit down by the chimney corner in ease and comfort while your comrades by thousands and hundreds of thousands are marching, struggling, fighting, and dying on battle fields and in prison pens to put down this wicked rebellion, and save the old Union. Stand by the old flag, boys! Let us stay and see this thing out! We're going to whip 'em in the end just as sure as God Almighty is looking down on us right now, and then we'll all go home together, happy and triumphant. And take my word for it, in after years it will be the proudest memory of your lives, to be able to say, "I stayed with the old regiment and the old flag until the last gun cracked and the war was over, and the Stars and Stripes were floating in triumph over every foot of the land!'"

"I can see him in my mind's eye, as plain as if it were yesterday. He stood firm and erect on his feet in the position of a soldier, and gestured very little, but his strong, sturdy frame fairly quivered with the intensity of his feelings, and we listened in the most profound silence.

"It was a raw, cold evening, and the sun, angry and red, was sinking behind the pine forests that skirted the ridges west of our camp when the Colonel concluded his address. It did not, I think, exceed more than ten minutes. The parade was dismissed, and the companies marched back to their quarters. As I put my musket on its rack and unbuckled my cartridge box, I said to one of my comrades, 'I believe the old Colonel is right; I am going right now down to the adjutant's tent and re-enlist;' and go I did, but not alone. Down to the adjutant's tent that evening streamed the boys by the score and signed the rolls, and the fruit of that timely and patriotic talk that Dan Grass made to us boys was that the great majority of the men re-enlisted, and the regiment retained its organization and remained in the field until the end of the war.

"But my letter is assuming rather lengthy proportions, and I must hasten to a close. I have related just one incident in the life of Col. Grass that illustrates his spirit of patriotism and love of country. I could speak of many more, but the occasion demands brevity. Of his career since the close of the war, in civil life here in Kansas, there are others better qualified to speak than I am. I will only say that my personal relations with him since he came to this State, dating away back in the early seventies, have continued to be, during all these years, what they were in the trying and perilous days of the war--of the most friendly and fraternal character. To me, at least, he was always Col. Dan Grass, my regimental commander; while he, as I am happy to believe, always looked upon and remembered me simply as 'Lee Stillwell, the little sergeant of Company D.'

"I remain very sincerely your friend,

"L. STILLWELL."

CHAPTER XV

LITTLE ROCK. EXPEDITIONS to AUGUSTA and SPRINGFIELD. MARCH, APRIL and MAY, 1864.

In the spring of 1864 it was determined by the military authorities to undertake some offensive operations in what was styled the "Red River country," the objective point being Shreveport, Louisiana. Gen. N. P. Banks was to move with an army from New Orleans, and Gen. Steele, in command of the Department of Arkansas, was to co-operate with a force from Little Rock. And here my regiment sustained what I regarded, and still regard, as a piece of bad luck. It was not included in this moving column, but was assigned to the duty of serving as provost guard of the city of Little Rock during the absence of the main army. To be left there in that capacity, while the bulk of the troops in that department would be marching and fighting was, from my standpoint, a most mortifying circumstance. But the duty that devolved on us had to be done by somebody, and soldiers can only obey orders. Our officers said at the time that only efficient and well-disciplined troops were entrusted with the position of provost-guards of a city the size of Little Rock, and hence that our being so designated was a compliment to the regiment. That sounded plausible, and it may have been true, probably was, but I didn't like the job a bit. It may, however, have all been for the best, as this Red River expedition, especially the part undertaken by Gen. Banks, was a disastrous failure. Gen. Steele left Little Rock about March 23rd, with a force, of all arms, of about 12,000 men, but got no further than Camden, Arkansas. Gen. Banks was defeated by the Confederates at the battle of Sabine Cross-Roads, in Louisiana, on April 8th, and was forced to retreat. The enemy then was at liberty to concentrate on General Steele, and so he likewise was under the necessity of retreating, and scuttling back to Little Rock just as rapidly as possible. But on this retreat he and his men did some good, hard fighting, and stood off the Confederates effectively.

About the first intimation we in Little Rock had that our fellows were coming back was when nearly every soldier in the city that was able to wield a mattock or a spade was detailed for fatigue duty and set to work throwing up breastworks, and kept at it, both day and night. I happened to see Gen. Steele when he rode into town on May 2nd, at the head of his troops, and he looked tough. He had on a battered felt hat, with a drooping brim, an oil-cloth "slicker," much the worse for wear, the ends of his pantaloons were stuck in his boots, and he was just splashed and splattered with mud from head to foot. But he sat firm and erect in his saddle, (he was a magnificent horseman,) and his eyes were flashing as if he had plenty of fight left in him yet. And the rank and file of our retreating army was just the hardest looking outfit of Federal soldiers that I saw during the war, at any time. The most of them looked as if they had been rolled in the mud, numbers of them were barefoot, and I also saw several with the legs of their trousers all gone, high up, socking through the mud like big blue cranes.

In view of the feverish haste with which Little Rock had been put in a state for defensive operations, and considering also all the reports in circulation, we fully expected that Price's whole army would make an attack on us almost any day. But the Confederates had been so roughly handled in the battle of Jenkins' Ferry, April 30th, on the Saline river, that none of their infantry came east of that river, nor any of their cavalry except a small body, which soon retired. The whole Confederate army, about May 1st, fell back to Camden, and soon all was again quiet along the Arkansas.

I will now go back about two weeks in order to give an account of a little expedition our regiment took part in when Gen. Steele's army was at Camden.

Late on the evening of April 19th, we fell in, marched to the railroad depot, climbed on the cars, and were taken that night to Devall's Bluff. Next morning we embarked on the steamboat "James Raymond," and started up White river. The other troops that took part in the movement were the 3rd Minnesota Infantry and a detachment of the 8th Missouri Cavalry. We arrived at the town of Augusta, (about eighty miles by water from Devall's

Bluff,) on the morning of the 21st. It was a little, old, dilapidated river town, largely in a deserted condition, situated on low, bottom land, on the east bank of White river. On arriving we at once debarked from the boat, and all our little force marched out a mile or so east of the town, where we halted, and formed in line of battle in the edge of the woods, with a large open field in our front, on the other side of which were tall, dense woods. As there were no signs or indications of any enemy in the town, and everything around was so quiet and sleepy, I couldn't understand what these ominous preparations meant. Happening to notice the old chaplain a short distance in the rear of our company, I slipped out of ranks, and walked back to him for the purpose of getting a pointer, if possible. He was by himself, and as I approached him, seemed to be looking rather serious. He probably saw inquiry in my eyes, and without waiting for question made a gesture with his hands towards the woods in our front, and said, "O Son of Jeremiah! Here is where we shall give battle to those who trouble Israel!" "What! What is that you say?" said I, in much astonishment. "It is even so," he continued; "the Philistines are abroad in the land, having among them, as they assert, many valiant men who can sling stones at a hair's breadth and not miss. They await us, even now, in the forest beyond. But, Son of Jeremiah," said he, "if the uncircumcised heathen should assail the Lord's anointed, be strong, and quit yourself like a man!" "All right, Chaplain," I responded; "I have forty rounds in the box, and forty on the person, and will give them the best I have in the shop. But, say! Take care of my watch, will you? And, should anything happen, please send it to the folks at home;"--and handing him my little old silver time-piece, I resumed my place in the ranks. After what seemed to me a most tiresome wait, we finally advanced, preceded by a line of skirmishers. I kept my eyes fixed on the woods in our front, expecting every minute to see burst therefrom puffs of white smoke, followed by the whiz of bullets and the crash of musketry, but nothing of the kind happened. Our skirmishers entered the forest, and disappeared, and still everything remained quiet. The main line followed, and after gaining the woods, we discovered plenty of evidence that they had quite recently been occupied by a body of cavalry. The ground was cut up by horses' tracks, and little piles of corn in the ear, only partly eaten, were scattered around. We advanced through the woods and swamps for some miles and scouted around considerably, but found no enemy, except a few stragglers that were picked up by our cavalry. We left Augusta on the 24th, on our steamboat, and arrived at Little Rock on the same day. I met the chaplain on the boat while on our return, and remarked to him that, "Those mighty men who could kill a jaybird with a sling-shot a quarter of a mile off didn't stay to see the show." "No," he answered; "when the sons of Belial beheld our warlike preparation, their hearts melted, and became as water; they gat every man upon his ass, and speedily fled, even beyond the brook which is called Cache." He then went on to tell me that on our arrival at Augusta there was a body of Confederate cavalry near there, supposed to be about a thousand strong, under the command of a General McRae; that they were bivouacked in the woods in front of the line of battle we formed, and that on our approach they had scattered and fled. The enemy's force really exceeded ours, but, as a general proposition, their cavalry was reluctant to attack our infantry, in a broken country, unless they could accomplish something in the nature of a surprise, or otherwise have a decided advantage at the start.

On May 16th we shifted our camp to Huntersville, on the left bank of the Arkansas river, and near our first location. We thus abandoned our log cabins, and never occupied them again. They were now getting too close and warm for comfort, anyhow. But they had been mighty good friends to us in the bitterly cold winter of '63-4, and during that time we spent many a cosy, happy day and night therein.

On May 19th we again received marching orders, and the regiment left camp that night on the cars, and went to Hicks' station, 28 miles from Little Rock. We remained here, bivouacking in the woods, until the 22nd, when, at 3 o'clock in the morning of that day, we took up the line of march, moving in a northerly direction. The troops that composed our force consisted of the 61st, 54th, and 106th Illinois, and 12th Michigan (infantry regiments), a battery of artillery, and some detachments of cavalry; Brig. Gen. J. R. West in command. We arrived at the town of Austin, 18 miles from Hicks' Station, about 2 o'clock on the afternoon of the 22nd. It was a little country village, situated on a rocky, somewhat elevated ridge. As I understand, it is now a station on the Iron Mountain railroad, which has been built since the war. I reckon if in May, 1864, any one had predicted that some day a railroad would be built and in operation through that insignificant settlement among the rocks and trees, he would have been looked on as hardly a safe person to be allowed to run at large.

Co. D started on the march with only one commissioned officer, Second Lieutenant Wallace. I have forgotten the cause of the absence of Capt. Keeley and Lieut. Warren, but there was doubtless some good reason. On the first day's march the weather was hot, and the route was through a very rough and broken country. Wallace was overcome by heat, and had to fall out, and wait for an ambulance. In consequence, it so happened that when we reached Austin, there was no commissioned officer with us, and I, as first sergeant, was in command of the company. And that gave rise to an incident which, at the time, swelled me up immensely. On arriving at the town, the regiment halted on some open ground in the outskirts, fell into line, dressed on the colors, and stood at ordered arms. Thereupon the adjutant commanded, "Commanding officers of companies, to the front and center, march!" I was completely taken by surprise by this command, and for a second or two stood, dazed and uncertain. But two or three of the boys spoke up at once and said, "You're our commanding officer, Stillwell; go!" The situation by this time had also dawned on me, so I promptly obeyed the command. But I must have been a strange looking "commanding officer." I was barefooted, breeches rolled up nearly to the knees, feet and ankles "scratched and tanned," and my face covered with sweat and dirt. The closest scrutiny would have failed to detect in me a single feature of the supposed "pomp and circumstance" of an alleged military hero. But I stalked down the line, bare feet and all, with my musket at a shoulder arms, and looking fully as proud, I imagine, as Henry of Navarre ever did at the battle of Ivry, with "a snow-white plume upon his gallant crest." By the proper and usual commands, the "commanding officers of companies" were brought up and halted within a few paces of Col. Ohr, who thereupon addressed them as follows:

"Gentleman, have your men stack arms where they now are, and at once prepare their dinner. They can disperse to get wood and water, but caution them strictly not to wander far from the gun stacks. We may possibly pass the night here, but we may be called on, at any moment, to fall in and resume the march. That's all, gentlemen."

While the Colonel was giving these instructions, I thought a sort of unusual twinkle sparkled in his eyes, as they rested on me. But, for my part, I was never more serious in my life. Returning to the company, I gave the order to stack arms, which being done, the boys crowded around me, plying me with questions. "What did the Colonel say? What's up, Stillwell?" I assumed a prodigiously fierce and authoritative look and said: "Say, do you fellows suppose that we commanding officers of companies are going to give away to a lot of lousy privates a confidential communication from the Colonel? If you are guilty of any more such impertinent conduct, I'll have every mother's son of you bucked and gagged." The boys all laughed, and after a little more fun of that kind, I repeated to them literally every word the Colonel said, and then we all set about getting dinner. About this time Lieut. Wallace rode up in an ambulance--and my reign was over. We resumed the march at 3 o'clock in the morning of the next day (May 23rd), marched 18 miles, and bivouacked that night at Peach Orchard Gap. This was no town, simply a natural feature of the country. Left here next morning (the 24th) at daylight, marched 18 miles, and bivouacked on a stream called Little Cadron. Left at daylight next morning (the 25th), marched 18 miles, and went into camp near the town of Springfield. By this time the intelligence had filtered down to the common soldiers as to the object of this expedition. It was to intercept, and give battle to, a force of Confederate cavalry, under Gen. J. O. Shelby, operating somewhere in this region, and supposed to have threatening designs on the Little Rock and Devall's Bluff railroad. But so far as encountering the Confederates was concerned, the movement was an entire failure. My experience during the war warrants the assertion, I think, that it is no use to send infantry after cavalry. It is very much like a man on foot trying to run down a jack-rabbit. It may be that infantry can sometimes head off cavalry, and thereby frustrate an intended movement, but men on horses can't be maneuvered into fighting men on foot unless the horsemen are willing to engage. Otherwise they will just keep out of the way.

We remained at Springfield until May 28th. It was a little place and its population when the war began was probably not more than a hundred and fifty, or two hundred. It was the county seat of Conway county, but there was no official business being transacted there now. About all the people had left, except a few old men and some women and small children. The houses were nearly all log cabins. Even the county jail was a log structure of a very simply and unimposing type. It has always been my opinion that this little place was the most interesting and romantic-looking spot (with one possible exception I may speak of later) that I saw in the South during all my army service. The town was situated on rather high ground, and in the heart of the primitive forest. Grand native trees were growing in the door-yards, and even in the middle of the main street,--and all around everywhere. And we were there at a season of the year when Nature was at its best, and all the scenery was most attractive and charming. I sometimes would sit down at the foot of some big tree in the center of the little village, and ponder on what surely must have been the happy, contented condition of its people before the war came along and spoiled all. Judging from the looks of the houses, the occupants doubtless had been poor people and practically all on the same financial footing, so there was no occasion for envy. And there was no railroad, nor telegraph line, nor daily papers, to keep them nervous and excited or cause them to worry. And they were far away from the busy haunts of congregated men,--

"Their best companions, innocence and health, And their best riches, ignorance of wealth."

Their trading point was Lewisburg, about fifteen miles southwest on the Arkansas river, and when that stream was at a proper stage, small steamboats would ply up and down, and bring to Lewisburg groceries and dry goods, and such other things as the country did not produce, which would then be wagoned out to Springfield and into the country generally. And judging from all that could be seen or heard, I think there were hardly any slaves at Springfield, or in the entire north part of Conway county, before the war. What few there may have been were limited to the plantations along the Arkansas river. I have never been at the little town since the occasion now mentioned, so personally I know nothing of its present appearance and condition. However, as a matter of general information, it may be said that after the war a railroad was built running up the Arkansas river valley, through the south part of the county. This road left Springfield out, so in course of time it lost the county seat, which went to a railroad town. And this road also missed Lewisburg, which has now disappeared from the map entirely.

When in camp at Springfield, many of the boys, in accordance with their usual habits, of their own motion at once went to scouting around over the adjacent country, after pigs, or chickens, or anything else that would serve to vary army fare. While so engaged two or three of our fellows discovered a little old whisky still. It was about two miles from Springfield, situated in a deep, timbered hollow, near a big spring. It was fully equipped for active operation, with a supply of "mash" on hands, and all other essentials for turning out whisky. Some of the 10th Illinois Cavalry found it first, and scared away the proprietor, then took charge of the still and proceeded to carry on the business on their own account. The boys of the 61st who stumbled on the place were too few to cope with the cavalrymen; thereupon they hastened back to camp and informed some trusty comrades of the delectable discovery. Forthwith they organized a strong party as an alleged "provost guard," and all armed, and under the command of a daring, reckless duty sergeant, hastened to the still. On arriving there, in their capacity as provost guards, they summarily arrested the cavalrymen, with loud threats of condign punishment, but after scaring them sufficiently, and on their solemn promise to at once return to camp and "be good" in the future, released them, and allowed them to depart. Then our bunch stacked arms, and started in to make whisky. Some of the number had served in the business before, and knew all about it, so that little still there in the hollow was then and there worked to its utmost capacity, day and night, and doubtless as it never had been before. Knowledge of this enterprise spread like wildfire among the enlisted men,--and oh, "how the whisky went down" at Springfield! Away along some hours after midnight, I would hear some of the boys coming in from the still, letting out keen, piercing whoops that could be heard nearly a mile. Like the festive Tam O'Shanter (with apologies to Burns),--

"The swats sae reamed in every noddle,
They cared na rebs nor guards a boddle."

I took just one little taste of the stuff, from Sam Ralston's canteen. It was limpid and colorless as water, and fairly burnt like fire as it went down my throat. That satisfied my curiosity, and after that many similar offers were declined, with thanks. Whether the officers at the time knew of this business or not, I do not know. If they did, they just "winked the other eye," and said nothing, for the boys ran the still, without restriction or interruption, until we left Springfield.

Telling of the foregoing episode causes many other incidents to come flocking to my memory that came under my notice during my army career, and in which whisky figured more or less. The insatiable, inordinate appetite of some of the men for intoxicating liquor, of any kind, was something remarkable, and the ingenious schemes they would devise to get it were worthy of admiration, had they been exerted in a better cause. And they were not a bit fastidious about the kind of liquor, it was the effect that was desired. One afternoon, a day or two after we arrived at Helena, Arkansas, a sudden yell, a sort of "ki-yip!" was heard issuing from one of the company tents, soon followed by others of the same tone. I had heard that peculiar yelp before, and knew what it meant. Presently I sauntered down to the tent from whence the sounds issued, and walked in. Several of the boys were seated around, in an exalted state of vociferous hilarity, and a flat, pint bottle, with the figure of a green leaf on one side, and labeled "Bay Rum" on the other, was promptly handed to me, with the invitation to "drink hearty." I did taste it. It was oily, greasy, and unpleasant, but there was no doubt that it was intoxicating. It was nothing but bay rum, the same stuff that in those days barbers were wont to use in their line of business. It finally came to light that the sutler of some regiment at Helena had induced the post-quartermaster at Cairo to believe that the troops stood in urgent need of bay rum for the purpose of anointing their hair, and thereupon he obtained permission to include several boxes of the stuff in his sutler supplies. When he got it to Helena he proceeded to sell it at a dollar a bottle, and his stock was exhausted in a few hours. What may have been done to this sutler I don't know, but that was the last and only time that I know of bay rum being sold to the soldiers as a toilet article, or otherwise. Of course, all sutlers and civilians were prohibited, under severe penalties, from selling intoxicating liquor to the enlisted men, but the profits were so large that the temptation was great to occasionally transgress, in some fashion. But, as a general rule, I think that the orders were scrupulously obeyed. The risk was too great to do otherwise.

I remember a little personal experience of my own, when once I tried to buy a drink of whisky. It is not a long story, so it will be told. It occurred at Devall's Bluff, in October, 1863, when our little furlough party was there, waiting the arrival of a boat from below on which to resume our homeward journey. One night in particular was quite cold. We slept in our blankets on the ground near the bank of the river, built good fires, and tried to keep as comfortable as possible. But the morning after this cold night I got up feeling wretched, both mentally and physically. I was weak from previous illness, my rheumatic pains were worse, and my condition in general was such as caused me to fear that I was liable to break down and not be able to go home. It occurred to me that a drink of whisky might brace me up some, so I started out to obtain one, if possible. There was a sort of a wharf-boat at the landing, moored to the bank, a stationary, permanent affair, with a saloon appurtenant. I went on the boat, walked up to the bar, and exhibiting a greenback to the bar-keeper, asked him if he would sell me a drink of whisky. "Can't do it," he answered, "the orders are strict against selling whisky to soldiers." I began moving away, and at that instant a big, greasy, colored deck-hand, or laborer of some sort, black as the ace of spades, crowded by me, brushing against me in the narrow passage on his way to the bar. "Boss," he called to the keeper, "want a dram!" A bottle and a glass were pushed towards him, he filled the glass to the brim, and drank the contents at a gulp. Then he smacked his big lips, rolled his eyes around, and with a deep breath exclaimed, "A-h-h! Dat whisky feels des pow'ful good dis cole mawnin'!" I looked at the darkey in bitterness of heart, and couldn't help thinking that it was all-fired mean, when a poor little sick soldier was not allowed to buy a drink of whisky, while a great big buck nigger roustabout had it handed out to him with cheerfulness and alacrity. But the orders forbidding the sale of intoxicating liquors to soldiers were all right, and an imperative military necessity. If the men had been allowed unlimited access to whisky, and the like, that would, in my opinion, simply have been ruinous to the good order, discipline, and efficiency of the army. That statement is based on events I saw myself while in the service, and which occurred when, in spite of the orders, the men managed to obtain liquor without let or hindrance. The scenes that would then ensue are too unpleasant to talk about, so they will be passed over in silence. It is only fair, however, to say that the same men who, when furiously drunk, were a disgrace to themselves and the organization to which they belonged, were, as a general rule, faithful and brave soldiers when sober.

At 4 o'clock on the morning of the 28th we broke camp at Springfield, and started back to Little Rock, marching in a south-easterly direction. We marched all that day, the 29th, 30th, and 31st, and arrived at our old camp at Huntersville at 9 o'clock in the evening of the last mentioned day. According to the official report the entire distance marched on the expedition, going and coming, was 190 miles, and we didn't see an armed Confederate on the whole trip. Our return route was through the wilderness, most of it primeval forest, and we didn't pass through a single town. But now there is a railroad that runs practically over all the course we followed during the last three days we were on this march. I haven't been in that region since we passed through there in May, 1864, but at that time it certainly was a very wild, rough, and broken country. We here had our first experience with scorpions and tarantulas, and soon learned that it was prudent, when bivouacking on the ground, to carefully turn over all loose rocks and logs in order to find and get rid of those ugly customers. The scorpions were about four or five inches long, the fore part of the body something like a crawfish, with a sharp stinger on the end of the tail. When excited or disturbed, they would curl their tails over their backs, and get over the ground quite rapidly. The tarantulas were just big hairy spiders, of a blackish-gray color, about as big as toads, and mighty ugly-looking things. The sting of the tarantula, and the bite of a spider, were very painful, but when that happened to any of us (which was seldom), our remedy was to apply a big, fresh quid of tobacco to the wound, which would promptly neutralize the poison.

CHAPTER XVI

DEVALL'S BLUFF; THE CLARENDON EXPEDITION. JUNE and JULY, 1864.

On June 20th we left Huntersville on the cars and went to Hicks' Station, hereinbefore mentioned, and there went into camp. In making this move, we left Little Rock for the last time, and from that day I have never seen the old town again. But our stay at Hicks' Station was brief. Marching orders came on June 24th, and on the next day we left on the cars and went to Devall's Bluff, and on reaching there filed on board the steamer "Kentucky," and started down White river, accompanied by several other boats also loaded with troops, all under the command of Gen. E. A. Carr. The object and purpose of this expedition was soon noised around among the men. The daring and enterprising Confederate General Shelby had on June 24th turned up at Clarendon, on White river, not far below Devall's Bluff, and here, with the aid of his artillery, had surprised and captured one of our so-called "tin-clad" gunboats, and had established a blockade of the river. As all our supplies came by way of that stream, it was necessary to drive Shelby away at once, hence our movement. We arrived at Clarendon on the morning of the 26th. Some of our gunboats were with us, in advance, and as soon as they came within range of the town began shelling it, and the woods beyond. The cannonade elicited no reply, and it was soon ascertained that the enemy had fallen back from the river. The transports thereupon landed, the men marched on shore, formed in line of battle, and advanced. The Confederates were found in force about two miles northeast of town, and some lively skirmishing and artillery practice began. But our regiment was stationed in the supporting line, (darn it!) and didn't get to pull a trigger. Cannon shot went over our heads now and then, but hurt nobody. While the racket was going on we were standing in line of battle, on the hither side of an extensive cotton field, and there was a big, tall cottonwood tree standing about a quarter of a mile in our front by the side of the road. I was looking in that direction when suddenly, as if by magic, a big forked branch of this tree quietly took leave of the trunk, as if it "didn't know how it happened." Before it struck the ground the shot from one of Shelby's guns that had done this pruning went screaming over our heads. It sounded just real good, like old times, with an effect, somehow, like a powerful tonic. But the affair didn't last long. Shelby had no stomach for fighting infantry, well supplied with artillery, and he soon fell back, and rapidly retreated in a northerly direction, leaving two pieces of his artillery in our possession. When the Confederates retired, we followed promptly and vigorously, but of course the infantry couldn't overhaul them, and neither could our cavalry bring them to a determined stand. Our route was largely through a low, swampy country, over a "corduroy" road. In many places there were large gaps in the corduroy, where the logs had rotted and disappeared, and the road was covered with green and slimy water about knee-deep. On encountering the first of these breaks, we took off our shoes and socks, tied them to the ends of the barrels of our muskets, rolled up our trousers, and waded in. As such places were numerous, it was not worth while to resume our foot-gear, so we just trudged on bare-footed. But the weather was warm, and it made no difference, and the boys would splash through the mud and water in great good humor, laughing and joking as they went. We followed hard after Shelby until the evening of the 27th, and it being impossible to catch up with him, we started back to Clarendon on the morning of the 28th. In the matter of rations I reckon "someone had blundered," when we started in pursuit of Shelby. We had left Clarendon with only a meager supply in our haversacks, and no provision train was with the command. So at the time we took the back track we were out of anything to eat. The country bordering on our route was wild, and thinly settled, and what people lived there were manifestly quite poor, hence there was very little in the shape of anything to eat that we could forage. On the first day of our return march our commissary sergeant, Bonfoy, did manage to capture and kill a gaunt, lean old Arkansas steer, and it was divided up among the men with almost as much nicety and exactness as if it was a wedding cake with a prize diamond ring in it; and we hadn't any salt to go with it, but in lieu of that used gun-powder, which was a sort of substitute. With that exception, (and a piece of hardtack, to be presently mentioned,) my bill of fare on the return march until we reached Clarendon consisted, in the main, of a green, knotty apple,--and some sassafras buds. About the middle of the afternoon on the second day the regiment made a temporary halt for some purpose, and we were sitting, or lying down, along the road side. There was a bunch of our cavalry on their horses, in column off the road a short distance, also at a halt, and I saw one of them munching a hardtack. I slipped out of ranks and approached the fellow, and when close to him said, "Partner, won't you give me a hardtack?" He looked at me a second or two without saying anything, and I was fearful that my appeal was going to be denied. But the look of ravenous hunger in my eyes probably gained the case, for at last he reached his hand into his haversack and handed me a tack, one of the big kind about four or five inches square. I was barely in time, for right then the cavalry moved on. I thrust the tack into my shirt bosom, gave a quick, furtive glance towards the company to see if anyone had observed me, and then started to get behind a big tree, where the precious morsel could be devoured without risk of detection. But John Barton had been watching, and was upon me before I could hide. "Hold on, Stillwell," said he, "that don't go! I divided with you as long as I had a crumb!" "That's so, John," I replied, heaving a mournful sigh, "here;" and breaking the hardtack in two, I gave him a fair half, and standing behind the tree we promptly gobbled down our respective portions.

We arrived at Clarendon on the evening of the 29th--having marched, in going and returning, about seventy miles. Here everybody got a square meal, which was heartily appreciated. As bearing on the above mentioned incident about the hardtack, it will be said here, basing my remarks on my experience in the army, and elsewhere, that I think there is nothing that will reduce human beings so much to the level of the brute creation as intense, gnawing hunger. All the selfishness there is in a man will then come to the surface, and to satisfy the well-nigh intolerable craving for something to eat, he will "go back" on his best friend. I could cite several instances in support of this statement that have come under my observation, but it is unnecessary.

Soon after reaching Clarendon, as above stated, fires burst forth, apparently simultaneously, all over the town, and soon every building was in ashes. It was a small place, and its population at the beginning of the war probably did not exceed three hundred. At this time the town had been abandoned by the residents, and so far as I know the houses were all vacant. The buildings were small frame or log structures, composed of cypress and pine lumber or logs, roofed with shingles, and highly combustible, and they made an exceedingly hot fire. I do not know the cause of the burning of the town. The soldiers were tired, mad, and out of sorts generally, and they may have fired it on their own motion, but it is more likely that it was done by order of the military authorities. The empty houses afforded excellent cover whereby the Confederates could slip up to the river bank and annoy our gunboats, even to the extent of capturing one, as they had done quite recently. So as a military measure the burning of the town was fully justified.

We left Clarendon on the evening of the 29th, on the steamer "Lillie Martin," arrived at Devall's Bluff some time during the night, debarked from the boat next morning, and went into camp near the river, where we enjoyed for a time an agreeable rest.

Before taking final leave of the Clarendon expedition I will, in the interest of the truth of history, indulge in a little criticism of the gallant and distinguished officer who was the Confederate commander in this affair. All who are conversant with the military career of General J. O. Shelby will readily concede that he was a brave, skillful, and energetic cavalry commander. He kept us in hot water almost continually in the Trans-Mississippi department, and made us a world of trouble. But I feel constrained to remark that, in reporting his military operations, he was, sometimes, a most monumental----well, I'll scratch out the "short and ugly" word I have written, and substitute "artist," and let it go at that. I have just been reading his reports of this Clarendon episode, as they appear on pages 1050-1053, Serial

Number 61, Official Records of the War of the Rebellion, and as he describes it, it is difficult to recognize it as being the same affair we took part in, in June, 1864. In the first place, he says that the loss of the Federals can "safely be put down at 250 killed and wounded," and that 30 will cover his own. On the other hand, our commander, Gen. Carr, says the Confederate loss, killed, wounded and captured, was "about" 74, and gives ours as 1 killed and 16 wounded. And from what I personally saw, I have no doubt that Gen. Carr's statements are correct. Shelby further asserts that "three times" he drove us "back to the river," and that later, while on his retreat, he "charged" us and "drove them (us) back three miles in confusion." Now, those statements are pure moonshine. I was there, and while, as previously stated, not on the firing line, was nevertheless in a position either to see or hear every thing of any material consequence that transpired. The force on each side was comparatively small, the field of active operations was limited, and it was not difficult for even a common soldier to have an intelligent idea of what was going on. And, for my part, with the natural curiosity of a boy, I was constantly on the alert to see or hear everything that was being done in the shape of fighting. In the operations near the town, we were not driven "back to the river," nor towards it, on any occasion. On his retreat, Shelby did make one or two feeble stands, the object being merely to delay us until his main body could get well out of the way, and when that was accomplished, his rear guard galloped after them as fast as they could. That it was mainly a race with him to get away is evident from a statement in his report, in which he says he was then (June 30th) "resting" his "tired and terribly jaded horses." But, in telling of his exploits, he says nothing about losing two pieces of his artillery. The saying of Bonaparte's, "False as a war bulletin," has passed into a proverb, and this bulletin of Gen. Shelby's is no exception.

CHAPTER XVII

DEVALL'S BLUFF. GRAND REVIEWS and INSPECTIONS. SURGEON J. P. ANTHONY. PRIVATE PRESS ALLENDER. JUNE and JULY, 1864.

I have said nothing so far about "grand reviews," or other functions of that sort, and here is as good a place as any to notice them. From some cause or other we had what seemed to us an undue proportion of grand reviews in Arkansas in the summer of 1864. They were not a bit popular with the common soldiers. It became a saying among us, when a grand review was ordered, that the reviewing officer had got a new uniform and wanted to show it--but, of course, that was only soldier talk.

On June 10th, while in camp at Huntersville, all the troops at Little Rock were reviewed by Maj. Gen. Daniel E. Sickles, late of the Army of the Potomac. He lost a leg at the battle of Gettysburg, which incapacitated him for active service, so President Lincoln gave him a sort of roving commission to visit and inspect all the western troops. In conducting the review at Little Rock, on account of his maimed condition he rode along the line in an open carriage. The day was exceedingly hot, the troops on our side of the river were reviewed on low grounds where the air was stifling, we wore our jackets tightly buttoned, and we all suffered fearfully from heat. One man in the line near me went over with a crash, all in a pile, from sunstroke, and I heard that there were several other such cases. Nine days later, (June 19th,) we had division grand review conducted by our division commander, Gen. C. C. Andrews, and on July 11th another grand review by the same officer. And interspersed with the reviews were several brigade inspections of arms. But as those did not involve any marching, they were not as fatiguing as the reviews. I will mention specifically but one of these inspections, and do so for the reason that there were some things connected with it I have always remembered with interest and pleasure. It was held on July 4th, at Devall's Bluff, the inspecting officer being Col. Randolph

B. Marcy, Inspector-General U.S. Army. He was a regular army officer, a graduate of West Point, and at this time was about fifty-two years of age. He was over six feet tall, straight as an arrow, and a splendid looking man in general. We had very short notice of this inspection, and having returned only a few days before from the Clarendon expedition, had not yet had time or opportunity to wash our shirts, and were in quite a rough and tough condition. And the fact that this inspection was to be conducted by the Inspector-General of the United States Army, an old regular, and a West Point graduate, made us nervous, and we apprehended all sorts of trouble. So far as I ever knew, the volunteers had not much love for the regular army officers. We regarded them as unreasonably strict and technical, and were of the impression that they were inclined to "look down" on volunteers. Whether this feeling was well founded, or not, I cannot say, but there is no question that it existed. On this occasion we went to work with a will, and soon had our muskets, bayonets, belt-plates, and accouterments in general, bright and shining, and in the very pink of condition. It was to be an inspection of arms only, and did not include knapsacks. About 9 o'clock on the morning of July 4th, we fell in on the regimental parade ground, broke into columns of companies, right in front, in open order, and the greatly feared Inspector-General entered on his duty. As already stated, we looked hard. Many of us were barefoot, and our clothes in general were dirty and ragged. But Col. Marcy knew we had just come off a march, he was a very sensible man, and capable of making some allowances. In accordance with the regulations, he passed in front of us, walking slowly and looking at us critically. As he came opposite each soldier, the latter brought his piece into the prescribed position for examination, but Col. Marcy contented himself with a sweeping glance, and did not take the musket in his hands. Then he passed to the rear of the ranks, and walked slowly along behind us, while we stood immovable, with eyes fixed to the front. It was soon all over. He then approached Col. Ohr, said something I did not hear, but which was evidently pleasant, for the Colonel smiled, then turned round facing us, and with a sweep of his arm in our direction said,--loud enough for many of us to hear, "Good soldiers!" whereupon we all felt much relieved and proud,--and the dreaded inspection was a thing of the past. Several years afterwards, when in civil life out in Kansas, I learned that Col. Marcy was not only a grand old soldier, but also a most interesting writer. I have two of his books in my library now, and have had for many years, one being his official report of the "Exploration of the Red River of Louisiana, in the year 1852;" the other, "Thirty Years of Army Life on the Border." Both are highly interesting, and I frequently take them from the shelf and look them over. And when I do so, there always rises up on about every page the recollection of the tall, imposing figure of Col. Marcy, as he stood beneath the oaks at Devall's Bluff, Arkansas, on the morning of July 4th, 1864, and waved his arm towards us, and said in a kind tone, and with approving look: "Good soldiers!"

There was in Company D an original sort of a character, by the name of Ambrose Pressley Allender,--for short, generally called "Press." He was at this time (1864) about thirty-five years old. He had been a private in a regiment of Kentucky infantry during the Mexican War, but what the length of his service may have been I do not know. But in his Mexican War experience he had at least learned every possible trick and device that could be resorted to in "playing off," as the boys called it; that is, avoiding duty on the plea of sickness or any other excuse that would serve. He was not a bad man, by any means, but a good-hearted old fellow. He had re-enlisted, along with the rest of us, when the regiment "veteranized." But his propensity for shirking duty, especially anything severe or unpleasant, seemed inveterate and incurable. He made me lots of trouble, for some time, after I became first sergeant. I was only a boy, and he was a man of mature age, about fifteen years my senior, and looking back to those days, I can see now where many times he pulled the wool over my eyes completely and induced me to grant him favors in the matter of details that he was not entitled to. But it was not long before I began to understand Press, and then, if he was excused from duty, or passed over for a lighter job, the authority had to come from the regimental surgeon. Dr. Julius P. Anthony, of Brown county, Illinois, was appointed surgeon of the regiment in September, 1863, and remained with us in that capacity until we were mustered out of the service. He was not a handsome man, by any means. He was hawk-nosed, with steel-blue eyes, and had a most peculiar sort of a high-keyed, nasal toned voice. But he was an excellent physician, and a shrewd, accurate judge of men. So, when Press bucked up against Dr. Anthony, he found a foeman worthy of his steel, and the keen-eyed old doctor was a different proposition from a boy orderly sergeant. Press would keep close watch of the details as they progressed down the company roll, and when he was next in turn, and the impending duty was one he did not fancy, would then retire to his tent or shack, and when wanted for picket, or some laborious fatigue duty, would be found curled up in his bunk and groaning dismally. When we were at Devall's Bluff, at a time about the last of July, 1864, I discovered him in this condition one morning before sick-call, when I went to apprise him (out of abundant caution) that he was next for duty, and not to wander from the camp. He forthwith told me he was very sick, hadn't slept a wink all night, and that I must pass over him for the time being. I replied that if he was sick, he must fall in at sick-call, and have the surgeon pass on his case, so he climbed out of his bunk, put on his trousers, and made ready. Sick-call was sounded pretty soon, and I went with Press and two or three of the other boys to the surgeon's tent. Press kept in the background until the other cases were disposed of, and then stepped forward. His breeches were unbuttoned down to nearly the last button, he was holding them up with his hands, and his stomach protruded like the belly of a brood-sow. "Well, Allender," inquired Dr. Anthony, "egad, what's the matter with you?" Press was careful to put on all the military frills at such a time, and he began thus: "Major Anthony, First Sergeant Stillwell has several times putten me on duty when I was not fitten for duty, and so I am now compelled to come to you, and----" "That'll do, Allender," interrupted the doctor, "what are your symptoms?" Press then began the story of his woes. He had racking pains in the stomach, headache, couldn't sleep, "all bloated up," he said, "as you can see for yourself;" with a comprehensive gesture towards his abdominal region,--and numerous other troubles, including "night sweats." Dr. Anthony heard him patiently, and without interruption, but scanned him closely all the time he was talking. Press at last stopped to take breath, and then the doctor, in his rasping voice, spoke as follows: "Allender, the trouble with you is simply exercising too little, and eating too much. And if you don't quit stuffing yourself, and get around more, I shall instruct Sergeant Stillwell to put you on fatigue duty every day until you are rid of that mass of fermenting fecal matter in your bowels, and your stomach is restored to normal condition. That's all." Then addressing me, he said: "Allender's able for duty;" and Press and I walked out. As soon as we were beyond the hearing of Dr. Anthony, Press turned loose. He was a terribly profane fellow when, in his opinion, ordinary language would not do the subject justice, and had accumulated a stock of the most unique and outrageous expressions that could be invented, and all these he now fired at the Doctor. Having no desire to put salt on a green wound, I said nothing. In perhaps an hour or so the first sergeant's call was sounded at the adjutant's tent, which meant a detail. I responded to the call, and the Sergeant-Major, consulting the regimental detail slip he held in his hand, told me he wanted a corporal and five privates from my company, with two days' rations, to help make up a scouting party going up White river on a steamboat, and for them to report in fifteen minutes. That caught old Press, and I went to his shack expecting a scene. He was found lying on his bunk, in his drawers and shirt--as usual in such emergencies. I proceeded to detail him as one of the scouting party, and told him to be all ready within fifteen minutes. In the meantime, the weather had changed, and a disagreeable, drizzling rain was falling. Press heaved a deep sigh when informed of his detail, and began to beg and protest. I told him that the doctor had refused to excuse him, that he was the next man on the roll for duty, that I had no discretion in the matter, and he would have to get ready and go. But, if he was feeling worse, I would go with him again to the doctor, and request him to look further into his case. Press sprang out of his bunk with a bound, and grabbed his trousers. "Before I'll ever go again," he said, "to that hawk-nosed old blankety-blank-blank, to get excused from duty, I'll see him in hell further than a pigeon can fly in a leap year. He hasn't got sense enough, anyhow, to doctor an old dominecker hen that is sick with a sore [anus], much less a civilized human being. You could let me off this detail, if you wanted to, and let me tell you,

Stillwell, if this trip kills me, which it probably will, I want you to remember, as long as you live, that the responsibility for my death lies on your head!" This last statement, I will confess, rather staggered me, and had it been delivered in a weak and pitiful tone, there is no telling what I might have done. But he didn't "roar" me "as gently as a sucking dove," by a long shot, for his voice was full and loud, and quivering with energy and power. So I made no response to this dire prediction; Press got ready, and went. The weather cleared up in a few hours, and was bright and pleasant, but nevertheless I became very uneasy about Press. If the old fellow really was sick, and if, by any possibility, this detail should result in his death, why, then, I felt that his last words would haunt me as long as I lived. I waited anxiously for the return of the scouting party, and when the whistle of the boat was heard on its arrival at the Bluff, went at once to the landing to learn the fate of Press, and stood on the bank where the men could be seen as they came ashore. Presently here came Press, very much alive, and looking fine! He bore, transfixed on his bayonet, a home-cured ham of an Arkansas hog; the tail feathers of a chicken were ostentatiously protruding from the mouth of his haversack, and which receptacle was also stuffed well-nigh to bursting with big, toothsome yams. And later the fact was developed that his canteen was full of sorghum molasses. As he trudged up the road cut through the bank, his step was springy and firm, his face was glowing with health, and beaded with perspiration. I felt greatly relieved and happy, and, inspired by the joy of the moment, called to him: "Hello, Press! You seem to be all right!" He glanced up at me, and in a sort of sheepish manner responded: "Ya-a-ss. As luck would have it, the trip 'greed with me." And from this time on, I had no more trouble with old Press. He turned over a new leaf, cut out completely his old-time malingering practices, and thenceforward was a good, faithful soldier. We were in some close places afterwards, and he never flinched, but stood up to the work like a man. He was mustered out with the rest of us in September, 1865, and after some going and coming, settled down in Peoria county, Illinois, where he died March 15, 1914, at the age of nearly eighty-five years.

CHAPTER XVIII

THE REGIMENT GOES HOME on VETERAN FURLOUGH.
INTERVIEW with GEN. W. T. SHERMAN AFTER the WAR.
A SHORT TOUR of SOLDIERING at CHESTER, ILLINOIS.
AUGUST, SEPTEMBER, OCTOBER, 1864.

After our return from the Clarendon affair, we remained in camp at Devall's Bluff, where nothing more important occurred than drilling, reviews, inspections, and the like. The summer was rapidly passing away, and still the regiment had not received the 30-day furlough promised us when we veteranized. Nearly all the other regiments in the department that had re-enlisted had received theirs, and it looked as if the poor old 61st Illinois had been "lost in the shuffle." The boys began to get a little impatient about this, and somewhat disposed to grumble, which was only natural. But on August 8th the paymaster made us a visit, paid us six months' pay and our veteran bounty, and then the prospect for the furlough began to brighten, and we were assured by our officers that we had not much longer to wait. And sure enough, on August 14th we started home. We left the recruits and non-veterans at Devall's Bluff, to which we expected to return on the expiration of our furlough, but the Fates willed otherwise, as will be seen later. When we filed on board the steamboat that August morning, the old regiment, as an organization, was leaving Arkansas forever.

I will say here that I have always regretted, and shall regret as long as I live, that after the capture of Vicksburg, the regiment happened to get switched off into Arkansas. We thereby were taken away from the big armies, and out of the main currents of the war, where great deeds were being done, and history made. Of course we couldn't help it; we had no choice; and, as I have remarked before, the common soldier can only do what those in authority direct. As connected with this subject, I will here tell the story of a little conversation I had with Gen. W. T. Sherman, at his office in Washington in February, 1883. I had gone to that city on a business matter, and while there met Col. P. B. Plumb, then one of the senators from Kansas. In the course of our conversation he asked if there were any of the "big bugs" in Washington I wanted to see,--if so, he would be glad to take me around and introduce me. I replied that there were only two; that just as a matter of curiosity I would like to see President Arthur, but I really was very desirous of having a little visit with Gen. Sherman. Plumb laughed, said that my desires were modest, and made a date with me when he would take me to see the President and Gen. Sherman. At the time appointed we went, first to the White House, where we met the President. I shook hands with him, and after a few commonplace remarks, retired to the background. The President and Plumb talked a minute or two about some public matter, and then we left. "Now," said Plumb, "we'll go and see 'Uncle Billy'." Sherman was then the General of the Army, and had his office, as I now remember, in the War Department building, near the White House. On entering his office, we found him seated at a desk, writing. I had seen him previously several times, but had no acquaintance with him whatever. Plumb introduced me to him, saying, as he gave my name, that I was one of his "boys." The General dropped his pen, shook hands with me heartily, and at once began talking. I think he was the most interesting talker I ever have known. He had lived a life of incessant activity, had done great things, and had mingled with great men, hence he was never at a loss for an engaging topic. After a while the monologue lulled, and gave me the opportunity for which I had been patiently waiting. "General," I began, "there is an incident connected with your military career during the Civil War that I have wanted for some time to speak to you about, and, if agreeable, will do so now." "Huh," said he, "what is it?" It was interesting, and a little amusing to me at the time, to see the instantaneous change that came over him. His face darkened, his eyes contracted, and a scowl appeared on his brow. His appearance and manner said, almost as plain as words: "Now here's a smart young Aleck, who never had a greater command than a picket post of three men, who is going to tell me how he thinks I should have fought a battle." Resuming, I said: "Some years ago I read Gen.

Badeau's 'Life of Grant,' and found published therein a letter from Gen. Grant to you, written some time in the fall of 1863, when you were marching across the country from Memphis to reinforce him at Chattanooga, in which Grant said, in substance, 'Urge on Steele the necessity of sending you Kimball's division of the Sixteenth Corps.' General," said I, "that meant us; it meant me; for my regiment was in Kimball's division, with Gen. Steele, in Arkansas. Now my point is, I am afraid that you didn't 'urge' Steele strongly enough, for we never got to you, and," I continued (in a tone of deep and sincere earnestness), "consequently we missed Missionary Ridge, the campaign of Atlanta, the March to the Sea, and the campaign of the Carolinas,--and I shall regret it as long as I live!" I noted with interest the change in the old General's countenance as I made my little speech. His face lighted up, his eyes sparkled, the scowl disappeared, and when I concluded he laughed heartily. "Didn't need you; didn't need you," he said; "had men enough,--and, let me tell you,--Steele needed every d--d man he had." It was quite evident that the General enjoyed the recital of my little alleged grievance, and he launched into a most interesting account of some incidents connected with the campaigns I had mentioned. I became fearful that I was imposing on his good nature, and two or three times started to leave. But with a word or gesture he would detain me, and keep talking. And when I finally did depart, he followed me out into the hall, and laying his hand on my shoulder in a most fatherly way, said, "Say! Whenever you are in Washington, come and see me! Don't be afraid! I like to see and talk with you boys!" and with a hearty shake of the hand he bade me good-by. He was a grand old man, and we common soldiers of the western armies loved him.

In going home on our veteran furlough, the regiment went by steamer down White river, thence up the Mississippi to Cairo, where we debarked and took the cars, and went to Springfield, Illinois, arriving there August 24th. The Mississippi was low, and our progress up the river was very slow. Two or three times our boat grounded on bars, and after trying in vain to "spar off," had to wait until some other boat came along, and pulled us off by main strength. Near Friar's Point, not far below Helena, where there was a long, shallow bar, the captain of the steamer took the precaution to lighten his boat by landing us all on the west bank of the river, and we walked along the river's margin for two or three miles to the head of the bar, where the boat came to the shore, and took us on again. Our officers assured us that our thirty days furlough would not begin until the day we arrived at Springfield, so these delays did not worry us, and we endured them with much composure.

On this entire homeward trip, on account of a matter that was purely personal, I was in a state of nervous uneasiness and anxiety nearly all the time. As heretofore stated, just a few days before starting home we were paid six months' pay, and our veteran bounty, the amount I received being $342.70. Several of the recruits and non-veterans whose homes were in my neighborhood gave me different amounts that had been paid them, with the request that I take this money home and hand it to their fathers, or other persons they designated. So, when we started, I had the most money on my person I ever had had before, and even since. The exact amount is now forgotten, but it was something over fifteen hundred dollars. Of nights I slept on the hurricane deck of the boat, with the other boys, and in the day time was mingling constantly with the enlisted men, and with all that money in my pocket. Of course, I said nothing about it, and had cautioned the boys who trusted me with this business also to say nothing, but whether they had all complied with my request I didn't know. I kept the money (which, except a little postal currency, was all in greenbacks) in my inside jacket pocket during the day time, didn't take off my trousers at night, and then stowed the bills on my person at a place--well, if a prowling hand had invaded the locality, it would have waked me quick! But I finally got home with all the money intact, duly paid the trust funds over to the proper parties, and then felt greatly relieved.

When the regiment arrived at Springfield we stored our muskets and accouterments in a public building, and then dispersed for our respective homes. I arrived at the Stillwell home the following day, August 25th, and received a hearty welcome.

But the admission must be made that I didn't enjoy this

furlough near as much as the individual one of the preceding autumn, for reasons I will state. You see, we were all at home now, that is, the veterans, and there were several hundred of us, and it seemed as if the citizens thought that they must do everything in their power to show how much they appreciated us. So there was something going on nearly all the time; parties, oyster suppers, and gatherings of all sorts. There was a big picnic affair held in the woods at the Sansom Spring which was attended by a crowd of people. A lawyer came down from Jerseyville and made us a long speech on this occasion, in which he refreshed our recollection as to our brave deeds and patriotic services in battle, and in camp and field generally, which was doubtless very fine. It is true, I spent several very happy days at home, with my own folks, but they were frequently broken in on by the neighbors, coming and going, who wanted to see and talk with "Leander." And the girls! bless their hearts! They were fairly ready to just fall down and worship us. But I was young, awkward, and exceedingly bashful, and can now see clearly that I didn't respond to their friendly attentions with the same alacrity and heartiness that would have obtained had I been, say, ten years older. The French have a proverb with a world of meaning in it, something like this: "If youth but knew--if old age could!" But probably it is best as it is.

When home on our veteran furlough a sad event occurred which directly affected the regiment, and which it can be truly said every member thereof sincerely deplored. This was the death of Lieut. Col. Simon P. Ohr. He never was a strong man, physically, and the hardships and exposures incident to army life were really the cause of his death. He died at his home, in Carrollton, Illinois, of a bronchial affection, on September 14th, 1864. He was a man of temperate habits, honest and upright, and a sterling patriot. As an officer, he was kind, careful as to the wants and necessities of his men, and in battle, cool, clear-headed, and brave. In due course of time Maj. Daniel Grass was appointed to the office of Lieutenant-Colonel, to fill the vacancy thus created by the lamented death of Col. Ohr.

The regiment rendezvoused at Springfield on September 26th, and left on the next day, on the cars, went to St. Louis, and were quartered in the Hickory Street Barracks, in the city. Another "Price Raid" was now on. Only a few days previously Gen. Sterling Price with a strong force, including, of course, Shelby's cavalry, entered southeast Missouri, and the day we arrived at St. Louis he showed up at Pilot Knob, only about 85 miles south of the city, where some sharp fighting occurred. There was now the biggest kind of a "scare" prevailing in St. Louis, and, judging from all the talk one heard, we were liable to hear the thunder of Price's cannon on the outskirts of St. Louis any day. We had been at Hickory Street Barracks only a day or two, when my company, and companies B and G, were detached from the regiment, embarked on a steamboat, and went down the Mississippi to the town of Chester, Illinois, which is situated on the Mississippi, at the mouth of the Kaskaskia river. We were sent here for the purpose, as we understood at the time, of guarding the crossing of the Mississippi at this place, and to prevent any predatory Confederate raid in that vicinity. We were quartered in some large vacant warehouses near the river, and had no guard duty to perform except a guard at the ferry landing, and a small one over our commissary stores. Altogether, it was the "softest" piece of soldiering that fell to my lot during all my service. We had roofs over our heads and slept at night where it was dry and warm, it was ideal autumn weather, and we just idled around, careless, contented, and happy. One lovely October day Bill Banfield and I in some way got a skiff, and early in the morning rowed over the river to the Missouri side, and spent the day there, strolling about in the woods. The country was wild and rough, and practically in a state of nature. We confined our rambling to the river bottom, which was broad and extensive, and densely covered with a primeval forest. Some of the trees, especially the sycamores and the cottonwoods, were of giant size. And the woods abounded in nuts and wild fruits; hickory nuts, walnuts, pecans, pawpaws, big wild grapes,--and persimmons, but the latter were not yet ripe. This locality was in Perry County, Missouri, and it seemed to be destitute of inhabitants; we saw two or three log cabins, but they were old, decayed, and deserted. We had brought some bacon and hardtack with us in our haversacks, and at noon built a fire and had an army dinner, with nuts and fruit for dessert. We got back to Chester about sundown, having had a most interesting and delightful time.

There was another little incident that happened while we were at Chester, which I have always remembered with pleasure. Between companies D and G of our regiment was a strong bond of friendship. Many of the boys of the two companies had lived in the same neighborhood at home, and were acquainted with each other before enlisting. The first sergeant of G was Pressley T. Rice, a grown man, and some five or six years my senior. He came to me one day soon after our arrival at Chester, and in his peculiar nasal tone said: "Stillwell, some of my boys think that when we are soldiering here in 'God's Country,' they ought to have soft bread to eat. If 'D' feels the same, let's go down to the mill, and buy a barrel of flour for each company, and give the boys a rest on hardtack." I heartily assented, but asked what should we do about paying for it, as the boys were now pretty generally strapped. Press responded that we'd get the flour "on tick," and settle for it at our next pay day. To my inquiry if we should take Company B in on the deal (the other company with us at Chester), Press dryly responded that B could root for themselves; that this was a "cahootnership" of D and G only. Without further ceremony we went to the mill, which was a fair-sized concern, and situated, as I now remember, in the lower part of the town, and near the river bank. We found one of the proprietors, and Press made known to him our business, in words substantially the same as he had used in broaching the matter to me, with some little additional explanation. He told the miller that the only bread we had was hardtack, that the boys accepted that cheerfully when we were down South, but that here in "God's Country," in our home State of Illinois, they thought they were entitled to "soft bread," so we had come to him to buy two barrels of flour; that the boys had not the money now to pay for it, but at our next pay day they would, and we would see to it that the money should be sent him. While thus talking, the miller looked at us with "narrowed eyes," and, as it seemed to me, didn't feel a bit delighted with the proposition. But maybe he thought that if he didn't sell us the flour, we might take it anyhow, so, making a virtue of necessity, he said he would let us have it, the price of the two barrels being, as I now remember, seven dollars. I produced my little memorandum book, and requested him to write the name and address of his firm therein, which he did, in pen and ink, and it is there yet, in that same little old book, now lying open before me, and reads as follows:

"H. C. Cole & Co.,
Chester, Ill."

Well, he sent us the flour, and D and G had soft bread the balance of the time we were at Chester.

I will now anticipate a few months, in order to finish the account of this incident. The spring of 1865 found the regiment at Franklin, Tennessee, and while there the paymaster made us a welcome visit. I then went to Press Rice, and suggested to him that the time had now come for us to pay the Chester miller for his flour, and he said he thought so too. We sat down at the foot of a tree and made out a list of all the boys of our respective companies who, at Chester, helped eat the bread made from the flour, and who were yet with us, and then assessed each one with the proper sum he should contribute, in order to raise the entire amount required. Of course the boys paid it cheerfully. Press turned over to me the proportionate sum of his company, and requested me to attend to the rest of the business, which I did. I wrote a letter to the firm of H. C. Cole & Co., calling their attention to the fact of our purchase from them of two barrels of flour in October of the previous year, and then went on to say that several of the boys who had taken part in eating the bread made from this flour had since then been killed in battle, or died of diseases incident to a soldier's life, but there were yet enough of us left to pay them for their flour, and that I here inclosed the proper sum. (I have forgotten in just what manner or form it was sent, but think it was by express.) In due course of time I received an answer, acknowledging receipt of the money, written in a very kind and complimentary vein. After heartily thanking us for the payment, the letter went on to state that in all the business dealings of H. C. Cole & Co. with Union soldiers the firm had been treated with fairness and remarkable honesty, and they sincerely appreciated it.

Many years later out in Kansas I met a man who had lived in Chester during the war, and told him the foregoing little story. He said he knew the milling firm of Cole & Co. quite well, and that during the war they were most intense and bitter Copperheads, and had no use whatever for "Lincoln hirelings," as Union soldiers were sometimes called by the "Butternut" element. My informant was a respectable, truthful man, so it is probable that his statement was correct. It served to throw some light on the grim conduct of the miller with whom Press and I dealt. But they treated us well, and if they were of the type above indicated, it is hoped that the little experience with us may have caused them to have a somewhat kindlier feeling for Union soldiers than the one they may have previously entertained.

CHAPTER XIX

EXPEDITION to NORTH MISSOURI. BACK in TENNESSEE ONCE MORE. MURFREESBORO. OCTOBER and NOVEMBER, 1864.

On October 14th we left Chester on the steamer "A. Jacobs," and went to St. Louis, where we arrived on the 15th, and marched out to Laclede Station, about six miles from St. Louis, on the Pacific railroad, where we found the balance of the regiment. There was a railroad bridge at this place, over a small stream, and I suppose that during the scare at St. Louis it was deemed prudent to have a force here to guard the bridge. On October 19th the regiment left Laclede, and went by rail on the North Missouri railroad, to Mexico, in Audrain county, Missouri, about 110 miles northwest of St. Louis. Here we reported to Col. Samuel A. Holmes, Colonel of the 40th Missouri Infantry. We left Mexico October 21st and marched northward 25 miles to Paris, the county seat of Monroe county. There was a body of irregular Confederate cavalry, supposed to be about 500 strong, under the command of a Col. McDaniel, operating in this region, and carrying on a sort of predatory and uncivilized warfare. We learned that it was our business up here to bring this gang to battle, and destroy them if possible, or, failing in that, to drive them out of the country. Our force consisted of about 700 infantry,--the 40th Missouri and the 61st Illinois, and a detachment of about 300 cavalry, whose state and regimental number I have forgotten. Our cavalry caught up with the Confederates at Paris, and had a little skirmish with them, but before the infantry could get on the ground the enemy lit out as fast as their horses could carry them. We lay that night at Paris, and the next day (the 22nd) marched to the little town of Florida, where we bivouacked for the night. It was a small place, situated on a high, timbered ridge, between the main Salt river and one of its forks. With the exception that it was not a county seat, it was practically a counterpart of the little village of Springfield, Arkansas, hereinbefore mentioned. It had only one street of any consequence, and all up and down this street, in several places right in the middle thereof, were grand, imposing native trees, such as oaks and hickories. But the place was now totally deserted, and looked lonesome and desolate. I ascertained several years later that it was the birthplace of Samuel L. Clemens, the author,--better known under his pen-name, "Mark Twain." It is also an interesting circumstance that the first military operation conducted by Gen. U. S. Grant was a movement in the summer of 1861 on this little village of Florida, with the intention and expectation of giving battle to a Confederate force in camp near the town.

The next day (the 23rd) we turned south, and marched to the little town of Santa Fe, and the next day thereafter back to Paris, where we remained a day. On the 26th we went to Middle Grove, and on the following day again reached the railroad at Allen, some distance northwest of Mexico, where we first started out. It would seem that this little station of Allen has, since the war, disappeared from the map,--at least, I can't find it. On this expedition the infantry never caught a glimpse of an armed Confederate, but the object of the movement was accomplished. We kept after our foes so persistently that they left that locality, crossed the Missouri river, joined Price's army, and with it left the State. At this time the section of country over which we marched in the pursuit of McDaniel's command is now all gridironed by railroads, but in 1864 there were only two, the North Missouri, running north-west from St. Louis to Macon, and the Hannibal and St. Joe, connecting those two places and extending from the Mississippi river on the east to the Missouri river on the west. We always remembered this scout up in north Missouri with feelings of comfort and satisfaction. Compared with some of our Arkansas marches, it was just a pleasure excursion. The roads were in good condition, and the weather was fine;--ideal Indian Summer days. And in the fruit and vegetable line we lived high. The country through which we passed abounded in the finest of winter apples, Little Romanites and Jennetings being the chief varieties. The farmers had gathered and piled them in the orchards in conical heaps and covered them with straw and earth sufficient to keep them from freezing. We soon learned what those little earth mounds signified, and, as a matter of course, confiscated the apples instanter. And the country was full of potatoes, cabbages, and turnips, on which we foraged with great liberality. If any apology for this line of conduct should be thought proper, it may be said that many of the farms were at this time abandoned, the owners having fled to the garrisoned towns to escape the Confederate raiders; further, if we hadn't taken this stuff our adversaries would, if by chance they happened again to infest that locality. Anyhow, a hungry soldier is not troubled, in such matters, by nice ethical distinctions. We remained at Allen on the 28th, and until the evening of the following day, when we left there on the cars for St. Louis. But sometime near midnight the train stopped at Montgomery City, about midway between Allen and St. Louis, we were roused up, and ordered to get off and form in line, which we did. Our officers then proceeded to give us careful instructions, to the effect that a band of Confederate cavalry was believed to be at Danville, out in the country a few miles south, and that we were going there to surprise and capture this party, if possible. We were strictly enjoined to refrain from talking and singing, and to remain absolutely silent in ranks. We then fell into column and marched for Danville, where we arrived an hour or so before dawn. But our birds (if there when we started from Montgomery) had flown--there were no Confederates there. A party of guerrillas had been in the town about two weeks before, who had murdered five or six unarmed citizens, (including one little boy about eight or ten years old,) and it was believed when we started to march out here that this gang, or some of them, had returned. The party that had previously raided Danville were under the command of one Bill Anderson, a blood-thirsty desperado, with no more humanity about him than an Apache Indian. He was finally killed in battle with some Union troops about the last of October, 1864. When killed there was found on his person a commission as Colonel in the Confederate army, signed by Jefferson Davis, and the brow-band of his horse's bridle was decorated with two human scalps. He was of that class of men of which Quantrell and the James and the Younger boys were fitting types, and who were a disgrace to mankind.

Sometime during the day (October 30th) we marched back to Montgomery City, got on the cars, and again started for St. Louis, where we arrived the next day, and marched out to old Benton Barracks, where we took up our quarters for the time being. So we were once more "tenting on the old camp ground," after an absence of nearly three years. But the place did not look as it did before. It seemed old and dilapidated and there were only a few troops there. As compared with the active, stirring conditions that obtained there in February and March, 1862, it now looked indescribably dejected and forlorn. But our stay here this time was short. We left on November 5th, marched into St. Louis, and down to the wharf, where we embarked on the steamer "David Tatum," and started up the Mississippi. We were puzzled for a while as to what this meant, but soon found out. We were told that the regiment was being sent home to vote at the ensuing presidential election, which would occur on November 8th, that we would take the cars at Alton and go to Springfield, and from there to our respective homes. We surely were glad that we were going to be granted this favor. The most of the States had enacted laws authorizing their soldiers to vote in the field, but the Illinois legislature since 1862 had been Democratic in politics, and that party at that time in our State was not favorably disposed to such a measure. Consequently the legislature in office had failed to pass any law authorizing their soldier constituents to vote when away from home. We arrived at Alton about 9 o'clock on the evening of the 5th, and found a train waiting us (box cars), which we at once climbed on. We had just got our guns and other things stowed away in corners, and were proceeding to make ourselves comfortable for a night ride to Springfield, when Lt. Wallace came down from the officers' caboose, and stopped at the Co. D car. "Boys," he called, "get out, and fall in line here by the track. The order to go to Springfield has been countermanded by telegraphic dispatch and we are ordered back to St. Louis." "What! What's that?" we exclaimed, in astonishment. "It's so," said Wallace, in a tone of deep regret; "get out." "Well, don't that beat hell!" was the next remark of about a dozen of us. But orders are orders, and there was nothing to do but obey. The curses of the disappointed soldiers in thus having this cup of satisfaction dashed from their lips were "not loud, but deep." But we all swung down from the cars, fell in, and marched back to and on board the "David Tatum," and were back at the wharf in St. Louis by next morning. We stacked arms on the levee, and the next morning, November 7th, left St. Louis on the steamer "Jennie Brown," headed down stream. So here we were again on the broad Mississippi, duplicating our beginning of March, 1862, and once more bound for "Dixie's Land." By this time we had become philosophical and indifferent in regard to the ups and downs of our career. If we had been ordered some night to be ready the next morning to start to California or Maine, the order would have been treated with absolute composure, and after a few careless or sarcastic remarks, we would have turned over and been asleep again in about a minute. We had made up our minds that we were out to see the war through, and were determined in our conviction that we were going to win in the end.

Election day, November 8th, was densely foggy, so much so that the captain of our steamboat thought it not prudent to proceed, so the boat tied up that day and night at the little town of Wittenburg, on the Missouri shore. Mainly to pass away the time, the officers concluded to hold a "mock" regimental presidential election. The most of the line officers were Democrats, and were supporting Gen. McClellan for President in opposition to Mr. Lincoln, and they were quite confident that a majority of the regiment favored McClellan, so they were much in favor of holding an election. An election board was chosen, fairly divided between the supporters of the respective candidates, and the voting began. As our votes wouldn't count in the official result, every soldier, regardless of age, was allowed to vote. But at this time I was a sure-enough legal voter, having attained my twenty-first year on the 16th of the preceding September. You may rest assured that I voted for "Uncle Abe" good and strong. When the votes were counted, to the astonishment of nearly all of us, Mr. Lincoln was found to have sixteen majority. As the regiment was largely Democratic when it left Illinois in February, 1862, this vote showed that the political opinions of the rank and file had, in the meantime, undergone a decided change.

We left Wittenburg on the forenoon of the 9th, but owing to the foggy conditions our progress was very slow. We reached Cairo on the 10th, and from there proceeded up the Ohio, and on the 11th arrived at Paducah, Kentucky, where we debarked, and went into camp. We remained here nearly two weeks, doing nothing but the ordinary routine of camp duty, so life here was quite uneventful. Paducah was then an old, sleepy, dilapidated, and badly decayed river town, with a population at the outbreak of the war of about four thousand. After our brief stay here terminated, I never was at the place again until in October, 1914, when I was there for about a day, which was devoted to rambling about the town. The flight of fifty years had made great changes in Paducah. It now had a population of about twenty-five thousand, four different lines of railroad, street cars, electric lights, and a full supply generally of all the other so-called "modern conveniences." On this occasion I hunted faithfully and persistently for the old camp ground of the regiment in 1864, but couldn't find it, nor even any locality that looked like it.

On the evening of November 24th the regiment left Paducah on the little stern-wheel steamboat "Rosa D," which steamed up the Ohio river as far as the mouth of the Cumberland, there turned to the right, and proceeded to ascend that stream. That move told the story of our probable destination, and indicated to us that we were doubtless on our way to Nashville to join the army of Gen. Thomas. There was another boat that left Paducah the same time we did, the "Masonic Gem," a stern-wheeler about the same size of our boat. It was also transporting a regiment of soldiers, whose State and regimental number I do not now remember. The captains of the two boats, for some reason or other, lashed their vessels together, side by side, and in this manner we made the greater part of the trip. In going up the Cumberland the regiment lost two men by drowning; Henry Miner, of Co. D, and Perry Crochett, of Co. G. There was something of a mystery in regard to the death of Miner. He was last seen about nine o'clock one evening on the lower deck of the boat, close to where the two boats were lashed together. It was supposed that in some manner he missed his footing and fell between the boats, and was at once sucked under by the current and drowned. His cap was discovered next morning on the deck near the place where he was last observed, but no other vestige of him was ever found. The other soldier, Perry Crochett, stumbled and fell into the river in the day time, from the after part of the hurricane deck of the boat. He was perhaps stunned by the fall, for he just sank like a stone. The boats stopped, and a skiff was at once lowered and manned, and rowed out to the spot where he disappeared, and which lingered around there a short time, in the hope that he might come to the surface. His little old wool hat was floating around on the tops of the waves, but poor Perry was never seen again. There was nothing that could be done, so the skiff came back to the boat, was hoisted aboard, the bells rang the signal "go ahead," and we went on. Miner and Crochett were both young men, about my own age, and had been good and brave soldiers. Somehow it looked hard and cruel that after over three years' faithful service they were fated at last to lose their lives by drowning in the cold waters of the Cumberland, and be devoured by catfish and snapping turtles,--but such are among the chances in the life of a soldier.

On our way up the Cumberland we passed the historic Fort Donelson, where Gen. Grant in February, 1862, gained his first great victory. There was, at that time, desperate and bloody fighting at and near the gray earthen walls of the old fort. Now there was only a small garrison of Union troops here, and with that exception, the place looked about as quiet and peaceful as some obscure country graveyard.

We arrived at Nashville after dark on the evening of the 27th, remained on the boat that night, debarked the next morning, and in the course of that day (the 28th) took the cars on what was then known as the Nashville and Chattanooga railroad, and went to Murfreesboro, about thirty miles southeast of Nashville. Here we went into camp inside of Fortress Rosecrans, a strong and extensive earthwork built under the direction of Gen. Rosecrans soon after the battle of Murfreesboro, in January, 1863.

CHAPTER XX

THE AFFAIR at OVERALL'S CREEK. MURFREESBORO. DECEMBER, 1864.

The invasion of Tennessee by the Confederate army under the command of Gen. J. B. Hood was now on, and only a day or two after our arrival at Murfreesboro we began to hear the sullen, deep-toned booming of artillery towards the west, and later north-west in the direction of Nashville. And this continued, with more or less frequency, until the termination, on December 16th, of the battle of Nashville, which resulted in the defeat of the Confederates, and their retreat from the State. About December 3rd, the Confederate cavalry, under the command of our old acquaintance, Gen. N. B. Forrest, swung in between Nashville and Murfreesboro, tore up the railroad, and cut us off from Nashville for about two weeks. The Union forces at Murfreesboro at this time consisted of about 6,000 men,--infantry, cavalry, and artillery, (but principally infantry,) under the command of Gen L. H. Rousseau.

December 4th, 1864, was a pleasant, beautiful day at old Murfreesboro. The sun was shining bright and warm, the air was still, and the weather conditions were like those at home during Indian summer in October. Along about the middle of the afternoon, without a single note of preliminary warning, suddenly came the heavy "boom" of cannon close at hand, in a northwesterly direction. We at once ran up on the ramparts, and looking up the railroad towards Nashville, could plainly see the blue rings of powder-smoke curling upwards above the trees. But we didn't look long. Directly after we heard the first report, the bugles in our camp and others began sounding "Fall in!" We hastily formed in line, and in a very short time the 61st Illinois and two other regiments of infantry, the 8th Minnesota and the 174th Ohio, with a section of artillery, all under the command of Gen. R. H. Milroy, filed out of Fortress Rosecrans, and proceeded in the direction of this cannonading. About four miles out from Murfreesboro we came to the scene of the trouble. The Confederates had opened with their artillery on one of our railroad block-houses, and were trying to demolish or capture it. The 13th Indiana Cavalry had preceded us to the spot, and were skirmishing with the enemy. Our regiment formed in line on the right of the pike, the Minnesota regiment to our right, and the Ohio regiment on the left, while our artillery took a position on some higher ground near the pike, and began exchanging shots with that of the enemy. The position of our regiment was on the hither slope of a somewhat high ridge, in the woods, with a small stream called Overall's creek running parallel to our front. We were standing here at ease, doing nothing, and I slipped up on the crest of the ridge, "to see what I could see." The ground on the opposite side of the creek was lower than ours, and was open, except a growth of rank grass and weeds. And I could plainly see the skirmishers of the enemy, in butternut clothing, skulking in the grass and weeds, and occasionally firing in our direction. They looked real tempting, so I hurried back to the regiment, and going to Capt. Keeley, told him that the Confederate skirmishers were just across the creek, in plain sight, and asked him if I couldn't slip down the brow of the ridge and take a few shots at them. He looked at me kind of queerly, and said: "You stay right where you are, and tend to your own business. You'll have plenty of shooting before long." I felt a little bit hurt at his remark, but made no reply, and resumed my place in the ranks. But he afterwards made me a sort of apology for his brusque reproof, saying he had no desire to see me perhaps throw my life away in a performance not within the scope of my proper and necessary duty. And he was right, too, in his prediction, that there would soon be "plenty of shooting." I had just taken my place in the ranks when a mounted staff officer came galloping up, and accosting a little group of our line officers, asked, with a strong German accent, "Iss ziss ze 61st Illinois?" and on being told that it was, next inquired for Col. Grass, who was pointed out to him. He rode to the Colonel, who was near at hand, saluted him, and said, "Col. Grass, ze Sheneral sends his compliments wiss ze order zat you immediately deploy your regiment as skirmishers, and forthwith advance on ze enemy, right in your front!" The recruits and non-veterans of the regiment being yet in Arkansas, its present effective strength hardly exceeded three hundred men, so there was just about enough of us to make a sufficient skirmish line, on this occasion, for the balance of the command. In obedience to the aforesaid order the regiment was promptly deployed as skirmishers, and the line advanced over the crest of the ridge in our front, and down the slope on the opposite side. At the bank of the creek a little incident befell me, which serves to show how a very trifling thing may play an important part in one's fate. I happened to reach the creek at a point opposite a somewhat deep pool. The water was clear and cold, and I disliked the idea of having wet feet on the skirmish line, and looked around for a place where it was possible to cross dry-shod. A rod or two above me the stream was narrow, and where it could be jumped, so I started in a run for that place. The creek bank on my side was of yellow clay, high and perpendicular, while on the other margin the bank was quite low, and the ground adjacent sloped upward gently and gradually. While running along the edge of the stream to the fording place, one of my feet caught on the end of a dead root projecting from the lower edge of the bank, and I pitched forward, and nearly fell. At the very instant of my stumble,--"thud" into the clay bank right opposite where I would have been, if standing, went a bullet fired by a Confederate skirmisher. He probably had taken deliberate aim at me, and on seeing me almost fall headlong, doubtless gave himself credit for another Yankee sent to "the happy hunting grounds." It is quite likely that owing to the existence of that old dead root, and my lucky stumble thereon, I am now here telling the story of this skirmish. By this time it was sunset, and darkness was approaching, but we went on. The Confederate skirmishers retired, but we soon developed their main line on some high ground near the edge of the woods,--and then we had to stop. We lay down, loaded and fired in that position, and nearly all of the enemy's balls passed over our heads. Presently it grew quite dark, and all we had to aim at was the long horizontal sheet of red flame that streamed from the muskets of the Confederates. In the mean time the artillery of both parties was still engaged in their duel, and their balls and shells went screaming over our heads. Occasionally a Confederate shell would explode right over us, and looked interesting, but did no harm. While all this firing was at its liveliest, I heard close by the heavy "thud" that a bullet makes in striking a human body, followed immediately by a sharp cry of "Oh!" which meant that someone had been hit. It proved to be Lieutenant Elijah Corrington, of Co. F. He was struck by the ball in the region of the heart, and expired almost instantly. He was a good man, and a brave soldier, and his death was sincerely mourned.

The affair was terminated by the 174th Ohio on our left getting around on the enemy's right flank, where it poured in a destructive volley, and the Confederates retired. We followed a short distance, but neither saw nor heard anything more of the enemy, so we finally retired also. We recrossed the creek, built some big fires out of dry chestnut rails, which we left burning, in order, I suppose, to make our foes believe we were still there, and then marched to Murfreesboro, where we arrived about midnight.

On the two following days, December 5 and 6, the Confederates showed themselves to the west of us, and demonstrated most ostentatiously against Murfreesboro. From where we stood on the ramparts of Fortress Rosecrans we could plainly see their columns in motion, with flags flying, circling around us as if looking for a good opening. They were beyond the range of musketry, but our big guns in the fortress opened on them and gave them a most noisy cannonading, but what the effect was I don't know,--probably not much. In the battles of the Civil War artillery playing on infantry at short range with grape and canister did frightful execution, of which I saw plenty of evidence at Shiloh; but at a distance, and firing with solid shot or shell, it simply made a big noise, and if it killed anybody, it was more an accident than otherwise.

Beginning about December 5th, and continuing for several days thereafter, we turned out at four o'clock every morning, fully armed, and manned the trenches in the rear of the breastworks, and remained there till after sunrise. It was a cold, chilly business, standing two or three hours in those damp trenches, with an empty stomach, waiting for an apprehended attack, which, however, was never made. For my part, I felt like I did when behind our big works in the rear of Vicksburg, and sincerely hoped that the other fellows would make an attempt to storm our defenses, and I think the other boys felt the same way. We would have shot them down just like pigeons, and the artillery in the corner bastions, charged with grape and canister, would have played its part too. But the Confederates had no intention of making any attempt of this nature. The Official Records of the Rebellion hereinbefore mentioned contain the correspondence between Hood and Forrest concerning this movement on Murfreesboro, and which clearly discloses their schemes. The plan was simply to "scare" Rousseau out of Murfreesboro, and cause him to retreat in a northerly direction towards the town of Lebanon, and then, having gotten him out of his hole, to surround him in the open with their large force of cavalry, well supported by infantry, and capture all his command. But Rousseau didn't "scare" worth a cent, as will appear later.

CHAPTER XXI

THE BATTLE of WILKINSON'S PIKE.
DECEMBER 7, 1864.

Early in the morning of December 7th, General Rousseau started out General Milroy with seven regiments of infantry, (which included our regiment,) a battery of artillery, and a small detachment of cavalry, to find out what Gen. Forrest wanted. Our entire force consisted of a trifle over thirty-three hundred men. We first marched south from Murfreesboro, on the Salem pike, but gradually executed a right wheel, crossed Stone river, and worked to the northwest. We soon jumped up the Confederate cavalry vedettes, and a portion of the 61st was thrown out as skirmishers, and acted with our cavalry in driving back these scattered outposts of the enemy. Finally, about noon, we ran up against the main line of the Confederates, on the Wilkinson pike, protected by slight and hastily constructed breastworks, made of dirt, rails, and logs. Their artillery opened on us before we came in musket range, and we halted and formed in line of battle in some tall woods, with an open field in front. We were standing here in line when Gen. Milroy with some of his staff rode up right in front of our regiment, and stopped on a little elevated piece of ground. Then the old man took out his field-glass, and proceeded carefully and deliberately to scrutinize the country before him. My place in the line was only two or three rods from him, and I watched his proceedings with the deepest interest. He would look a while at the front, then sweep his glass to the right and scan that locality, then to the left and examine that region. While he was thus engaged, we all remained profoundly silent, his staff sat near him on their horses, also saying nothing. His survey of the country before him could not have lasted more than five minutes, but to me it seemed terribly long. At last he shut up his glass, returned it to its case, gave his horse a sort of a "haw" pull, and said something in a low tone to the different members of his staff, who forthwith dispersed in a gallop up and down our line. "Now," thought I, "something is going to happen." One of the staff stopped and said something to Col. Grass, and then came the command: "Attention, battalion! Shoulder arms! Face to the rear! Battalion, about face! Right shoulder shift arms! Forward, guide center, march!" And that, I thought, told the story. The other fellows were too many for us, and we were going to back out. They probably had someone up a tree, watching us, for we had hardly begun our rearward movement before their artillery opened on us furiously, and the cannon balls went crashing through the tree tops, and bringing down the limbs in profusion. But, as usual, the artillery hurt nobody, and we went on, quietly and in perfect order. After retiring through the woods for some distance, we gradually changed the direction of our march to the left, the result being that we executed an extensive left wheel, and pivoted towards the left flank of the enemy. Here our entire regiment was deployed as skirmishers, and we again advanced. We later learned that the enemy had made all their preparations to meet us at the point where we first encountered their line, so they were not fully prepared for this new movement.

Gen. Milroy, in his official report of the battle, in describing this advance, says:

"The Sixty-first Illinois was deployed as skirmishers in front of the first line, [and the] line advanced upon the enemy through the brush, cedars, rocks, and logs, under a heavy fire of artillery. Skirmishing with small arms began soon after commencing my advance, but my skirmish line advanced, rapidly, bravely, and in splendid order, considering the nature of the ground, driving the rebels before them for about a mile," [when their main line was struck].

As we were advancing in this skirmish line across an old cotton field, the Confederates ran forward a section of artillery, placed it on some rising ground and opened on us a rapid fire. The shot and shell fell all around us, throwing up showers of red dirt, but doing no harm. While these guns were thus engaged, I noticed a large, fine-looking man, mounted on an iron gray horse, near one of the pieces, and who was intently watching our advance across the field. He evidently was a Confederate officer, and I thought possibly of high rank; so, taking careful aim each time, I gave him two shots from "Trimthicket," (the pet name of my old musket,) but without effect, so far as was perceivable. After each shot he remained impassive in his saddle, and soon after galloped away. After the battle I talked about the incident with some of the Confederates we captured, and they told me that this officer was Gen. Forrest himself. He was probably too far away when I fired at him for effective work, but he doubtless heard the bullets and perhaps concluded that he had better not expose himself unnecessarily.

Our skirmish line continued to advance across the cotton field before mentioned. In our front was a dense thicket of small cedars occupied by the Confederate skirmishers, and as we approached these woods our progress was somewhat slow. I happened to notice in the edge of the thicket, and only a few rods in my front, a big, heavy log, which was lying parallel to our line, and would afford splendid protection. Thereupon I made a rush, and dropped behind this log. It was apparently a rail-cut, and had been left lying on the ground. A little fellow of Co. H, named John Fox, a year or two my junior, saw me rush for this log, he followed me, and dropped down behind it also. He had hardly done this when he quickly called to me--"Look out, Stillwell! You'll get shot!" I hardly understood just what caused his remark, but instinctively ducked behind the log, and at that instant "whis-sh" went a bullet from the front through the upper bark of the log, right opposite where my breast was a second or two before, scattering worm-dust and fragments of bark over my neck and shoulders. "I seed him a-takin' aim," dryly remarked little Fox. "Where is he?" I quickly inquired. "Right yander," answered Fox, indicating the place by pointing. I looked and saw the fellow--he was a grown man, in a faded gray uniform, but before I could complete my hasty preparations to return his compliment he disappeared in the jungle of cedar.

An incident will now be described, the result of which was very mortifying to me at the time, and which, to this day, I have never been able to understand, or account for. We had passed through the cedar woods before mentioned, and entered another old cotton field. And right in the hither edge of that field we came plump on a Confederate cavalry vedette, seated on his horse. The man had possibly been on duty all the previous night, and perhaps was now dozing in his saddle, or he never would have stayed for us to slip up on him as we did. But if asleep, he waked up promptly at this stage of the proceedings. All along our line the boys began firing at him, yelling as they did so. The moment I saw him, I said to myself, with an exultant thrill, "You're my game." He was a big fellow, broad across the back, wearing a wool hat, a gray jacket, and butternut trousers. My gun was loaded, I was all ready, and what followed didn't consume much more than two seconds of time. I threw my gun to my shoulder, let the muzzle sink until I saw through the front and rear sights the center of that broad back--and then pulled the trigger. Porting my musket, I looked eagerly to the front, absolutely confident that my vision would rest on the horse flying riderless across the field, and the soldier lying dead upon the ground. But to my utter amazement, there was the fellow yet on his horse, and, like John Gilpin of old, going,

"Like an arrow swift
Shot by an archer strong."

He had a small gad, or switch, in his right hand, with which he was belaboring his horse every jump, and the upshot of the matter was, he reached and disappeared in the woods beyond, without a scratch, so far as any of us on our side ever knew. How my shot happened to miss that man is just one of the most unaccountable things that ever happened to me in my life. I was perfectly cool and collected at the time, and my nerves were steady as iron; he was a splendid mark, at close range, and I took a deadly aim. And then to think that all our other fellows missed him too! It was certainly a thing that surpasses all comprehension.

At the time I am now writing these lines, a little over half a century has passed away since this incident occurred, and it will here be recorded that now I am sincerely thankful that I failed to kill that man. Considering his marvelous escape on this occasion, the presumption is strong that he lived through the war, married some good woman, and became the father of a family of interesting children, and likely some one of his boys fought under the old flag in the Spanish-American War,--so it is probably all for the best.

But,--how in the world did I happen to miss him?

Only a few minutes after this incident I experienced the closest call (so far as can be stated with certainty) that befell me during my service. On this day it so happened that Co. D was assigned a position on the extreme right of the skirmish line. This was not the regulation place for the company in the regimental line, and just how this came about I don't know, but so it was. As the first sergeant of D, my position was on the extreme right of the company, consequently I was the right hand man of the whole skirmish line. We were continuing our advance across the field where we came on the vedette just mentioned, and all in high spirits. I had on a broad-brimmed felt hat, my overcoat, and beneath that what we called a "dress-coat," with the ends of my trouser legs tucked in my socks; was carrying my gun at a ready, and eagerly looking for something to shoot at. There was a little bunch of Confederates in the woods on our right that were sort of "pot-shooting" at us as we were moving across the field, but we paid no attention to them, as the main force of the enemy was in our front. Suddenly I was whirled around on my feet like a top, and a sensation went through me similar, I suppose, to that which one feels when he receives an electric shock. I noticed that the breast of my overcoat was torn, but saw no blood nor felt any pain, so it was manifest that I wasn't hurt. It was clear that the ball which struck me had come from the right, so some of us paid attention to those fellows at once, and they soon disappeared. At the first opportunity after the battle was over I examined my clothes to find out what this bullet had done. As stated, it came from the right, and first went through the cape of my overcoat, then through the right-arm sleeves of my overcoat and dress coat, thence through the right breast of both those coats, and then through the left breast thereof, and from thence went on its way. All told, it made nine holes in my clothes, but never touched my flesh. But it was a fine line-shot and had it been two inches further back all would have been over with me.

Just after this episode, as we approached a rise in the field we came in sight of the main line of the enemy, in the edge of the woods on the opposite side of the field. The right wing of our skirmish line then took ground to the right and the other wing to the left in order to uncover our main line. It then marched up, and the action became general. The musketry firing on both sides was heavy and incessant, and, in addition, the enemy had a battery of artillery, which kept roaring most furiously. We also had a battery, but it was not now in evidence, the reason being as we afterwards learned, that it had exhausted its ammunition during the previous course of the day, and had returned to Fortress Rosecrans for a further supply, but before it got back the fight was over. The engagement had lasted only a short time, when the command was given to charge, and our whole line went forward. And thereupon I witnessed the bravest act that I ever saw performed by an officer of the rank of general. The regiment immediately on the left of the right wing of our regiment was the 174th Ohio. It was a new regiment, and had never been under fire but once before, that occasion being the affair at Overall's creek three days previous. So, when we started on this charge, I anxiously watched this big, new Ohio regiment, for it was perfectly plain that if it faltered and went back, our little right wing of the 61st Illinois would have to do likewise. And presently that Ohio regiment stopped!--and then we stopped too. I looked at those Ohio fellows; there was that peculiar trembling, wavy motion along their line which precedes a general going to pieces, and it seemed like the game was up. But just at that supreme moment, old Gen. Milroy appeared, on his horse, right in front of that Ohio regiment, at a point opposite the colors. He was bareheaded, holding his hat in his right hand, his long, heavy, iron-gray hair was streaming in the wind, and he was a most conspicuous mark. The Confederates were blazing away along their whole line, yelling like devils, and I fairly held my breath, expecting to see the old General forthwith pitch headlong from his horse, riddled with bullets. But he gave the enemy very little time to practice on him. I was not close enough to hear what he said, but he called to those Ohio men in a ringing tone, and waved his hat towards the enemy. The effect was instantaneous and sublime. The whole line went forward with a furious yell, and surged over the Confederate works like a big blue wave,--and the day was ours!

The Confederates retreated on a double quick, but in good order. We captured two pieces of their artillery, a stand of colors, and about two hundred prisoners. We followed them a short distance, but saw them no more, and about sundown we marched back to Fortress Rosecrans. But before finally passing from this affair, a few other things connected therewith will be mentioned.

As we went over the Confederate works on our charge, I saw lying on the ground, inside, a dead Confederate lieutenant-colonel. He was on his back, his broad-brimmed hat pulled over his face, and a pair of large gauntlet gloves tucked in his belt. His sword was detached from the belt, in the scabbard, and was lying transversely across his body. As I ran by him I stooped down and with my left hand picked up the sword, and carried it along. I brought it to camp with me, kept it until we were mustered out, and then brought it home. Later a Masonic lodge was organized in Otterville, and some of the officers thereof borrowed from me this sword for the use of the tyler of the lodge, in his official duties. In 1868 I came to Kansas, leaving the sword with the lodge. After the lapse of some years there came a time when I desired to resume possession of this relic of the war, but on taking action to obtain it, it was ascertained that in the meantime the lodge building, with all its furniture and paraphernalia, including the sword in question, had been accidentally destroyed by fire. And thus passed away the only trophy that I ever carried off a battlefield. Many years later I met here in Kansas the late Confederate Gen. John B. Gordon, of Georgia, and had a long and interesting conversation with him. I told him the facts connected with my obtaining this sword, and of its subsequent loss, as above stated. He listened to me with deep attention, and at the close of my story, said he was satisfied from my general description of the dead Confederate officer that the body on which I found the sword was that of W. W.

Billopp, lieutenant-colonel of the 29th Georgia, who was killed in this action. Gen. Gordon also said that he was well acquainted with Col. Billopp in his life time, and that he was a splendid gentleman and a brave soldier. It has always been a matter of regret with me that the sword was destroyed, for I intended, at the time I sought to reclaim it from the Masonic lodge, to take steps to restore it to the family of the deceased officer, in the event that it could be done.

When the Confederates retired from this battlefield of December 7th, they left their dead and severely wounded on the field, as it was impossible for them to do otherwise. I walked around among these unfortunates, and looked at them, and saw some things that made me feel sorrowful indeed. I looked in the haversacks of some of the dead to see what they had to eat,--and what do you suppose was found? Nothing but raw, shelled corn! And many of them were barefooted, and judging from appearances, had been so indefinitely. Their feet were almost as black as those of a negro, with the skin wrinkled and corrugated to that extent that it looked like the hide of an alligator. These things inspired in me a respect for the Confederate soldiers that I never had felt before. The political leaders of the Davis and Toombs type who unnecessarily brought about the war are, in my opinion, deserving of the severest condemnation. But there can be no question that the common soldiers of the Confederate army acted from the most deep-seated convictions of the justice and the righteousness of their cause, and the fortitude and bravery they displayed in support of it are worthy of the highest admiration.

After the engagement of December 7th, the Confederates still remained in our vicinity, and showed themselves at intervals, but made no aggressive movement. Cold weather set in about this time, the ground was covered with sleet, and our situation, cooped up in Fortress Rosecrans, was unpleasant and disagreeable. We had long ago turned in our big Sibley tents, and drawn in place of them what we called "pup-tents." They were little, squatty things, composed of different sections of canvas that could be unbuttoned and taken apart, and carried by the men when on a march. They were large enough for only two occupants, and there were no facilities for building fires in them, as in the case of the Sibleys. Owing to the fact that the Confederates were all around us, we were short of fire-wood too. Stone river ran through the fortress, and there were some big logs in the river, which I suppose had been there ever since the work was constructed, and we dragged them out and used them to eke out our fires. They were all water-soaked, and hardly did more than smoulder, but they helped some. At night we would crowd into those little pup-tents, lie down with all our clothes on, wrap up in our blankets and try to sleep, but with poor success. I remember that usually about midnight I would "freeze out," and get up and stand around those sobbing, smouldering logs,--and shiver. To make matters worse, we were put on half rations soon after we came to Murfreesboro, and full rations were not issued again until the Confederates retreated from Nashville after the battle of December 15-16.

CHAPTER XXII

THE FIGHT ON THE RAILROAD NEAR MURFREESBORO, DECEMBER 15, 1864.

On the afternoon of December 12th the regiment fell in and we marched to the railroad depot at Murfreesboro, climbed on a train of box cars, and started for Stevenson, Alabama, about 80 miles southeast of Murfreesboro. The number of the regiment who participated in this movement, according to the official report of Maj. Nulton, was 150 men, and we were accompanied by a detachment of about forty of the 1st Michigan Engineers. (See Serial No. 93, Official Records of the War of the Rebellion, p. 620.) We soon learned that the train was going to Stevenson to obtain rations for the troops at Murfreesboro, and that our province was to serve as guards for the train, to Stevenson and on its return. We had not gone more than eight or ten miles from Murfreesboro before we ran into the Confederate cavalry vedettes who were scattered along at numerous points of observation near the railroad. However, on our approach they scurried away like quails. But in many places the track had been torn up, and culverts destroyed, and when we came to one of these breaks, the train had to stop until our engineers could repair it, and then we went on. Right here I will say that those Michigan Engineers were splendid fellows. There was a flat car with our train, and on this car was a supply of extra rails, spikes, and other railroad appliances, with all the tools that the engineers used in their work, and it was remarkable to see how quick those men would repair a break in the road. They also were provided with muskets and accouterments the same as ordinary soldiers, and when the necessity arose, (as it did before we got back to Murfreesboro,) they would drop their sledges and crowbars, buckle on their cartridge boxes and grab their muskets, and fight like tigers. It was "all the same to Joe" with them. After getting about thirty-five miles from Murfreesboro we saw no more of the enemy, the railroad from thereon was intact, and we arrived at Stevenson about 10 o'clock on the morning of the 13th. The train was loaded with rations and early on the morning of the 14th we started back to Murfreesboro, having in addition to the force with which we left there, a squad of about thirty dismounted men of the 12th Indiana Cavalry, who joined us at Stevenson. The grade up the eastern slope of the Cumberland Mountains was steep, a drizzling rain had fallen the night before, making the rails wet and slippery, and the train had much difficulty in ascending the grade, and our progress was tedious and slow. This delay probably was the cause of our undoing, as will be revealed later. We didn't get over the mountains until some time in the afternoon, and went along slowly, but all right; and about dark reached Bell Buckle, 32 miles from Murfreesboro. Here trouble began on a small scale. A Confederate cavalry vedette was on the alert, and fired at us the first shot of the night. The bullet went over us near where I was sitting on top of a car, with a sharp "ping," that told it came from a rifle. But we went on, proceeding slowly and cautiously, for the night was pitch dark, and we were liable to find the railroad track destroyed at almost any place. At 2 o'clock in the morning, just after leaving Christiana, about 15 miles from Murfreesboro, our troubles broke loose in good earnest. We encountered the Confederate cavalry in force, and also found the track in front badly torn up. We got off the cars, formed in line on both sides of the road and slowly advanced, halting whenever we came to a break in the road, until our Michigan Engineers could repair it. As above stated, they were bully boys, and understood their business thoroughly, and very soon would patch up the breaks so that the train could proceed. But it went only about as fast as a man could walk, and during the balance of that cold, dark night, we marched along by the side of the track, skirmishing with the enemy. On one occasion we ran right up against their line, they being on their horses, and evidently awaiting our approach. Luckily for us, their guns must have been wet; they nearly all missed fire, with no result save a lively snapping of caps along substantially their entire line. But our guns went off, and we gave the fellows a volley that, at least, waked up all the owls in the neighborhood. It was so intensely dark that accurate shooting was out of the question, and whether we hurt anybody or not I don't know, but our foes galloped off in great haste, and disappeared for a while. Shortly before daylight, when we were within about six miles of Murfreesboro, we came to the worst break in the track we had yet encountered. It was at the end of a short cut in the road that was perhaps four or five feet deep. In front of this cut the track was demolished for several rods, and a deep little culvert was also destroyed. We sat down on the ground near the track, and our engineers went to work. The situation was like this: In our front, towards Murfreesboro, and on our right and left rear were corn fields, with the stalks yet standing, and on our left front was a high rocky ridge, heavily timbered with a dense growth of small cedars, and which ridge sloped abruptly down to the railroad track. A small affluent of Stone river, with a belt of willow along its banks, flowed in a winding course along our right, in the general direction of Murfreesboro. While we were sitting here on the ground, half asleep, waiting for the engineers to call out "All right!"--there came a volley of musketry from the woods of the rocky ridge I have mentioned. We sprang to our feet, formed in the cut facing the ridge, and began returning the fire. After this had continued for some time, a party of the enemy moved to our rear, beyond gunshot, and began tearing up the track there, while another party took up a position on the opposite side of the little stream on our right, and opened fire on us from that direction. A portion of our force was shifted to the right of the train to meet the attack from this quarter, and the firing waxed hot and lively. Our engineers had seized their guns, and were blazing away with the rest of us, and our bunch of dismounted cavalry men were also busy with their carbines. This state of things continued for fully an hour, and I think some longer, when suddenly, coming from our left rear, a cannon ball screamed over our heads, followed by the roar of the gun. The commanding officer of Co. D in this affair (and the only officer of our company present) was Lieut. Wallace, and he was standing near me when the cannon ball went over us. "What's that?" he exclaimed. "It means they have opened on us with artillery," I answered. "Well," he responded, "let 'em bang away with their pop-guns!" and I think we all felt equally indifferent. We had become familiar with artillery and knew that at long range it was not very dangerous. But the enemy's cannon kept pounding away, and pretty soon a shot struck somewhere on the engine with a resounding crash. About this time Col. Grass gave the order to retreat. There was only one way of escape open, and that was down the track towards Murfreesboro. We hastily formed in two ranks, and started down the right side of the track in a double quick. As we passed out of the cut a body of dismounted cavalry came out of the woods on the ridge to our left and gave us a volley of musketry. But, being on higher ground than we were, they overshot us badly, and did but little harm. We answered their fire, and their line halted. The command quickly went along our column to load and fire as we went, and "keep firing!" and we did so. We kept up a rattling, scattering fire on those fellows on our left which had the effect of standing them off, at any rate, and in the meantime we all did some of the fastest running down along the side of the railroad track that I have ever seen. Speaking for myself, I am satisfied that I never before surpassed it, and have never since equaled it. But we had all heard of Andersonville, and wanted no Confederate prison in ours. To add to our troubles, an irregular line of Confederate cavalry charged on us through the corn field in our rear, firing and yelling at the top of their voices, "Halt! Halt! you G---- d---- Yankee sons of ----!"--their remarks closing with an epithet concerning our maternal ancestors which, in the words of Colonel Carter of Cartersville, was "vehy gallin', suh." But, as said by the French soldier, old Peter, in "The Chronicles of the Drum,"

"Cheer up! 'tis no use to be glum, boys,--
'Tis written, since fighting begun,
That sometimes we fight and we conquer
And sometimes we fight and we run."

Occasionally we would send a bullet back at these discourteous pursuers, and possibly on account of that, or maybe some other reason, they refrained from closing in on us.

About half a mile from where we left the train the railroad

crossed on a high trestle the little stream I have mentioned, which here turned to the left, and we had to ford it. It was only about knee-deep, but awful cold. The Confederates did not attempt to pursue us further after we crossed the creek, and from there we continued our retirement unmolested. I fired one shot soon after we forded the stream, and I have always claimed, and, in my opinion, rightfully, that it was the last shot fired in action by the regiment during the war. I will briefly state the circumstances connected with the incident. In crossing the creek, in some manner I fell behind, which it may be said was no disgrace, as the rear, right then, was the place of danger. But, to be entirely frank about it, this action was not voluntary on my part, but because I was just about completely played out. Firing had now ceased, and I took my time, and soon was the tail-end man of what was left of us. Presently the creek made a bend to the right, and circled around a small elevated point of land on the opposite side, and on this little rise I saw a group of Confederate cavalrymen, four or five in number, seated on their horses, and quietly looking at us. They maybe thought there was no more fight left in us, and that they could gaze on our retreat with impunity. They probably were officers, as they had no muskets or carbines, and were apparently wearing better clothes than private soldiers. I noted especially that they had on black coats, of which the tails came down to their saddle-skirts. They were in easy shooting distance, and my gun was loaded. I dropped on one knee behind a sapling, rested my gun against the left side of the tree, took aim at the center of the bunch, and pulled the trigger. "Fiz-z-z--kerbang!" roared old Trimthicket with a deafening explosion, and a kick that sent me a-sprawling on my back! There were two loads in my gun! My last preceding charge had missed fire, and in the excitement of the moment and the confusion and uproar around me, I had failed to notice it, and rammed home another load. But I regained my feet instantly, and eagerly looked to see the effect of my shot. Nobody was lying on the ground, but that entire party was leaving the spot, in a gallop, with their heads bent forward and their coat tails flying behind them. Their curiosity was evidently satisfied. There is no mistake that I sent two bullets through the center of that squad, but whether they hit anybody or not I don't know.

At a point about a mile or so from where we left the train, we reached one of our railroad block houses, held by a small garrison. Here we halted, and reformed. As I came slowly trudging up to Co. D, Bill Banfield was talking to Lieut. Wallace, and said: "I guess Stillwell's gone up. Haven't seen him since we crossed that creek." I stepped forward and in a brief remark, containing some language not fitting for a Sunday-school superintendent, informed Bill that he was laboring under a mistake.

Soon after we arrived at the blockhouse a strong force of our troops, having marched out that morning from Murfreesboro, also appeared on the ground. Gen. Rousseau had learned that we were attacked, and had sent these troops to our assistance, but they were too late. He had also sent a detachment to this point the evening before, to meet us, but on account of our being delayed, as before stated, we did not appear, so this party, after waiting till some time after sunset, marched back to Murfreesboro.

In this affair we lost, in killed, wounded, and prisoners, about half the regiment, including Col. Grass, who was captured. He was a heavy-set man, somewhat fleshy, and at this time a little over forty years old. He became completely exhausted on our retreat, (being on foot,) tumbled over, and the Confederates got him. Many years later, when we were both living in Kansas, I had an interesting conversation with him about this affair. He told me that his sole reason for ordering the retreat was that he had ascertained shortly before the artillery opened on us, that our cartridges were almost exhausted. Then, when our assailants brought their artillery into play, he realized, he said, that the train was doomed, that it would soon be knocked to pieces, and also set on fire by the balls and shells of the enemy, and that we were powerless to prevent it. Under these circumstances he deemed it his duty to give up the train, and save his men, if possible. Col. Grass was a good and brave man, and I have no doubt that he acted in this matter according to his sincere convictions of duty.

The Confederate commander in this action was Gen. L. S. Ross of Texas, who, after the war, served two terms as governor of that State. All his men were Texans, (with the possible exception of the artillery,) and, according to the official reports, were more than three times our number. I think it is permissible to here quote a small portion of the official report made by Gen. Ross of this engagement, as found on page 771, Serial No. 93, Official Records of the War of the Rebellion. Speaking of our defense of the train, he says:

"The men guarding it fought desperately for over an hour, having a strong position in a cut of the railroad, but were finally routed by a most gallant charge of the Sixth Texas, supported by the Third Texas."

While the tribute thus paid by Gen. Ross to the manner of our defense is appreciated, nevertheless I will say that he is absolutely wrong in saying that we were "routed" by the charge he mentions. We retreated simply and solely in obedience to the orders of Col. Grass, our commander, and neither the Sixth Texas nor the Third Texas had a thing to do in bringing that about. I don't deny that they followed us pretty closely after we got started.

Among our casualties in this affair was Lt. Lorenzo J. Miner, of Co. B, (originally of Co. C,) a splendid young man, and a most excellent officer. In addition to his other efficient soldierly qualities he deservedly had the reputation of being the best drill-master in the regiment. I happened to see him on our retreat, shortly before we arrived at the blockhouse. He was being helped off the field by Sergt. Amos Davis of Co. C and another soldier, one on each side, supporting him. They were walking slowly. Miner's eyes were fixed on the ground, and he was deathly pale. I saw from his manner that he was badly hurt, but did not learn the extent of it till later. He was shot somewhere through the body. The wound proved mortal and he died a few days after the fight.

And so it was, that after more than three years of brave and faithful service he was fated to lose his life in the last action the regiment was in--a small, obscure affair among the rocks and bushes, and which, when mentioned in the general histories at all, is disposed of in a paragraph of about four lines. But a soldier in time of war has no control over his fate, and no option in the selection of the time when, nor the place where, it may be his lot to "stack arms" forever.

I will now resume the account of what occurred after we

reached the blockhouse. It will be brief. We formed in line with the reinforcements that had come from Murfreesboro, and advanced toward the train. We encountered no opposition; the enemy had set fire to the cars, and then had hastily and entirely disappeared.

I have recently discovered in a modern edition of the Reports of the Adjutant-General of Illinois, (the date on the title page being 1901,) that in the revised sketch of our regiment a recital has crept in stating that in our subsequent advance we "recaptured the train in time to prevent its destruction." How that statement got into the sketch I do not know, and I am sorry to be under the necessity of saying that it is not true. When we got back to the scene of the fight the train was a mass of roaring flame, the resulting consequence being that every car was finally consumed. No matter how much it may hurt, it is always best to be fair, and tell the truth.

In the course of the day our troops all returned to Murfreesboro. Maj. Nulton, who was now our regimental commander, gave us of the 61st permission to march back "at will." That is, we could start when we got ready, singly or in squads, and not in regimental formation. So Bill Banfield and I started out to get something to eat, as we were very hungry. Since leaving Stevenson on the morning of the 14th, we had had no opportunity to cook anything, and had eaten nothing but some hardtack and raw bacon. Then that night we had left our haversacks on top of the cars when we got off the train to skirmish with the enemy, and never saw them again. And this was a special grievance for Bill and me. We each had a little money, and on the morning we left Stevenson had gone to a sutler's, and made some purchases to insure us an extra good meal when we got back to Murfreesboro. I bought a little can of condensed milk, (having always had a weakness for milk in coffee,) while Bill, with a kind of queer taste, invested in a can of lobsters. One time that night, while sitting on the ground, in the cold and dark, tired, hungry, and sleepy, waiting while our engineers patched a break in the railroad, Bill, with a view, I reckon, to cheering us both up, delivered himself in this wise: "This is a little tough, Stillwell, but just think of that bully dinner we'll have when we get to Murfreesboro! You've your can of condensed milk, and I've mine of lobsters; we'll have coffee with milk in it, and then, with some hardtack, we'll have a spread that will make up for this all right." But, alas!

"The best laid schemes o' mice and men
Gang aft a-gley."

My precious condensed milk, and the crustaceans aforesaid of Bill's, doubtless went glimmering down the alimentary canal of some long-haired Texan, to his great satisfaction. My wish at the time was that the darned lobsters might make the fellow sick,--which they probably did. So Bill and I were now at the burning train, looking for something to take the place of our captured Belshazzar banquet. We found a car that was loaded with pickled pork in barrels, and getting a fence rail, we finally succeeded, after some peril and much difficulty, in prying off one of the barrels, and it fell to the ground, bursting open as it did so, and scattering the blazing pieces of pork all around. We each got a portion, and then sat down on a big rock, and proceeded to devour our respective chunks without further ceremony. The outside of the meat was burned to a coal, but we were hungry, all of it tasted mighty sweet, and we gnawed it just like dogs. At the close of the repast, I took a look at Bill. His face was as black as tar from contact with the burnt pork, and in other respects his "tout ensemble" "left much to be desired." I thought if I looked as depraved as Bill certainly did it would be advisable to avoid any pocket looking-glass until after a thorough facial ablution with soft water and plenty of soap. Dinner over, we were soon ready for the march to camp, (there being no dishes to wash,) and started down the railroad track for Murfreesboro. We took our time, and didn't reach camp till about sundown. We were the last arrivals of Co. D, and, as there were all sorts of rumors afloat, we afterwards learned that Capt. Keeley had become quite anxious about us. As we turned down our company street I saw the Captain standing in front of his tent, looking in our direction. After the affairs of the 4th and the 7th, I had taken much satisfaction, in speaking to him of those events, in adopting the phraseology of the old chaplain, and had expressed myself several times in language like this: "And we smote them, hip and thigh, even as Joash smote Boheel!" But it was now necessary to amend my boastful statement, so as I approached Capt. Keeley, and before anything else had been spoken, I made to him this announcement: "And they smote us, hip and thigh, even as Joash smote Boheel!" Keeley laughed, but it was a rather dry laugh, and he answered: "Well, I'm glad they didn't smite you boys, anyhow--but, great God! go wash your faces, and clean up generally. You both look like the very devil himself." We passed on, complied with the Captain's directions, and then I curled up in my dog tent and slept without a break until next morning.

In concluding my account of this affair it will be stated that the most of our boys who were captured in the fight, and (I think) all the line officers who had the same bad luck, made their escape, singly, or in little parties, not long thereafter. Their Confederate captors, on or about the day after our encounter, had hurriedly joined the army of Gen. Hood, taking their prisoners with them. In their retreat from Tennessee on this occasion, the Confederates had a hard and perilous time. The guards of the captured Yankees were probably well-nigh worn out, and it is likely that, on account of their crushing defeat at Nashville, they had also become discouraged and careless. Anyhow, the most of our fellows got away while Hood was yet on the north side of the Tennessee river. He crossed that stream with the wreck of his army on the 26th and 27th of December, and fell back into Mississippi.

CHAPTER XXIII

MURFREESBORO. WINTER of 1864-1865. FRANKLIN. SPRING and SUMMER of 1865.

After the retreat of Hood from Nashville, matters became very quiet and uneventful with us at Murfreesboro. The regiment shifted its camp from the inside of Fortress Rosecrans out into open ground on the outskirts of the town, and proceeded to build winter quarters. These consisted of log cabins, like those we built at Little Rock the previous winter, only now the logs were cedar instead of pine. There were extensive cedar forests in the immediate vicinity of Murfreesboro, and we had no difficulty whatever in getting the material. And we had plenty of nice, fragrant cedar wood to burn in our fire-places, which was much better than soggy Arkansas pine. And I remember with pleasure a matter connected with the rations we had in the fore part of the winter. For some reason or other the supply of hardtack became practically exhausted, and we had but little in the line of flour bread, even for some weeks after Hood retreated from Nashville. But in the country north of Murfreesboro was an abundance of corn, and there were plenty of water-mills, so Gen. Rousseau sent out foraging parties in that region and appropriated the corn, and set the mills to grinding it, and oh, what fine cornbread we had! We used to make "ash-cakes," and they were splendid. The method of making and cooking an ash-cake was to mix a quantity of meal with proper proportions of water, grease, and salt, wrap the meal dough in some dampened paper, or a clean, wet cloth, then put it in the fire and cover it with hot ashes and coals. By testing with a sharp stick we could tell when the cake was done, then we would yank it from the fire, scrape off the fragments of the covering and the adhering ashes,--and then, with bacon broiled on the cedar coals, and plenty of good strong coffee, we would have a dinner better than any (from my standpoint) that Delmonico's ever served up in its palmiest days.

On February 4th, 1865, the non-veterans and recruits of the regiment came to us from Arkansas, and so we were once more all together, except a few that were in the Confederate prisons down South. We were all glad to see each other once more, and had many tales to "swap," about our respective experiences during our separation.

On February 10th, Lieutenant Wallace resigned, and returned to his home in Illinois. The chief reason for his resignation was on account of some private matter at home, which was giving him much anxiety and trouble. Further, the war in the region where we were was practically over, and there was nothing doing, with no prospect, so far as we knew, of any military activity for the regiment in the future. Wallace's resignation left Co. D without a second lieutenant, as we then did not have enough enlisted men in the company to entitle us to a full complement of commissioned officers, and the place remained vacant for some months.

On March 21st, we left Murfreesboro by rail and went to Nashville, and thence to Franklin, about twenty miles south of Nashville, and on what was then called the Nashville and Decatur railroad. A desperate and bloody battle occurred here between our forces under the command of Gen. Schofield and the Confederates under Gen. Hood, on November 30th, only two days after our arrival at Murfreesboro. I have often wondered why it was that Gen. Thomas, our department commander, did not send our regiment, on our arrival at Nashville, to reinforce Schofield, instead of to Murfreesboro, for Gen. Schofield certainly needed all the help he could get. But it is probable that Gen. Thomas had some good reason for his action.

When we arrived at Franklin we relieved the regiment that was on duty there as a garrison, and it went somewhere else. It was the 75th Pennsylvania, and the officers and men composing it, so far as I saw, were all Germans. And they were fine, soldierly looking fellows, too. From this time until we left Franklin in the following September, our regiment comprised all the Union force that was stationed at the town. Maj. Nulton was in command of the post, and, subject only to higher authorities at a distance, we were "monarchs of all we surveyed." When we came to Franklin the signs of the battle of November 30th were yet fresh and plentiful. As soon as time and opportunity afforded, I walked over the whole field, (in fact, several times,) looking with deep interest at all the evidences of the battle. I remember especially the appearance of a scattered grove of young locust trees which stood at a point opposite the right center of the Union line. For some hours the grove was right between the fire of both the Union and the Confederate lines, and the manner in which the trees had been riddled with musket balls was truly remarkable. It looked as if a snowbird could not have lived in that grove while the firing was in progress.

General William A. Quarles, of Tennessee, was one of the Confederate generals who were wounded in this battle, and after incurring his wound was taken to the house of a Tennessee planter, Col. McGavock, about a mile from Franklin, near the Harpeth river. Two or three other wounded Confederate officers of less rank were taken to the same place. When the Confederates retreated from Nashville, Gen. Quarles and these other wounded officers were unable to accompany the army. They remained at McGavock's, and were taken prisoners by our forces. They were put under a sort of parole of honor, and allowed to remain where they were, without being guarded. They had substantially recovered from their wounds at the time our regiment arrived at Franklin, and not long thereafter Capt. Keeley came to me one day, and handed me an order from Maj. Nulton, which directed me to take a detail of four men, with two ambulances, and go to McGavock's and get Gen. Quarles and the other Confederate officers who were there, and bring them into Franklin, for the purpose of being sent to Nashville, and thence to the north to some military prison. I thereupon detailed Bill Banfield and three other boys, told them what our business was, and instructed them to brush up nicely, and have their arms and accouterments in first class condition, and, in general, to be looking their best. Having obtained the ambulances, with drivers, we climbed aboard, and soon arrived at the fine residence of old Col. McGavock. I went into the house, met the lady of the establishment, and inquired of her for Gen. Quarles, and was informed that he was in an upper room. I requested the lady to give the general my compliments, and tell him that I desired to see him. She disappeared, and soon the general walked into the room where I was awaiting him. He was a man slightly below medium stature, heavy set, black hair, piercing black eyes, and looked to be about thirty years old. He was a splendid looking soldier. I stepped forward and saluted him, and briefly and courteously told him my business. "All right, sergeant," he answered, "we'll be ready in a few minutes." Their preparations were soon completed, and we left the house. I assigned the general and one of the other officers to a seat near the front in one of the ambulances, and Bill Banfield and I occupied the seat behind them, and the remaining guards and prisoners rode in the other conveyance. There was only one remark made on the entire trip back to Franklin, and I'll mention it presently. We emerged from the woods into the Columbia pike at a point about three-quarters of a mile in front of our main line of works that had been charged repeatedly and desperately by the Confederates in the late battle. The ground sloped gently down towards the works, and for fully half a mile was as level as a house floor. I noticed that at the moment we reached the pike Gen. Quarles began to take an intense interest in the surroundings. He would lean forward, and look to the right, to the front, to the left, and occasionally throw a hasty glance backward,--but said nothing. Finally we passed through our works, near the historic "cotton-gin," and the general drew a deep breath, leaned back against his seat, and said: "Well, by God, the next time I fight at Franklin, I want to let the Columbia pike severely alone!" No one made any response, and the remainder of the journey was finished in silence. I duly delivered Gen. Quarles and his fellow-prisoners to Maj. Nulton, and never saw any of them again.

Early in April, decisive military operations took place in Virginia. On the 3rd of that month our forces marched into Richmond, and on the 9th the army of Gen. Lee surrendered to Gen. Grant. At Franklin we were on a telegraph line, and only about twenty miles from department headquarters, so the intelligence of those events was not long in reaching us. I am just unable to tell how profoundly gratified we were to hear of the capture of Richmond, and of Lee's army. We were satisfied that those victories meant the speedy and triumphant end of the war. It had been a long, desperate, and bloody struggle, and frequently the final result looked doubtful and gloomy. But now,--"there were signs in the sky that the darkness was gone; there were tokens in endless array"; and the feeling among the common soldiers was one of heart-felt relief and satisfaction. But suddenly our joy was turned into the most distressing grief and mourning. Only a few days after we heard of Lee's surrender came the awful tidings of the foul murder of Mr. Lincoln. I well remember the manner of the men when the intelligence of the dastardly crime was flashed to us at Franklin. They seemed dazed and stunned, and were reluctant to believe it, until the fact was confirmed beyond question. They sat around in camp under the trees, talking low, and saying but little, as if the matter were one that made mere words utterly useless. But they were in a desperate frame of mind, and had there been the least appearance of exultation over the murder of Mr. Lincoln by any of the people of Franklin, the place would have been laid in ashes instanter. But the citizens seemed to understand the situation. They went into their houses, and closed their doors, and the town looked as if deserted. To one who had been among the soldiers for some years, it was easy to comprehend and understand their feelings on this occasion. For the last two years of the war especially, the men had come to regard Mr. Lincoln with sentiments of veneration and love. To them he really was "Father Abraham," with all that the term implied. And this regard was also entertained by men of high rank in the army. Gen. Sherman, in speaking of Mr. Lincoln, says this:

"Of all the men I ever met, he seemed to possess more of the elements of greatness, combined with goodness, than any other."

For my part, I have been of the opinion, for many years, that Abraham Lincoln was the greatest man the world has ever known.

In the latter part of June the recruits of the 83rd, the 98th, and the 123rd Illinois Infantry were transferred to the 61st, making the old regiment about nine hundred strong. Co. D received forty-six of the transferred men, all of these being from the 83rd Illinois. And they were a fine set of boys, too. Their homes were, in the main, in northwestern Illinois, in the counties of Mercer,

Rock Island, and Warren. They all had received a good common school education, were intelligent, and prompt and cheerful in the discharge of their duties. They were good soldiers, in every sense of the word. It is a little singular that, since the muster-out of the regiment in the following September, I have never met a single one of these boys.

The ranks of the regiment now being filled nearly to the maximum, the most of the vacancies that existed in the line of commissioned officers were filled just as promptly as circumstances would permit. Lieut. Col. Grass had been discharged on May 15th, 1865, and Maj. Nulton, who was now our ranking field officer, was, on July 11th, promoted to the position of Colonel. He was the first, and only, colonel the regiment ever had. The vacancy in the lieutenant-colonelcy of the regiment was never filled, for what reason I do not know. Capt. Keeley was promoted Major, and first Lieutenant Warren to Captain of Co. D in Keeley's stead. And thus it came to pass that on July 11th I received a commission as second lieutenant of our company, and on August 21st was promoted to first lieutenant. Soon after receiving my commission, Capt. Warren was detailed on some special duty which took him away from Franklin for some weeks, and consequently during his absence I was the commanding officer of Co. D. So far as ever came to my knowledge, I got along all right, and very pleasantly. It is a fact, at any rate, that I presented a more respectable appearance than that which was displayed during the brief time I held the position at Austin, Arkansas, in May, 1864.

CHAPTER XIV

THE SOLDIER'S PAY. RATIONS; ALLUSIONS to SOME of the USEFUL LESSONS LEARNED by SERVICE in the ARMY in TIME of WAR. COURAGE in BATTLE.

This story is now drawing to a close, so I will here speak of some things of a general nature, and which have not been heretofore mentioned, except perhaps casually.

One important feature in the life of a soldier was the matter of his pay, and a few words on that subject may not be out of place. When I enlisted in January, 1862, the monthly pay of the enlisted men of a regiment of infantry was as follows: First sergeant, $20; duty sergeants, $17; corporals and privates, $13. By act of Congress of May 1st, 1864, the monthly pay of the enlisted men was increased, and from that date was as follows: First sergeant, $24; duty sergeants, $20; corporals, $18; privates, $16. That rate existed as long, at least, as we remained in the service. The first payment made to our regiment was on May 1st, 1862, while we were in camp at Owl Creek, Tennessee. The amount I received was $49.40, and of this I sent $45 home to my father at the first opportunity. For a poor man, he was heavily in debt at the time of my enlistment, and was left without any boys to help him do the work upon the farm, so I regarded it as my duty to send him every dollar of my pay that possibly could be spared, and did so as long as I was in the service. But he finally got out of debt during the war. He had good crops, and all manner of farm products brought high prices, so the war period was financially a prosperous one for him. And, to be fair about it, I will say that he later repaid me, when I was pursuing my law studies at the Albany, New York, Law School, almost all the money I had sent him while in the army. So the result really was that the money received by me, as a soldier, was what later enabled me to qualify as a lawyer.

I have heretofore said in these reminiscences that the great "stand-bys" in the way of the food of the soldiers of the western armies were coffee, sow-belly, Yankee beans, and hardtack. But other articles of diet were also issued to us, some of which we liked, while others were flat failures. I have previously said something about the antipathy I had for rice. The French General, Baron Gourgaud, in his "Talks of Napoleon at St. Helena", records Napoleon as having said, "Rice is the best food for the soldier." Napoleon, in my opinion, was the greatest soldier that mankind ever produced,--but all the same, I emphatically dissent from his rice proposition. His remark may have been correct when applied to European soldiers of his time and place,--but I know it wouldn't fit western American boys of 1861-65.

There were a few occasions when an article of diet was issued called "desiccated potatoes." For "desiccated" the boys promptly substituted "desecrated," and "desecrated potatoes" was its name among the rank and file from start to finish. It consisted of Irish potatoes cut up fine and thoroughly dried. In appearance it much resembled the modern preparation called "grape nuts." We would mix it in water, grease, and salt, and make it up into little cakes, which we would fry, and they were first rate. There was a while when we were at Bolivar, Tennessee, that some stuff called "compressed vegetables" was issued to us, which the boys, almost unanimously, considered an awful fraud. It was composed of all sorts of vegetables, pressed into small bales, in a solid mass, and as dry as threshed straw. The conglomeration contained turnip-tops, cabbage leaves, string-beans (pod and all), onion blades, and possibly some of every other kind of a vegetable that ever grew in a garden. It came to the army in small boxes, about the size of the Chinese tea-boxes that were frequently seen in this country about fifty years ago. In the process of cooking, it would swell up prodigiously,--a great deal more so than rice. The Germans in the regiment would make big dishes of soup out of this "baled hay," as we called it, and they liked it, but the native Americans, after one trial, wouldn't touch it. I think about the last box of it that was issued to our company was pitched into a ditch in the rear of the camp, and it soon got thoroughly soaked and loomed up about as big as a fair-sized hay-cock. "Split-peas" were issued to us, more or less, during all the time we were in the service. My understanding was that they were the ordinary garden peas. They were split in two, dried, and about as hard as gravel. But they yielded to cooking, made excellent food, and we were all fond of them. In our opinion, when properly cooked, they were almost as good as Yankee beans.

When our forces captured Little Rock in September, 1863, we obtained possession, among other plunder, of quite a quantity of Confederate commissary stores. Among these was a copious supply of "jerked beef." It consisted of narrow, thin strips of beef, which had been dried on scaffolds in the sun, and it is no exaggeration to say that it was almost as hard and dry as a cottonwood chip. Our manner of eating it was simply to cut off a chunk about as big as one of our elongated musket balls, and proceed to "chaw." It was rather a comical sight to see us in our cabins of a cold winter night, sitting by the fire, and all solemnly "chawing" away, in profound silence, on the Johnnies' jerked beef. But, if sufficiently masticated, it was nutritious and healthful, and we all liked it. I often thought it would have been a good thing if the government had made this kind of beef a permanent and regular addition to our rations. As long as kept in the dry, it would apparently keep indefinitely, and a piece big enough to last a soldier two or three days would take up but little space in a haversack.

Passing from the topic of army rations, I will now take leave to say here, with sincerity and emphasis, that the best school to fit me for the practical affairs of life that I ever attended was in the old 61st Illinois during the Civil War. It would be too long a story to undertake to tell all the benefits derived from that experience, but a few will be alluded to. In the first place, when I was a boy at home, I was, to some extent, a "spoiled child." I was exceedingly particular and "finicky" about my food. Fat meat I abhorred, and wouldn't touch it, and on the other hand, when we had chicken to eat, the gizzard was claimed by me as my sole and exclusive tid-bit, and "Leander" always got it. Let it be known that in the regiment those habits were gotten over so soon that I was astonished myself. The army in time of war is no place for a "sissy-boy;" it will make a man of him quicker, in my opinion, than any other sort of experience he could undergo. And suffice it to say, on the food question, that my life as a soldier forever cured me of being fastidious or fault-finding about what I had to eat. I have gone hungry too many times to give way to such weakness when sitting down in a comfortable room to a table provided with plenty that was good enough for any reasonable man. I have no patience with a person who is addicted to complaining or growling about his food. Some years ago there was an occasion when I took breakfast at a decent little hotel at a country way-station on a railroad out in Kansas. It was an early breakfast, for the accommodation of guests who would leave on an early morning train, and there were only two at the table,--a young traveling commercial man and myself. The drummer ordered (with other things) a couple of fried eggs, and that fellow sent the poor little dining room girl back with those eggs three times before he got them fitted to the exact shade of taste to suit his exquisite palate. And he did this, too, in a manner and words that were offensive and almost brutal. It was none of my business, so I kept my mouth shut and said nothing, but I would have given a reasonable sum to have been the proprietor of that hotel about five minutes. That fool would then have been ordered to get his grip and leave the house,--and he would have left, too.

I do not know how it may have been with other regiments in the matter now to be mentioned, but I presume it was substantially the same as in ours. And the course pursued with us had a direct tendency to make one indifferent as to the precise cut of his clothes. It is true that attention was paid to shoes, to that extent, at least, that the quartermaster tried to give each man a pair that approximated to the number he wore. But coats, trousers, and the other clothes were piled up in separate heaps, and each man was just thrown the first garment on the top of the heap; he took it and walked away. If it was an outrageous fit, he would swap with some one if possible, otherwise he got along as best he could. Now, in civil life, I have frequently been amused in noting some dudish young fellow in a little country store trying to fit himself out with a light summer coat, or something similar. He would put on the garment, stand in front of a big looking glass, twist himself into all sorts of shapes so as to get a view from every possible angle, then remove that one, and call for another. Finally, after trying on about every coat in the house, he would leave without making a purchase, having found nothing that suited the exact contour of his delicately moulded form. A very brief experience in a regiment that had a gruff old quartermaster would take that tuck out of that Beau Brummell, in short order.

Sometimes I have been, at a late hour on a stormy night, at a way-station on some "jerk-water" railroad, waiting for a belated train, with others in the same predicament. And it was comical to note the irritation of some of these fellows and the fuss they made about the train being late. The railroad, and all the officers, would be condemned and abused in the most savage terms on account of this little delay. And yet we were in a warm room, with benches to sit on, with full stomachs, and physically just as comfortable as we possibly could be. The thought would always occur to me, on such episodes, that if those kickers had to sit down in a dirt road, in the mud, with a cold rain pelting down on them, and just endure all this until a broken bridge in front was fixed up so that the artillery and wagon train could get along,--then a few incidents of that kind would be a benefit to them. And instances like the foregoing might be multiplied indefinitely. On the whole, life in the army in a time of war tended to develop patience, contentment with the surroundings, and equanimity of temper and mind in general. And, from the highest to the lowest, differing only in degree, it would bring out energy, prompt decision, intelligent action, and all the latent force of character a man possessed.

I suppose, in reminiscences of this nature, one should give his impressions, or views, in relation to that much talked about subject,--"Courage in battle." Now, in what I have to say on that head, I can speak advisedly mainly for myself only. I think that the principal thing that held me to the work was simply pride; and am of the opinion that it was the same thing with most of the common soldiers. A prominent American functionary some years ago said something about our people being "too proud to fight." With the soldiers of the Civil War it was exactly the reverse,--they were "too proud to run";--unless it was manifest that the situation was hopeless, and that for the time being nothing else could be done. And, in the latter case, when the whole line goes back, there is no personal odium attaching to any one individual; they are all in the same boat. The idea of the influence of pride is well illustrated by an old-time war story, as follows: A soldier on the firing line happened to notice a terribly affrighted rabbit running to the rear at the top of its speed. "Go it, cotton-tail!" yelled the soldier. "I'd run too if I had no more reputation to lose than you have."

It is true that in the first stages of the war the fighting qualities of American soldiers did not appear in altogether a favorable light. But at that time the fact is that the volunteer armies on both sides were not much better than mere armed mobs, and without discipline or cohesion. But those conditions didn't last long,--and there was never but one Bull Run.

Enoch Wallace was home on recruiting service some weeks in the fall of 1862, and when he rejoined the regiment he told me something my father said in a conversation that occurred between the two. They were talking about the war, battles, and topics of that sort, and in the course of their talk Enoch told me that my father said that while he hoped his boy would come through the war all right, yet he would rather "Leander should be killed dead, while standing up and fighting like a man, than that he should run, and disgrace the family." I have no thought from the nature of the conversation as told to me by Enoch that my father made this remark with any intention of its being repeated to me. It was sudden and spontaneous, and just the way the old backwoodsman felt. But I never forgot it, and it helped me several times. For, to be perfectly frank about it, and tell the plain truth, I will set it down here that, so far as I was concerned, away down in the bottom of my heart I just secretly dreaded a battle. But we were soldiers, and it was our business to fight when the time came, so the only thing to then do was to summon up our pride and resolution, and face the ordeal with all the fortitude we could command. And while I admit the existence of this feeling of dread before the fight, yet it is also true that when it was on, and one was in the thick of it, with the smell of gun-powder permeating his whole system, then a signal change comes over a man. He is seized with a furious desire to kill. There are his foes, right in plain view, give it to 'em, d---- 'em!--and for the time being he becomes almost oblivious to the sense of danger.

And while it was only human nature to dread a battle,--and I think it would be mere affectation to deny it, yet I also know that we common soldiers strongly felt that when fighting did break loose close at hand, or within the general scope of our operations, then we ought to be in it, with the others, and doing our part. That was what we were there for, and somehow a soldier didn't feel just right for fighting to be going on all round him, or in his vicinity, and he doing nothing but lying back somewhere, eating government rations.

But, all things considered, the best definition of true courage I have ever read is that given by Gen. Sherman in his Memoirs, as follows:

"I would define true courage," (he says,) "to be a perfect sensibility of the measure of danger, and a mental willingness to endure it." (Sherman's Memoirs, revised edition, Vol. 2, p. 395.) But, I will further say, in this connection, that, in my opinion, much depends, sometimes, especially at a critical moment, on the commander of the men who is right on the ground, or close at hand. This is shown by the result attained by Gen. Milroy in the incident I have previously mentioned. And, on a larger scale, the inspiring conduct of Gen. Sheridan at the battle of Cedar Creek, Virginia, is probably the most striking example in modern history of what a brave and resolute leader of men can accomplish under circumstances when apparently all is lost. And, on the other hand, I think there is no doubt that the battle of Wilson's Creek, Missouri, on August 10, 1861, was a Union victory up to the time of the death of Gen. Lyon, and would have remained such if the officer who succeeded Lyon had possessed the nerve of his fallen chief. But he didn't, and so he marched our troops off the field, retreated from a beaten enemy, and hence Wilson's Creek figures in history as a Confederate victory. I have read somewhere this saying of Bonaparte's: "An army of deer commanded by a lion is better than an army of lions commanded by a deer." While that statement is only figurative in its nature, it is, however, a strong epigrammatic expression of the fact that the commander of soldiers in battle should be, above all other things, a forcible, determined, and brave man.

CHAPTER XXV

FRANKLIN, SUMMER of 1865. MUSTERED OUT, SEPTEMBER 8, 1865. RECEIVE FINAL PAYMENT at SPRINGFIELD, ILLINOIS, SEPTEMBER 27, 1865. THE REGIMENT "BREAKS RANKS" FOREVER.

Soldiering at Franklin, Tennessee, in May, June, July, and August, 1865, was simply of a picnic kind. The war was over in that region, and everything there was as quiet and peaceful as it was at home in Illinois. Picket guards were dispensed with, and the only guard duty required was a small detail for the colors at regimental headquarters, and a similar one over our commissary stores. However, it was deemed necessary for the health of the men to maintain company drills to a certain extent, but they were light and easy. Near the camp was a fine blue-grass pasture field, containing in a scattered, irregular form numerous large and magnificent hard maples, and the drilling was done in this field. Capt. Warren was somewhat portly, and not fond of strenuous exercise anyhow, so all the drilling Co. D had at Franklin was conducted by myself. But I rather liked it. With the accession of those 83rd Illinois men, the old company was about as big and strong as it was at Camp Carrollton, and it looked fine. But, to tell the truth, it is highly probable that we put in fully as much time lying on the blue grass under the shade of those grand old maples as we did in company evolutions.

Sometime during the course of the summer a middle aged widow lady named House began conducting a sort of private boarding establishment at her residence in the city, and Col. Nulton, Maj. Keeley, and several of the line officers, including myself, took our meals at this place during the remainder of our stay at Franklin. Among the boarders were two or three gentlemen also of the name of House, and who were brothers-in-law of our hostess. They had all served in Forrest's cavalry as commissioned officers, and were courteous and elegant gentlemen. We would all sit down together at the table of Mrs. House, with that lady at the head, and talk and laugh, and joke with each other, as if we had been comrades and friends all our lives. And yet, during the four years just preceding, the Union and the Confederate soldiers thus mingled together in friendship and amity had been doing their very best to kill one another! But in our conversation we carefully avoided anything in the nature of political discussion about the war, and in general each side refrained from saying anything on that subject which might grate on the feelings of the other.

On September 4th, 1865, the regiment left Franklin and went by rail to Nashville for the purpose of being mustered out of the service. There were some unavoidable delays connected with the business, and it was not officially consummated until September 8th. In the forenoon of the following day we left Nashville on the cars, on the Louisville and Nashville railroad, for Springfield, Illinois, where we were to receive our final payment and certificates of discharge.

Early on Sunday morning, September 10th, we crossed the Ohio river at Louisville, Kentucky, on a ferry boat, to Jeffersonville, Indiana. This boat was provided with a railroad track extending from bow to stern, and so arranged that when the boat landed at either bank, the rails laid along the lower deck of the boat would closely connect with the railroad track on the land. This ferry transferred our train in sections, and thus obviated any necessity for the men to leave the cars. The ferrying process did not take long, and we were soon speeding through southern Indiana. As stated, it was Sunday, and a bright, beautiful autumn day. As I have hereinbefore mentioned, our train consisted of box cars, (except one coach for the commissioned officers,) and all the men who could find room had taken, from preference, seats on top of the cars. Much of southern Indiana is rugged and broken, and in 1865 was wild, heavily timbered, and the most of the farm houses were of the backwoods class. We soon began to see little groups of the country people, in farm wagons, or on foot, making their way to Sunday school and church. Women, young girls, and children predominated, all dressed in their "Sunday-go-to-meeting" clothes. And how the women and girls cheered us, and waved their handkerchiefs! And didn't we yell! It was self-evident that we were in "God's Country" once more. These were the first demonstrations of that kind the old regiment had seen since the girls of Monticello Seminary, in February, 1862, lined the fences by the road side and made similar manifestations of patriotism and good will.

We arrived at Indianapolis about noon, there got off the cars and went in a body to a Soldiers' Home close at hand, where we had a fine dinner; thence back to the old train, which thundered on the rest of the day and that night, arriving at Springfield the following day, the 11th. Here we marched out to Camp Butler, near the city, and went into camp.

And now another annoying delay occurred, this time being in the matter of our final payment. What the particular cause was I do not know; probably the paymasters were so busy right then that they couldn't get around to us. The most of us (that is, of the old, original regiment) were here within sixty or seventy miles of our homes, and to be compelled to just lie around and wait here at Camp Butler was rather trying. But the boys were patient, and on the whole endured the situation with commendable equanimity. "But the day it came at last," and in the forenoon of September 27th we fell in line by companies, and each company in its turn marched to the paymaster's tent, near regimental headquarters. The roll of the company would be called in alphabetical order, and each man, as his name was called, would answer, and step forward to the paymaster's table. That officer would lay on the table before the man the sum of money he was entitled to, and with it his certificate of discharge from the army, duly signed by the proper officials. The closing of the hand of the soldier over that piece of paper was the final act in the drama that ended his career as a soldier of the Civil War. Now he was a civilian, free to come and go as he listed. Farewell to the morning drum-beats, taps, roll-calls, drills, marches, battles, and all the other incidents and events of a soldier's life.

"The serried ranks, with flags displayed,
The bugle's thrilling blast,
The charge, the thund'rous cannonade,
The din and shout--were past."

The scattering-out process promptly began after we received our pay and discharges. I left Springfield early the following day, the 28th, on the Chicago, Alton, and St. Louis railroad, and went to Alton. Here I luckily found a teamster who was in the act of starting with his wagon and team to Jerseyville, and I rode with him to that place, arriving there about the middle of the afternoon. I now hunted diligently to find some farm wagon that might be going to the vicinity of home, but found none. While so engaged, to my surprise and great delight, I met the old Chaplain, B. B. Hamilton. As heretofore stated, he had resigned during the previous March and had been at home for some months. His greeting to me was in his old-fashioned style. "Son of Jeremiah!" he exclaimed, as he extended his hand, "why comest thou down hither? And with whom hast thou left those few sheep in the wilderness?" I promptly informed him, in effect, that my coming was regular and legitimate, and that the "few sheep" of the old regiment were forever through and done with a shepherd. Hamilton did not reside in Jerseyville, but had just arrived there from his home in Greene county, and, like me, was trying to find some farmer's conveyance to take him about five miles into the country to the home of an old friend. I ascertained that his route, as far as he went, was the same as mine, so I proposed that we should strike out on foot. But he didn't entertain the proposition with much enthusiasm. "Son of Jeremiah," said he, "you will find that a walk of nine miles" (the distance to my father's) "will be a great weariness to the flesh on this warm day." But I considered it a mere pleasure walk, and was determined to go, so he finally concluded to do likewise. I left my valise in the care of a Jerseyville merchant, and with no baggage except my sword and belt, we proceeded to "hit the dirt." I took off my coat, slung it over one shoulder, unsnapped my sword, with the scabbard, from the belt, and shouldered it also. Our walk was a pleasant and most agreeable one, as we had much to talk about that was interesting to both. When we arrived at the mouth of the lane that led to the house of the Chaplain's friend, we shook hands and I bade him good-by, but fully expected to meet him many times later. But our paths in life diverged,--and I never saw him again.

I arrived at the little village of Otterville about sundown. It was a very small place in 1865. There was just one store, (which also contained the post-office,) a blacksmith shop, the old "Stone school house," a church, and perhaps a dozen or so private dwellings. There were no sidewalks, and I stalked up the middle of the one street the town afforded, with my sword poised on my shoulder, musket fashion, and feeling happy and proud. I looked eagerly around as I passed along, hoping to see some old friend. As I went by the store, a man who was seated therein on the counter leaned forward and looked at me, but said nothing. A little further up the street a big dog sprang off the porch of a house, ran out to the little gate in front, and standing on his hind legs with his fore paws on the palings, barked at me loudly and persistently,--but I attracted no further attention. Many of the regiments that were mustered out soon after the close of the war received at home gorgeous receptions. They marched under triumphal arches, decorated with flags and garlands of flowers, while brass bands blared, and thousands of people cheered, and gave them a most enthusiastic "Welcome Home!" But the poor old 61st Illinois was among the late arrivals. The discharged soldiers were now numerous and common, and no longer a novelty. Personally I didn't care, rather really preferred to come back home modestly and quietly, and without any "fuss and feathers" whatever. Still, I would have felt better to have met at least one person as I passed through the little village who would have given me a hearty hand-shake, and said he was glad to see me home, safe from the war. But it's all right, for many such were met later.

I now had only two miles to go, and was soon at the dear old boyhood home. My folks were expecting me, so they were not taken by surprise. There was no "scene" when we met, nor any effusive display, but we all had a feeling of profound contentment and satisfaction which was too deep to be expressed by mere words.

When I returned home I found that the farm work my father was then engaged in was cutting up and shocking corn. So, the morning after my arrival, September 29th, I doffed my uniform of first lieutenant, put on some of father's old clothes, armed myself with a corn knife, and proceeded to wage war on the standing corn. The feeling I had while engaged in this work was "sort of queer." It almost seemed, sometimes, as if I had been away only a day or two, and had just taken up the farm work where I had left off.

Here this story will close.

In conclusion I will say that in civil life people have been good to me. I have been honored with different positions of trust, importance, and responsibility, and which I have reason to believe I filled to the satisfaction of the public. I am proud of the fact of having been deemed worthy to fill those different places. But, while that is so, I will further say, in absolute sincerity, that to me my humble career as a soldier in the 61st Illinois during the War for the Union is the record that I prize the highest of all, and is the proudest recollection of my life.

Printed in Great Britain
by Amazon

83559646R00150